Soviet Hieroglyphics

Soviet Hieroglyphics

Visual Culture in
Late Twentieth-Century Russia

Edited by
Nancy Condee

Indiana University Press
Bloomington and Indianapolis

BFI PUBLISHING

BFI Publishing
London

First published in 1995 by
Indiana University Press
601 North Morton Street, Bloomington, Indiana 47404
and the
British Film Institute
21 Stephen Street, London W1P 1PL, England

The paper used in this publication meets the minimum requirements of
American National Standard for Information Sciences—Permanence of Paper
for Printed Library Materials, ANSI Z39.48-1984.

Manufactured in the United States of America

British Library Cataloguing in Publication Data
A catalogue record for this book is available from the British Library.
BFI ISBNs: 0-85170-458-1 (cl)—0-85170-459-X (pa)

Library of Congress Cataloging-in-Publication Data

Soviet hieroglyphics : visual culture in late twentieth-century Russia
/ edited by Nancy Condee.
p.   cm.
Compilation of seven articles translated from Russian.
Includes bibliographical references and index.
ISBN 0-253-31402-X (cl : acid-free paper).—ISBN 0-253-20945-5 (pa : acid-free
paper)
1. Arts, Soviet.   2. Arts and society—Soviet Union.   3. Arts,
Russian.   4. Arts and society—Russia (Federation).   5. Allegories.
I. Condee, Nancy.
NX556.A1S66   1995
700'.1'03094709049—dc20 94-22839

1 2 3 4 5 00 99 98 97 96 95

Contents

Introduction

Nancy Condee

The chapters of this volume are all concerned in one way or another with visual culture, with objects or texts that engage us in a primarily visual apprehension. These include documentary and feature film; television news, game shows, advertisements, and soap operas; billboards, painting, board games, statues, cartoons, and currency.

De-Sovietization and rapid, recent Westernization have profoundly affected these texts in recent years; indeed, until quite recently, some of them did not even exist as cultural categories. Yet it must be remembered that Communism had its own visual display that has also shaped the present moment: its multistoried propaganda frames, its banners and posters, its Lenin dirigibles, the gestic performances of its political leaders, its parades and spectacles. One of many things that Communism did not have was effective marketing skills, with the result that the "billboards of communism" touting socialism's endurance were themselves endured and devisualized by a public that had no earthly reason to look at them.[1]

As one Russian critic has remarked, Soviet cultural symbols now seem somehow closer, simpler, and even more understandable than the newest democratic slogans and reborn ancient emblems (Novikov). Within the words "Soviet" and "cultural" there is, of course, enormous variety. The mentality of War Communism coveted very different artifacts, treasured different texts, enforced different codes of decorum (or anti-decorum) from those that were coveted, treasured, or enforced a decade later, after the celebrations of Stalin's fiftieth birthday in 1929, when the cozy concern for "culturedness" [*kul'turnost'*] became of increasing importance. Nevertheless, the CPSU hammer and sickle, the Red Army's five-pointed star, the KGB's sword and shield, the Soviet red banner, and Lenin's earnest, decapitated head, whether stamped in pig iron or embroidered on the cover of a family album, number among the determining icons of the twentieth century, no less than such Western contributions as Coca-Cola's dynamic curve or McDonald's golden arches.

Indeed, the very fact that these Soviet symbols, *unlike* the seemingly transhistorical dynamic curve, now belong to a discrete historic past contributes to their particular cultic significance. And unlike Russia's older symbols—the double-headed eagle, which faithfully served both Byzantine and Hapsburg rule before being adopted by Ivan III; the Russian merchant's *tricouleur*, now the flag of the Russian Federation; or the endlessly self-reviving Saint George and the Dragon—Soviet symbols are inextricably and specifically embedded in this one century. The Russian variant of the twentieth century reserved a mere decade on either end—more precisely, seventeen years on one end, nine on the other—for alternative economic systems of sign production. Hence, it is difficult *not* to discern an internal tension in the new slogans, as if they were a new culture's early drafts, still cast in the handwriting of Soviet experience. If "continuity"—for decades a topic of debate among Sovietologists—was once a link between prerevolutionary Russia and the postrevolutionary Soviet Union, it has now become a series of possible link-ages, each of which must in some way reckon with the lengthy but transitory twentieth-century instantiation known as the Soviet period.[2]

For those who do not work in this field, two interrelated features of the Soviet period bear mention here: its strong tendency toward a fixed hier-archy of cultural production and the particular way that it fetishized high culture. Briefly put, from 1932 until the late 1980s, Soviet culture—and in particular here, high culture—was guided by the firm hand of the Party in accordance with the dominant aesthetic canon, socialist realism; literature played a key part in mapping out the terrain of Soviet cultural production. Socialist realism was conceived in reference to and extrapolated on the basis of prose, above all the long biographical novel.[3] To the extent that one could speak of a keystone of Soviet culture, the object holding up that triumphal arch was the book, preferably the big book or "brick" [*kirpich*], the conceptual building block of the new high culture.

Many cultural observers, therefore, were taken by surprise in May 1986, as the system was falling apart, when elections within the Union of Cine-matographers played a pivotal role in redefining the potential of the crea-tive union as a lever for reform. And yet the fact that the most sweeping early manifestation of perestroika in the cultural sphere should occur in visual culture, rather than within the community of dissident writers whose every utterance had been tracked for years by Radio Liberty and the BBC, was (in retrospect, as always) no surprise at all.

The Union of Writers was in no position to undertake a similar palace revolt. Literature, the sepulchral reserve of Stalinist legitimacy, certainly *had* oppositional forces within its own union; unfortunately, those opposi-tional forces were even more conservative than the Union Secretariat itself. For a variety of reasons, having in part to do with the technical conditions of the film industry (Condee and Padunov, "Frontiers"), the liberal cine-matographers had more at stake in seizing the administrative structure of

Introduction

their union and more likelihood of success than had the liberal writers. Thus, while "quiet revolutions" were carried out in other arenas of the culture industry (international music exchanges, for example, managed to circumvent Goskontsert and the Union of Composers, whose administration was one of the last to reform), the most publicized, influential, and striking model of systemic industry reform took place in the arena of visual culture, specifically cinema. The fact that the creative unions subsequently became an irrelevant model altogether does not obscure either their crucial role as a measure of cultural reform in the early years of the perestroika period or the significance of cinema in doing what literature could not accomplish, namely, breaking the geriatocratic administration of culture.

The irony and ideological logic to this usurpation of literature's leading role did not escape the liberal filmmakers. Given Lenin's legendary blessing of cinema as "the most important of all the arts," they could challenge literature's supremacy while still remaining politically correct. This strategy was well timed, since the neo-Leninism of early perestroika was to last only a brief period; by 1988, it had already given way to anti-Leninism. Here, once again, cinema was to play a role in generating a key text—Marina Goldovskaia's 1988 film *Solovki Power* [*Solovetskaia vlast'*]—in bringing this issue into the open.

The collapse of high culture in the Soviet Union, which corresponded more or less to the collapse of totalitarianism, was thus played out most vividly in the rapidly changing fortunes of the film and book industries. While it may be argued that these two industries are a key measure in the West as well, the history of their relations to each other had been constructed differently in the Soviet Union, according to the terms of totalitarianism, rather than those of the marketplace. To choose a small example, a Soviet filmscript based on a published novel or story might generally have had greater prospects of success than an original filmscript, not because the public had in any sense already been sold on the product, but because the book, already being in print, had therefore already been vetted by the censor, increasing the likelihood that the filmscript would proceed with fewer impediments than an entirely new script. This mechanism was one of many ways that film (and theater productions, in a somewhat different fashion) was indentured to literature as the master canon in ways largely unrecognized and absent in the West. Cultural perestroika disrupted this set of relations, setting film "free" from literature and ultimately leading to the impoverishment of both.

An apparently minor result of the changing fortunes within the book industry was the re-emergence of authors' books, self-consciously "made" objects to be handled and contemplated as things in themselves.[4] The fact that this process happened simultaneously with an explosion in mass literature (including the visual genres of comics and pornography) does not detract from the success of the author's book in salvaging some kind of élite status for the book, now no longer the pinnacle of a unitary artistic system. The rare, expensive author's book had retrieved some of its privilege by resituating itself in a culture that now valued "the look" over "the read," visual display over the verbal imaginary. The author's book "achieved" in literature's high culture what comics and pornography did in literature's mass culture: it rescued the industry by acquiescing to a set of cultural priorities that stressed visuality. Thus, in the shift from book culture to visual culture, even the book itself becomes retrospectively "visualized."[5]

In this respect, this volume engages the notion of visual culture somewhat differently from other recent texts, which have delineated a specific range for their analysis, such as photography (Dagognet), statuary (Llewellyn), television (Kruger), or art and art theory (Adler, Crary, Krauss, Stafford). While individual chapters in this book may make such delineations, the volume as a whole does not; its polemical inclusion of the book as a largely unrecognized participant in visual culture—whether as the object itself, as a collection of images, or as an industry generating its own forms of visual display (book covers, bookstand displays, kiosks)—suggests that visual culture is a process and not a thing, a particular way of perceiving the object and not the particular object perceived.

The significance of this process as it has emerged in the arena of literature over the last several decades can perhaps best be articulated by comparing two central texts from the Soviet cultural opposition: *Pages from Tarusa [Tarusskie stranitsy,* 1961] and *Metropol [Metropol',* 1979]. Both are literary texts that include images. Contrary to what one might expect, *Pages from Tarusa* contains considerably more images than *Metropol.* Its images fall roughly into four categories: (1) illustrations to stories (usually imaginary "portraits" of a story's protagonist); (2) previously unreproduced sketches by well-known, late-nineteenth-century artists from the holdings of Tarusa's Polenov Museum; (3) photographs of leading cultural figures (Vsevolod Meyerhold, Konstantin Stanislavskii, Marina Tsvetaeva, and Nikolai Zabolotskii); and (4) ephemera of the rich and famous, such as Ivan Turgenev's calling card, or a collection of origami cranes folded by Lev Tolstoi for the Polenov children and dutifully dated (18 November 1896) and described by several members of the Polenov family (250).

Metropol, by contrast, has only three sets of images: Boris Messerer's famous gramophone frontispiece, which soon became a symbol of late Soviet oppositional culture; Andrei Voznesenskii's graphic poem "Mother" [*Mat*]; and Anatolii Brusilovskii's erotic drawings, significantly unlisted in the original table of contents (so that they could, presumably, be omitted if politically necessary). While it remains a literary text, *Metropol*'s concept of literature abandons both *Pages from Tarusa's* homage to late nineteenth-century high culture and that work's reverence for the word as "begetter" of the image. Instead, *Metropol's* images point the way to a gradual process of greater equilibrium between word and image that reaches its full expression more than a decade later. Thus, paradoxically, the process of visualization not only does not exclude literature, it is played out most vividly in literature, precisely the medium with the greatest resistance to (and, arguably, the most to lose from) the ascendancy of visual culture.

It is at this point that we must return briefly to Communism's visual display, because, as the Moscow Conceptualists accurately demonstrated, that display usually included a verbal text, often explicitly taken from a book and intended to instruct and exhort, to shape the visual experience along proper ideological lines. This was true not only of Communism's posters, but also of its paintings, the titles of which were, in a sense, the prompter's hiss, delivering to us the lines we were supposed to have learned already. Whatever Conceptualism's amendments of Communism's image,[6] its amendment of Communism's verbal text was an interruption of the citation and the substitution of an ironic, contemplative silence, an appreciation of the verbal as limpid, visual spectacle. For all this, Communism is involuntarily indebted to the Conceptualists, whose revolutionary vanguard began to rescue Communism's pictographs long before the political system showed serious signs of collapse.

Conceptualism is, of course, a broader artistic enterprise than its most familiar subgenre, a kind of "Communist chic," but it was this Communist chic, of all the Conceptualists' preoccupations, that most captured the imagination of the educated, Westernized, urban population; the result was that Communist chic itself quickly became a cultural tendency reaching far beyond Conceptualism.[7] Imposed, one might argue, violently and unsuccessfully by the Soviet régime, Communist chic met with success only under capitalism, most evidently in the areas of art, advertising, photography, and fashion design. Contrary to the oft-heard claims that it was a brief fad, Communist chic continues to reappear because it draws upon the common memory of tortuous experience now safely filed in the dustbin of history, a little like a visit to Jurassic Park. The appropriation of Soviet symbols by the fashion and advertising industries in particular promises a tempting reversal of the experience of appropriation, acted out in a twofold fantasy:

the opportunity, through ownership, of dominating the dominators; and the cleansing skepticism of post-utopian consumption, thereby neutralizing any resistance to capital's own proffered utopia. Thus, while the déluge of materials chronicling Soviet atrocities has long passed, it is specifically *chronicles* that have passed. Soviet atrocities, of necessity adorned with the familiar trinkets of totalitarianism, still produce a marketable frisson. Meanwhile, the collapse of the massive political apparatus has left a product-hungry population ideally suited for grand-scale visual extravaganza, mass spectacle, and universal invitation to join the world in choosing Coke, smoking Marlboro, and eating Mars bars. This, despite the vague resemblance, is not a new totalitarian world order; this is "freedom," but a freedom deeply indebted to its predecessor for preparing a public with understandable and unreasonable expectations of immediately meeting massive physical and material needs.

Hieroglyphics—in a metaphoric sense, the subject of these essays—are sacred writings in picture form, a fusion of verbal and visual texts. Whether the contributors here are writing about the moving image (film, video, television), the still image (paintings, billboards, medals, cartoons, currency), or the inscribed, three-dimensional object (bridges, monuments, books, pedestals, buildings, and statues), their concern is largely the constituent elements present or absent from any particular example of visual display. An assumption common to many chapters is that visual display sets into action a kind of contemplation fundamentally different from the verbal imagination inspired by the book. Thus, for example, our memory of the "narrative resolution" of the Soviet Union, for example, cannot be recalled without a familiar set of images signalling its closure (e.g., Yeltsin on the tank, Gorbachev reading his farewell speech). The story must be rendered visually. Where the verbal text exists, it must be imbedded into those images, as into any hieroglyph.

This volume comes out of the Working Group on Contemporary Russian Culture, which held its fourth meeting at the School of Slavonic Studies (University of London) in July 1993, together with a weeklong screening of Stalin films and parodies at the National Film Theatre (London). The Working Group, which met annually from 1990 to 1993, focused its research efforts on contemporary culture, with particular emphasis on popular culture, about which there was, as might be expected, little consensus. As a general rule, we took "contemporary" to mean post-1985, Russia's years of perestroika and post-perestroika. Although the Working Group's research turned at times to the distant past—1932, for example, or even 1905—its analysis of that past was grounded in the coherence (or incoherence) of late twentieth-century Russia. The essays included in this volume continue to reflect that orientation in their historical analysis.

Research coming out of this group has appeared over the past several years in the *Harriman Institute Forum, October,* and *New Left Review,* as well as the Russo-Soviet periodicals *Znamia* [*The Banner*], *Iskusstvo kino* [*Cinema Art*], *Voprosy literatury* [*Problems of Literature*], *Nezavisimaia gazeta* [*Independent Gazette*], and *Obshchestvennye nauki i sovremennost'* [*Social Sciences and Contemporaneity*]. Work presented at the first two annual meetings has been collected in an issue of *Stanford Slavic Studies.* The group's work has formed the basis of polemics in the journals *Novyi mir* [*New World*], *Voprosy literatury,* and *Literaturnoe obozrenie* [*Literary Review*].

Similar in some respects to such collections as *Bolshevik Culture, Russia in the Era of NEP, Cultural Revolution in Russia, 1928–1931,* and *The Culture of the Stalin Period,* this volume differs in its more extensive use of specific texts, chosen as primary heuristic tools in a larger discussion of cultural processes. Its contributors work largely in film, literature, and cultural studies rather than in the social sciences.

Key questions, stated or implied, in the above-mentioned volumes might be, to quote Hans Günther, "what is the common denominator?" and "what type of culture?" (*Culture of the Stalin Period* xvi); here the questions are different. Instead of seeking a common base or typological similarity, the contributors seek to understand the ways in which incompatible cultural texts are intershuffled, such that the call for a free market system, for example, reverberates with an enduring Leninist optimism.

Thus, the texts under discussion here are examined less as utterance than as iteration: the citation of a song, the visual rhetoric of statuary, the recapitulation of a slogan, the way an image may retrace a familiar pattern from a different ideological camp. One question here, then, might seem a restatement of an early twentieth-century question ("how is this made?"), except that the curiosity is focused more on textual provenance than on the formal elements of a text's construction; more on its resultant incongruity than on its congruity as the sum of individual parts.

If *Bolshevik Culture,* to choose another scholarly cousin, examines the transition from Russian to Soviet culture, then this volume examines the impossibility of simple reversal now that the Great Experiment has failed. Any discussion of the transition from Soviet to Russian culture (or Russian culture 2) is pointless without an integrated assessment of its indenture to Soviet ceremony and performance rites; its badges, emblems, and totems;

its fables, parables, and myths as they are re-enacted across the surface of present-day Russia.

Given the volume's focus on visual culture, it might seem curious to begin the selection of essays with Katerina Clark's wide-ranging contribution on the ways in which sound—and music in particular—in recent Russo-Soviet films attempts to redefine and temper the visual hegemony of cinema. Yet if cultural coherence is indeed increasingly expressed through visuality (as, if nothing else, a more profitable, wide-reaching, and marketable range of potential commodities than provided by verbal texts), then indeed sound as an organizing component within the visual media (film, television, video) is exhibiting a correspondingly broader range of choices. Moving away from its traditional function of enhancing the visual text—a legacy of the movie-hall piano player who accompanies the silent image—the sound text in the films of Vitalii Kanevskii, Kira Muratova, and others examined in Clark's work serves as a device that brakes or impedes our rush to involvement with the image, reminding us that it is a constructed object, a punctuated sign.

Song is particularly effective in bringing about this disjuncture because it was through the common memory of song that the Soviet utopia had been most eloquently celebrated.[8] The act of singing becomes, in the post-utopian tenor of these films, a coming to terms with the failure of the Soviet *Gesamtkunstwerk*, even in recent cinema seeking to rekindle the allure and *Gemütlichkeit* of the Stalin era. Clark polemically discards her own terminology ("Aural Hieroglyphics?"), which self-consciously plays off against the volume as a whole, as not so much a false choice as an overly restrictive enterprise. She looks instead at the ways in which the historical effectiveness of song to express a vision of the rosy future also conditioned the potential to debunk such a vision.

Outside the arena of cinema and beyond the moment of Clark's writing, I might add, the "war of music" has continued. During the armed standoff between troops loyal to President Boris Yeltsin and conservative parliamentarians in early October 1993, as the *New York Times* reports, the two sides assaulted each other with musical manifestos: the Yeltsin forces amplified old patriotic songs and rock music (thus symbolically "bracketing" the Soviet period on either side) in order to drown out efforts at political agitation by the parliamentarians. In response, the conservative defenders gathered outside the parliament sang back Soviet military songs, such as "Afghanistan, You Are the Fate of Our Generation" (2 October 1993). The "performance" of this politico-musical duet—spontaneous, unrehearsed, and free to the public—was the warm-up number to a bloody conflagration that made the August 1991 putsch seem innocent by comparison.

The conflicts of October 1993 and its precursor, August 1991, are, of course, striking in both their similarities and their differences. Two aspects of this complex topic bear mentioning here, the first of which concerns the parliament building itself. A rubber-stamp institution of Soviet power (its first redaction), with very little independent authority even in the perestroika years (its second redaction), the parliament became in August 1991 the "Russian White House," site of citizen rebirth (its third redaction). By October 1993, however, it had become the fortress of new conservative resistance (its fourth redaction), before going up in smoke (its fifth redaction). Of these, the contrast between the liberal White House of 1991 and the burnt-out black house of 1993 was a stunning visual example of the radical mutability of cultural symbols that has been characteristic of Russia since Gorbachev's first efforts in early 1986 at appropriating and redefining Soviet symbology.[9]

A second point of striking comparison is provided by Ostankino, the television tower that was a secondary site of conflict in both instances. In August 1991, Ostankino was "taken from within"—that is, the conditions of its seizure had been set up long before the putsch itself, with Leonid Kravchenko's appointment to head Gosteleradio. In October 1993, the new conservatives remained outside the walls of television, battling unsuccessfully to get in. Television was thus, in some sense, a critical measure of social control, a fact not lost on the 1991 putsch leaders, despite their failure to manipulate adequately the televised image.

Of the two conflicts, August 1991 is unquestionably of greater significance as a founding myth of modern-day Russia. Not only was the putsch attempted and defeated in that year, Gorbachev resigned the presidency and the Soviet Union ceased to exist, thus marking the formal moment when *Homo sovieticus* reverted to *Homo russicus*.[10]

In their analysis of the "script, blood, and image" of the August 1991 putsch, Victoria E. Bonnell and Gregory Freidin trace Russia's uneasy transition to citizenry. The right to transmit over Soviet television at Ostankino during 19 through 22 August in fact became the area of fiercest debate, so that the event changed its name ("state of emergency," "coup"), even as the battle waged over the control of its image.

This battle was fought on terms that would have been unrecognizable to the dissident community a decade earlier, for the shift of battle terrain from *samizdat* to satellite dish is implicitly also a shift away from their particular understanding of high culture to a broader notion of cultural discourse. In Western Europe and the United States, high culture had been crashing since the early twentieth century, a victim, as Alexander Solzhenitsyn so quaintly (but so accurately) put it, of the "relentless cult of novelty."[11] Yet the cult of novelty was *not* a part of the Soviet experience: at least two generations of the Soviet intelligentsia recited the signature verses of their own unofficial culture, silently or aloud, long before they dared entrust the words to *samizdat*; *samizdat* itself was, in essence, the secret copying of alternative canonical texts. In official culture, decrepit leaders insisted that the same rites of hierarchy be observed in all aspects of life, ranging from the order atop the Mausoleum to the Leninist opening citation in scholarship. The disaffected intelligentsia had *Hamlet*; official culture had *Swan Lake*; they shared a regard for cultural monuments.

Characteristic of the Soviet experience, then, was not the relentless cult of novelty but the relentless novelty of cult, the endless capacity to organize experience anew into a highly codified, overdetermined order, the significance of which could only be understood as an altered form of other cults. As every Soviet schoolchild knew, Pushkin was carried close to the heart of Gogol', who was carried close to the heart of Belinskii, who was carried close to the heart of Chernyshevskii, who was carried close to the heart of Lenin, who was carried close to the heart of us all (along with Pushkin, of course, who was the Lenin of poetry).[12]

As Eric Naiman and Anne Nesbet discuss in their analysis of Stanislav Govorukhin's film trilogy, Solzhenitsyn himself was precisely one such cult figure, a fate of which he was not unaware when he issued the artistic manifesto mentioned above.[13] Thus, the fact that Solzhenitsyn's son, Stepka, apparently prefers and is best versed in the work of Nikolai Gogol' may simply be a matter of the boy's tastes; yet it may also be, given Solzhenitsyn's highly determined cultic universe, that Stepka "chooses" Gogol' as a source of commentary on Russia's social mores because Stepka knows he *must not choose* Tolstoi or Dostoevskii. To choose these two is to acknowledge the constructed quality of the cult; to choose *between* the two is to destroy the syncretic quality of the cult's evolution. Thus, there is an uneasy, self-conscious quality to Solzhenitsyn's self-presentation to filmmaker Govorukhin, as if the writer sensed he might momentarily be relegated to Krymskii Val with the other statuary.

As Helena Goscilo discusses in her contribution to this volume, Pushkin may be the lone surviving cult within high culture,[14] and even he stands in lonely and dubious confrontation with the golden arches across the city square. Goscilo's "gendered trinity" relies upon a close reading of specific

Introduction

texts (Viacheslav Krishtofovich's film *Adam's Rib* [*Rebro Adama*, 1991], Liudmila Petrushevskaia's story *Night Time* [*Vremia noch'*, 1992], and Galina Shcherbakova's *The Ubiquists* [*Ubikvisty*, 1992]) to provide an interpretive model of enduring cultural values. I have placed her argument, more concerned with continuity than change, between the two articles on fallen idols: Solzhenitsyn, a man of stature who has lost his pedestal, and Feliks Dzerzhinskii, a pedestal that has lost its statue.

Mikhail Yampolsky's piece on statuary proceeds from Riegl's observation that "intentional monuments," as opposed to ruins, are constructed from the outset as objects of admiration and contemplation. Despite their massive, tangible bulk, they belong in the arena of a visual culture, such that tactile engagement constitutes a virtual act of transgression. Their elevation, Yampolsky argues, puts them visually and ideologically beyond the reach of the quotidian. A curious if temporary consequence, I might add, was the frequency throughout 1992 with which toppled statuary became for a time the standard on-camera location for television news reporting, a vengeful reminder by the most quotidian of all media that the minutes of Communism's eternal statuary have ticked irretrievably away. Broadening his analysis to currency and official documents, Yampolsky raises interesting questions about the fictions that must be imprinted on these texts to render them legal.

A different sort of fiction constitutes the subject of Susan Larsen's contribution on Kira Muratova's film *A Change of Fate* [*Peremena uchasti*, 1987]. While Larsen's focus is, in one sense, the tightest of those essays included in this volume, it engages a text that is crucial not only to an understanding of Muratova's work as a whole, but also to a larger European discussion of colonial discourse, the intercutting of race and gender, carried out in this film through its many displacements. Based on W. Somerset Maugham's story "The Letter," Muratova's film is no longer about British colonialism, but certainly not about Soviet colonialism; filmed in Tadzhikistan, it is not about Central Asia, but no longer about Singapore; deliberately unfaithful to its setting in the second decade of the twentieth century, it conjures up images from the closing years of the century, ironically "de-Sovietized" by a filmmaker whose work was systematically destroyed by Soviet bureaucrats.

The final contribution, written with my co-author, Vladimir Padunov, is the last of our four related articles tracing the period of transition from perestroika to early consumer culture. Specifically, this article is concerned with kiosks, advertising strategies, bookstores, philanthropy, property battles, board games, pornography, and rituals honoring high culture (openings, receptions, and so-called *prezentatsii*). In a larger sense, the article continues the discussion of the changing status of cultural objects and practices in an economic order that has collapsed and is slowly in the process of inventing something we have not seen before: postsocialist capitalism.

What links these essays, apart from their common focus on contemporary Russia, is their interest in the extreme instability of its cultural texts, the extreme disjuncture between the original significance ascribed to an object at the time of its recent construction and the (often antonymical) meanings that accrue to it over a relatively short span of time.

The alternative definition of hieroglyphics—"illegible," that which can be looked at but not deciphered—seems at times to be the most apt description of these texts, produced in conditions of an almost unrecognizable market. Although we may disagree about many features, there is no question about the fact that "market" (like "socialism") must be conceived in a radically different fashion as a result of the passage through the Soviet period.

In certain arenas of cultural manipulation (advertising and rock video, for example) we see rapid, even futuristic acceleration, combined with studious neglect of both legislative and distribution infrastructures.[15] Elsewhere, this weird anachronia seems to work in reverse: late twentieth-century archeology in Russia, for example, loses its identity as an academic project and reverts to something akin to early twentieth-century bargain hunting.[16] These changes must not be reduced only to a matter of better or worse, however tempting it may be to do so. The louder we lament the death of the book, for example, the less we fathom the accompanying shifts within Russia's long-established cult of the dead writer. If I may indulge myself in a distant example from beyond the boundaries of present-day Russia, the Uzbek exhibition of economic achievements (Tashkent's VDNKh) is the proposed future site of a Central Asian Disneyland. Who cares whether such a transformation is better or worse, when the proposal itself is so inadvertently articulate about the functions of socialist utopias and Western theme parks?[17]

Those of us working in the contemporary Russian period, which used to be called (among other things) Sovietology, are repeatedly warned nowadays not to "date" our research by situating it too firmly in any one set of historical coordinates or assumptions (such as Sovietology, for example), lest we be swept out to sea by the tides of change. I would like to close this introduction by taking precisely that risk, if for no other reason than a perverse curiosity about the experience of being swept out to sea.

At the time of this writing, debates rage in Moscow about the final dispensation, seventy years late, of Lenin's remains. It is an interesting problem, since, as a dead leader, he cannot be buried without ritual, yet no appropriate ritual remains. So far the debate has focused on kinship and geography, on whether he is to be buried—as he had wished—beside his mother in Saint Petersburg (formerly Leningrad, after his revolutionary pseudonym) or beside his father in Simbirsk (formerly Ulianovsk, after his family name), or even whether he is to be left alone in the Mausoleum, also under threat of removal from Red Square. However these issues are resolved (and they may indeed be resolved by the time this volume reaches its readers' hands), they are perhaps less interesting than the ritual itself, for the burial cannot proceed without ritual, if only that ritual by which state, political, religious, civic, and other institutions dissociate themselves rhetorically from that burial process. As Russian political leaders and recovering Sovietologists have learned the hard way, no political act in Russia is without broad cultural significance and no single significance is exempt from usurpation. My hope is that the readers of this collection—by then, perhaps, informed of how this final Leninist conundrum is resolved—will appreciate with me both the ceremony and the silence that will inevitably accompany the event.[18]

I wish to thank my colleagues and members of the Working Group, as well as those who worked to bring about the London meeting: Alastair Brison, Colin MacCabe, Radojka Miljevich, Deac Rossell, and Kate Stables. The School of Slavonic Studies (University of London) provided unstinting support in hosting our meeting. Special thanks are extended to Helena Goscilo, who organized the London meeting, and Vladimir Padunov, who served with me as director of the four-year project. The Russian and East European Studies Center of the University of Pittsburgh provided generous support in the preparation of the manuscript.

The Working Group on Contemporary Russian Culture was supported by the Joint Committee on the Soviet Union and Its Successor States (American Council of Learned Societies/Social Science Research Council) with funds from the Mellon Foundation. Additional funding and support for the Working Group was provided by the John D. and Catherine T. MacArthur Foundation, the Soros Foundation, the British Film Institute, and the National Film Theatre, the journal Ogonek [Little Flame], the Diagilev Center, and Russkoe Kino [Russian Cinema].

The editor owes a special debt of gratitude to Christiane Loch Dutton, Rebecca Einhorn, Carol Leonard, and Sherrie Windish for their help and encouragement, as well as to Kira and Nikolai, two small and very patient children, for their drawings of our family on the back of earlier drafts of this manuscript.

Notes

1. Greta Slobin initiated the first of several brief but fruitful exchanges on this subject and Alla Efimova's presentation at the University of California, Berkeley in June 1991 revived my interest in Communism's visual display. For a further development of Efimova's work, see her *Tekstura*.

2. For the purposes of this essay, I define this as extending from 7 November 1917 through 25 December 1991. Clearly, we can argue to our hearts' content about either end of this spectrum; more specifically, some literary scholars might prefer 1932 as a starting point, in order better to tell the story of Communism's betrayal of the avant-garde. Regardless of its accuracy, this story is also narratively convenient, since it proposes a model whereby two distinct and separate entities—politics and culture—resituate themselves *vis-à-vis* each other: politics precedes culture in choosing the wrong path; culture thereby has implicitly less fundamental culpability for what followed next, being itself a hostage and a victim to the accomplished fact of 1917. This position, admittedly reduced here to absurd schematism, is no longer convincing; indeed it would be more sensible to suggest that neither politics nor culture underwent any radical shift in 1917. We miss much if we "count" Soviet culture only from 1932. Beginning there not only destroys significant cultural modulations within the 1920s; it implicitly encourages a truncation of post-1953 culture by its reduction of "Soviet" to "Stalinist," a position that is polemically appealing but wrongheaded.

3. Some of the key texts in this discussion are by Clark, Dunham, and James.

4. Both visuality and authors' books are discussed at greater length by Vladimir Padunov in Chapter 7 of this volume and in Condee and Padunov, "Proigrannyi rai" 75–77.

5. An interesting example of several processes simultaneously present in the production of a single text (or set of related texts) is the six-video cassette series *Shakespeare: The Animated Tales* (Random House Home Video), which makes use of (much less expensive) Russian animators from Soiuzmul'tfil'm and includes a *Hamlet* using Russian glass-painting techniques virtually unknown in the West. Lightyear Entertainment also makes extensive use of Russian animators from the elegantly named Klassika Studio in Moscow. Here may be discerned the redefinition of book as visual text, the recasting of high culture into a "low" medium, and the use of the Russian as an impoverished but highly trained artisan who still retains skills needed by the Western culture industry.

6. See Epshtein, Prater, Tupitsyn, and Zinik, as well as articles by Bakshtein, Sussman, Tupitsyn, and Wollen in Ross, *Between Spring and Summer* for some of the best work on Moscow Conceptualism.

7. Nor was its potential export value—i.e., its hard-currency [*valiuta*] value—left solely to benefit the Conceptualist pocket. "The exotica of Communist totalitarianism," Groys remarks, "is, like oil and caviar, one of the few goods the country can export to the West" ("On the Ethics" 112).

8. The linking of the Stalin years to debates on utopia is itself an assailable position, of course. Richard Stites has argued most eloquently against this linkage in his contri-

Introduction

bution to *The Culture of the Stalin Period* and elsewhere; Boris Groys has offered the most exhaustive interpretation of Stalin culture as a utopia sharing certain features with that of the avant-garde. However much the Stalin years were indeed marked by a frenzied attempt to dismantle utopian models of the 1920s, those efforts were fueled by a state scheme of a different order. Reduced to its simplest components, the point of contention was not utopia versus something else (dystopia, totalitarianism) but between individual and state utopias. The 1930s witnessed, to use Hans Günther's term, the *Verstaatlichung* of utopian construction.

9. As if this were not enough, the Russian parliament's central position as the key image on the Russian 10,000-ruble voucher note was an inadvertently eloquent reminder of the risks of citizen investment in Russia's economic future.

10. One could argue, of course, that the reversion process actually began six years earlier in 1985, in both the political and cultural arenas, and is still incomplete today, for not only does *Homo sovieticus* still walk the earth, the Soviet Union still exists, if only as a vision (like monarchy) of the future. Like Gagarin in his spaceship, the Soviet Union has simply become more utopian than we had previously thought possible.

11. Of the many responses to this manifesto, Aleksandr Genis's article is the most interesting and provocative.

12. For brevity's sake, I have left out Dmitrii Aleksandrovich Prigov, who is also Pushkin (see Works Cited).

13. Director Stanislav Govorukhin, an outspoken anti-Yeltsin patriot with strong political ambitions (currently focused on the Democratic Party of Russia), is also well aware that Solzhenitsyn still has the potential to draw upon dissatisfied conservatives and yet has no political aspirations to office that might conflict with Govorukhin's own.

14. For an extensive treatment of this phenomenon, see Gasparov, Hughes, and Paperno.

15. Over thirteen major advertising firms already exist in Russia, including Premier, Begemot, NTD, ESCART, OK, Solidarnost' [Solidarity], Capital, Gratis, and Sasha. Avrora [Aurora] is the largest and oldest company. Other Western ad agencies, such as BBDO, have aggressively hired Russian staff. In addition to its own professional journals, *Reklama* [*Advertisement*] and *Prism*, the industry has also organized itself around four advertising associations: the Association of Advertising Workers, the Foundation for Support of Advertising Producers, the Russian Association of Advertisers, and the Russian Association of Advertising Agencies. A newly founded lobbying organization, the Coalition for Objective Information, works to rescind and limit laws governing advertising, such as Article 19 ("Basic Principles of the Russian Federation's Legislation on the Protection of Citizens' Health"), which forbids the advertisement of cigarettes and alcohol in the mass media. On rock video and the video clip industry, see "Generation '93," *Gumanitarnyi fond* [*Humanities Foundation*].

16. For an exception to this trend, see coverage of the team working on the Manezh project under Aleksandr Veksler of the Archaeological Research Institute in, inter alia, the *New York Times* 14 October 1993.

17. A variation on the socialist utopia/Western theme park is already in the making in Prenden, a former army base located twenty miles north of Berlin in the former German Democratic Republic. The entrepreneurs, a Berlin investment concern, plan to transform the base into a totalitarian microculture complete with police, spies, and informers, as well as a hard-currency hotel, Trabants, and GDR consumer items, bought for GDR "currency." The expectation of success in the venture, which requires an anticipated investment of $32 million to $62 million, is based in part on the success of a work-

ing museum in Berlin, located in the former Communist youth league's headquarters, which currently attracts hundreds of visitors daily (*New York Times* 9 November 1993). The principal cause for concern is that the theme park will become either a political gathering point for extreme right-wing Stalinists or a target of hostility for former dissidents, both of whom "confuse" fantasy dystopia with something else.

18. At stake, so to speak, is not just the fate of Lenin's body, but also that of the other political leaders buried in the Kremlin wall, including Leonid Brezhnev, Iurii Andropov, Konstantin Chernenko, and, of course, Joseph Stalin himself.

Works Cited

Adler, Kathleen, ed. *The Body Imagined: The Human Form and Visual Culture Since the Renaissance.* New York: Cambridge UP, 1993.

Clark, Katerina. *The Soviet Novel: History as Ritual.* 2nd ed. Chicago: U of Chicago P, 1985.

Condee, Nancy, and Vladimir Padunov. "Frontiers of Soviet Culture: Reaching the Limits?" *The Harriman Institute Forum* 1.5 (1988): 1–8.

———. "Proigrannyi rai: ruletka sotsializma, rynochnyi determinizm i postmodernizm po ob'iazatel'noi programme." *Iskusstvo kino* 9 (1992): 72–81.

Crary, Jonathan. *Techniques of the Observer: On Vision and Modernity in the Nineteenth Century.* Boston: MIT P, 1990.

Dagognet, François. *Etienne-Jules Marey: A Passion for the Trace.* New York: Zone, 1992.

Dunham, Vera S. *In Stalin's Time: Middleclass Values in Soviet Fiction.* Enlarged and updated. Durham, NC: Duke UP, 1990.

Efimova, Alla, and Lev Manovich, eds. and trs. *Tekstura: Russian Essays on Visual Culture.* Chicago: U of Chicago P, 1993.

Èpshtein, Mikhail. "Tezisy o metarealizme i kontseptualizme." Unpublished essay, 8 June 1983.

Fitzpatrick, Sheila, ed. *Cultural Revolution in Russia, 1928–1931.* Bloomington: Indiana UP, 1984.

Fitzpatrick, Sheila, Alexander Rabinowitch, and Richard Stites, eds. *Russia in the Era of NEP: Explorations in Soviet Society and Culture.* Bloomington: Indiana UP, 1991.

Gasparov, Boris, Robert Hughes, and Irina Paperno, eds. *Cultural Mythologies of Russian Modernism: From the Golden Age to the Silver Age.* Berkeley: U of California P, 1992.

"Generation '93," *Gumanitarnyi fond* 1 (23–178) (1993): 8.

Genis, Aleksandr. "Solzhenitsyn protiv postmodernistov." *panorama* 10–16 March 1993.

Gleason, Abbott, Peter Kenez, and Richard Stites, eds. *Bolshevik Culture: Experiment and Order in the Russian Revolution.* Bloomington: Indiana UP, 1985.

Groys, Boris. "On the Ethics of the Avant-Garde." *Art in America* (May 1993): 110–13.

———. *The Total Art of Stalinism: Avant-Garde, Aesthetic Dictatorship, and Beyond.* Tr. Charles Rougle. Princeton: Princeton UP, 1992.

Günther, Hans, ed. *The Culture of the Stalin Period.* New York: St. Martin's P, 1990.

———. *Die Verstaatlichung der Literatur: Entstehung und Funktionsweise des sozialistisch-realistischen Kanons in der sowjetischen Literatur der 30er Jahre.* Stuttgart: Metzler, 1984.

James, C. Vaughn. *Soviet Socialist Realism: Origins and Theory.* New York: Saint Martin's P, 1973.

Krauss, Rosalind E. *The Optical Unconscious.* Boston: MIT P, 1993.

Introduction

Kruger, Barbara. *Remote Control: Power, Cultures, and the World of Appearances*. Boston: MIT P, 1993.

Llewellyn, Nigel. *The Art of Death: Visual Culture and the English Death Ritual c. 1500–c. 1800*. London: Reaktion, 1991.

Metropol'. Ed. Vasilii Aksenov, Andrei Bitov, Viktor Erofeev, et al. Facsimile edition. Ann Arbor: Ardis, 1979. English translation: *Metropol: Literary Almanac*. New York: Norton, 1982.

New York Times 2 October 1993.

New York Times 14 October 1993.

New York Times 9 November 1993.

Novikov, Vladimir. "Iz sora vyrastut stikhi," *Rossiiskie vesti* 24 July 1993.

Prater, Scott. "Socialist Realism is Dead . . . Long Live Socialist Realism! or The Murder of Socialist Realism by Postmodernism and Its Conceptualist Wake." Unpublished essay, 19 April 1991.

"Prigov kak Pushkin." Conversation between Dmitrii Prigov and Andrei Zorin. *Teatr* 1 (1993): 116–43.

Riegl, Alois. "The Modern Cult of Monuments: Its Character and Its Origin." *Oppositions* 24 (Fall 1982): 21–51.

Ross, David A., ed. *Between Spring and Summer: Soviet Conceptual Art in the Era of Late Communism*. Cambridge, MA: MIT P, 1990.

Solzhenitsyn, Alexander. "The Relentless Cult of Novelty and How It Wrecked the Century." *New York Times Book Review* 7 February 1993.

Stafford, Barbara Maria. *Body Criticism: Imaging the Unseen in Enlightenment Art and Medicine*. Boston: MIT P, 1991.

Stanford Slavic Studies. Russian Culture in Transition: Selected Papers of the Working Group for the Study of Contemporary Russian Culture, 1990–1991. Vol. 7 (1993). Ed. Gregory Freidin.

Stites, Richard. "Stalin: Utopian or Antiutopian?" *The Cult of Power: Dictators in the Twentieth Century. East European Quarterly* 10 (1983); East European Monograph 140. Ed. Joseph Heid. 77–93.

———. "Stalinism and the Restructuring of Revolutionary Utopianism." See Günther, *The Culture of the Stalin Period*, 78–94.

Tarusskie stranitsy: literaturno-khudozestvennyi illiustrirovannyi sbornik. Ed. V. Koblikov, N. Otten, N. Panchenko, et al. Kaluga: Kaluzhskoe knizh. izd., 1961. English translation: *Pages from Tarusa: New Voices in Russian Writing*. Ed. Andrew Field. Boston: Little, Brown, 1964.

Tupitsyn, Margarita. "From Sots Art to SovArt: A Story of the Moscow Vanguard." *Flashart* (November/December 1987): 75–80.

Zinik, Zinovy. "vitaly komar-alexandr melamid." Tr. Jamey Gambrell. *A-Ya* 7 (1986): 18–24.

Note on Transliteration, Translation, and Citation

In transliterating from Russian into English, I have generally used the modified Library of Congress Transliteration System, also known as System II in J. Thomas Shaw's *The Transliteration of Modern Russian for English-Language Publications* (New York: MLA, 1979). Where English-language custom has overwhelmingly dictated a particular spelling ("Bolshevik" instead of "Bol'shevik," "Tchaikovsky" instead of "Chaikovskii," "Yeltsin" instead of "El'tsin"), I have accommodated that usage.

Because this volume is intended for both specialist and nonspecialist, quotations are given in English, with Russian in brackets only where absolutely necessary to clarify or specify original intent. Likewise, titles of films, television shows, board games, books, stories, poems, plays, and spectacles, as well as foundations, are given in English, with Russian in brackets when first mentioned. Unless otherwise noted, the translations are by the scholars themselves.

Periodicals, television series, publishers, and stores, many of which are more familiar to the educated reader in the original Russian, are cited in Russian with English translation in brackets at first mention: *Pravda* [*Truth*], *Vremia* [*Time*], Moskovskii rabochii [Moscow Worker Publishing], and Dom knigi [House of Books]. Subsequent references are in the original only: *Pravda.*

The notes, presumably of greater interest to the Russian-speaking specialist, cite sources in their original language only.

Soviet Hieroglyphics

One

Aural Hieroglyphics?
Some Reflections on the Role of Sound in Recent Russian Films and Its Historical Context

Katerina Clark

Toward the end of Vitalii Kanevskii's *Freeze, Die, Come to Life* [*Zamri, umri, voskresni,* 1990], the two pre-teenage protagonists, Valerka and Galiia, are walking home along a railroad track after barely escaping from a bandit gang who want to kill them because they believe the children may report them. It is the late Stalin period, and it is a strange home to which the friends are returning, the settlement attached to a prison camp and mine in Suchan in the Soviet Far East. Galiia's father is a truck driver who works with the prisoners, while Valerka's single mother who mans the buffet at the miners' club frequently locks him out of their squalid barracks room while she gives easy sexual favors to local men, many of them camp guards. But it is home, nevertheless. As they walk along the sleepers, Valerka sings to Galiia one of those sentimental romances that were popular among children of that age (allegedly taught him by one of the bandits). It tells of a young pair who loved each other so strongly even though they "were still children" that they vowed never to forget each other.

There is a break, and the song resumes with its young man, now a pilot, saying, "If you don't love me, it's no use." He turns away from the controls and "the motor races to the ground," the propeller sticks up motionless as the dying man whispers his last words, "If you don't love me, it's no use." When the girl of the song learns that her old love has been killed in a plane crash she, having in the meantime trained as a pilot herself, takes her plane high into the skies and then throws herself out without a parachute.

Valerka's song is the closest he and Galiia have come to declaring their deep attachment to each other; until this point, their exchanges have followed the patterns of the dog-eat-dog adult world around them. Galiia asks Valerka to sing the song again, and the camera leaves the pair and pans around a landscape of gentle hills and woods; this is, essentially, the first time that the camera has abandoned its relentless focus on the mud and dereliction so typical of recent Russian cinema. The Edenic stillness is broken by the sounds of running, a shout, two almost muffled bangs and then an "*Oi*"; the bandits, whom the audience (but not the children) sees leering out of a freight train that had passed earlier, had come back to kill them. In the next scene, Galiia's body is brought back to the settlement on a railway trolley and we learn that Valerka is in hospital. Galiia's mother, naked and with her hair streaming behind her, rushes around aimlessly on a broomstick, screaming in her crazed grief as two anonymous small children among the bystanders stare impassively at the scene.

Such, then, is the dramatic climax with all its tragic elements—young life snuffed out, a love that can never see fulfillment, a mother's inconsolable grief, and children who grow up in a place where the joys of childhood are denied them. But I want to focus here on the song about the two lovers that prefigures and heightens the tragic dénouement. The story of the woman pilot who, in her crazed grief, throws herself out of her plane without a parachute represents an inversion of a key myth of High Stalinism, capsulely present in "The March of the Aviators" [*Avia-marsh* or *Vse vyshe*], a song that every former Soviet who grew up in the 1930s or 1940s remembers from those times and that, with its specific mention of the motor and the propeller, is probably an intended referent here[1]:

> We were born that fairy tales might become reality,
> To conquer the vastness of space.
> Reason gave us steel wings for arms,
> And, in place of a heart, a fiery motor.
>
> Ever higher and higher and higher
> We urge on our bird's flight,
> And in every propeller there breathes
> Peace for our borders.

The lovers were not meant to crash down to their deaths, but to go ever "higher." Nor were they meant to have experienced such compelling love and desperate grief ("in place of a heart, a fiery motor"). Their raison d'être was to reach for the heights and thereby guard the borders. Rather than wilfully crash to the ground, the woman aviator should have descended as a crack paratrooper, another group inscribed in the key myths of Stalinist culture. The paratroopers are, for example, celebrated in the famous "Busby Berkeley" sequences at the end of Grigorii Aleksandrov's *The Circus* [*Tsirk*, 1936], while in Dziga Vertov's *Lullaby* [*Kolybel'naia*, 1937] the ultimate in

Aural Hieroglyphics?

women's liberation promised by the new society was that baby girls could grow up to become parachutists.

The Icarian tragedy is caught most economically in the discrepancy between the events of Valerka's song and the opening line of "The March of the Aviators": "We were born that fairy tales might become reality." The point in Kanevskii's cryptic inversion of this myth is not that there was a tragedy; Soviet official culture is redolent with tales of tragic deaths, the bread and butter of most legitimating myth systems (consider the principal exemplum for Soviet children: the young boy Pavel Morozov, who died a martyr's death in 1932 at the hands of the "kulaks," after he denounced his own father to the authorities). Rather, the tragedy consists in the fact that the heroic grandeur of the promised genre (the "fairy tale") was never achieved, a point hammered home in this film in a variety of ways, including the insistent foregrounding of mud and dilapidation.

I focus here on the role of a song in a recent film not merely to decode it in terms of hidden political commentary, or "aural hieroglyphics"; I am suggesting a historical context for the fact that—in recent Russian films—songs, music, and, as we shall see, sound generally have played a particularly crucial role. Many movies today have very little musical sound track in the conventional sense.[2] Music does not fulfill its usual film function of setting a mood or suggesting the import of a scene: swelling music for the welling emotions; music that forebodes danger; the solo saxophone to suggest melancholy or loneliness; fast music to emphasize the hectic pace of the chase. In some recent films, snatches of songs, generally sung by one of the protagonists, punctuate the narrative; background music may provide a wordless version of a recognizable song.[3]

Thus the music on the sound track does not have an auxiliary or casual function; it is a medium through which some of the main points are made. Commonly, songs well known from the Stalin era have been used as an aural equivalent of such visual bric-a-brac as posters with slogans, portraits or busts of Stalin and Lenin, and even the telltale cornices of the Stalinist apartment block[4], as a cryptic subtext suggesting the hollow, crude or sinister nature of Stalinist culture. Thus, in one of the more heavy-handed uses of music in *Freeze, Die, Come to Life*, for instance, a parade of schoolchildren marching to mark a revolutionary holiday (presumably May Day) keeps balking and refusing to go on because the route before them is awash with effluent from the school sewers, which overflowed when someone (Valerka, as it turns out) put yeast in them. As the children keep balking, their school director orders them to march and sing the lines of the patriotic anthem, "Ebullient, mighty [*moguchaia*] . . . my country. . . . " Inevitably some of the children sneak in an "Ebullient, stinky [*voniuchaia*—i.e., it rhymes] . . . ," which leads to an investigation by the school director.

In many films, music and song appear less as a code per se than as an emblem of a worldview.[5] Most frequently, rock music and jazz—forms that have had, and continue to have, a problematical status in the Soviet Union/ Russia—are foregrounded as emblems of the eccentric and nonconformist, of the carnival,[6] or of Western sensibilities.[7] The rock movie itself, one of the most common genres since perestroika, I have largely excluded from my purview here for reasons of space. With increasing frequency, however, whether a film is set in the present or the past, the old songs play a crucial role in it.

The films that use the old songs depend on the audience's ability to recognize them and to know their significance. A great variety is represented: official songs; outright propagandistic songs; songs from the revolutionary era; songs from the Second World War; popular songs from the old films; other genuinely popular songs from the Stalin era (mostly of love); prerevolutionary or émigré romances; songs from the camps or underworld; and songs from verses by classical writers. Sometimes simulations of one or another genre are composed for a given film, but more often directors are concerned to present authentic and widely known songs.[8] In some instances, however, songs of one type are sung in a film with the style or inflection of another. In *Freeze, Die, Come to Life*, for instance, some war songs are sung in the style of the camp songs. Thus, the shadings can be quite subtle.[9]

Arguably, such songs do not function merely as part of the political subtext, as hieroglyphs, which must be decoded by an initiated audience. Nor is the function of the songs purely thematic. The prominence of the old songs in so many recent films has to do with the centrality and function of song and music in the Soviet era.

As Richard Stites and others have pointed out, songs played a crucial role in the culture of the Stalin years.[10] Even today they represent, as it were, the common treasury in the cultural memory of the populace—workers, bureaucrats, farmers, and intellectuals alike; in large degree, attachment to the old songs even cuts across the hardening political lines. Old musical films of the 1930s, 1940s, and 1950s are still shown on television, and the audience often knows the words of the songs and sings along, with nostalgia.[11] Such songs provide less complicated filiations going back into the past than could be provided by literature or art. Even people who were born after the Stalin era often treasure these songs and have memorized them. Old and even cracked records from the 1930s remain treasured objects to be shared with friends at a high point of a party.

Thus, many still love to sing the songs that a Western observer might see as somewhat propagandistic, yet almost everyone draws a line somewhere between "a good song" and "sheer propaganda." (Or, in the case of the more diehard and nationalist zealot, the line might be between good old songs and those clearly tainted with some kind of Westernism or moral laxness). Many Soviet mothers not necessarily enamored of the regime have sung their children to sleep with its lullaby, which is about how someone from an ethnic minority need not fear persecution in (Stalin's) Soviet Union, where all the nationalities live in harmony. Sung with similar affection is Liubov' Orlova's song as she swings on a "moon" high above the circus crowd. But some draw a line at the film's main song, "Broad Is My Native Land" [*Shiroka strana moia rodnaia*], also known as "Song of the Motherland" [*Pesnia o rodine*], placing it in that totally separate category of "sheer propaganda." (After all, the last two lines of the refrain proclaim that nowhere else does one breathe so freely). In the 1930s, however, the song was one of the decade's greatest hits and also functioned as, de facto, an auxiliary national anthem.

In a sense, the music of Stalinist culture, especially the popular songs, is the element of greatest ambiguity. It comes from such a problematical time; yet it continues to be popular and to suggest a take on the 1930s to which many subscribed at the time: as the slogan ran, "Life has become better, Life has become gayer." Indeed, some recent films have formed part of a wave of reaction against the depiction of the Stalin era in only the most grim colors (as it is depicted in *Freeze, Die, Come to Life*).

One of the most prominent of them, Ivan Dykhnovichnyi's *Moscow Parade* [*Prorva*, 1992] celebrates what critics are calling "the Stalinist *belle époque*," as a time with its own aesthetic and (for the privileged) distinct charm (Zorkaia 3–9). *Moscow Parade* presents the era of the Great Purge as a sort of belated "Jazz Age," complete with sexual hedonism, tennis creams, parties, cruise ships and smoky cafés with *chanteuses* and jazz orchestras. Indeed, in its choice for the film's leading role (the wife of an NKVD official) of the German *chanteuse* Ute Lemper—who lives in England, frequently performs in France (and recently in America), and sings in the film in German, English, French, and Russian—the film even suggests that the "new class" of this singularly xenophobic country partook of an international culture of the leisured. Lemper's own repertoire includes Brecht, Piaf, and, of course, Marlene Dietrich, on whom she is particularly stylized,

Katerina Clark

as was the heroine of Aleksandrov's *The Circus*, which also culminates in a parade on Red Square (Dobrotvorskaia 30).

But the celebration of "totalitarian kitsch" is not sustained. The film's very Russian title—*Prorva*—means both "an excessively large amount" of something (suggesting the grotesque aspect of Stalinist monumentalism) and "the abyss" at the edge of which all were standing (and into which many of the protagonists fell in a roundup at the end). The sparkling white of the clothing and decorations in the film, the exuberant fountains by which the protagonists meet, the popping champagne corks, and so forth all have a dark aspect as well.

"Totalitarian kitsch" is not merely a matter of stylization and spectacular photography. It alludes to the way the 1930s aspired to achieve an aesthetic system.

Music in the films of the 1930s and 1940s functioned not merely as soft-sell propaganda (much of which still "sells" today, after the regime it was supporting melted away). There is a reason why music played such an important role in films of the Stalin era, one which cannot be accounted for solely in terms of the necessity of providing a "gay" counterpoint to Stalinist repressiveness, or in terms of the fact that Boris Shumiatskii (for most of the 1930s, the head of Soviet cinema), director Grigorii Aleksandrov, and others believed in the potential of "transcoding" the American musical to the Soviet context (the 1930s equivalent of the "Red Pinkerton,"—i.e., the officially sponsored attempt by writers of the early to middle 1920s at transcoding the conventions of popular Western adventure and detective fiction to a Soviet context).

The pivotal role of music in Soviet film of the 1930s was not just for crudely propagandistic purposes. It is no accident that some of the major names of creative life were involved in working in some way on musical films, music for films, or on film theories that gave music a prominent role (names that come to mind include Grigorii Kozintsev and Leonid Trauberg (the leaders of an avant-gardist group of the 1920s known as FEKS), Dmitrii Shostakovich, Sergei Prokofiev, Nikolai Erdman, Il'f and Petrov, Isaak Babel'—and Sergei Eisenstein himself. To some degree, this can be accounted for in terms of the necessity for each of earning income, or of state-sponsored policies, but by no means entirely. Not all interpretations of the role and kind of "music" appropriate to Soviet culture were acceptable to the state. One hardly needs to be reminded that the central document of the anti-Formalist official campaign of the 1930s was the 1936 attack on a Shostakovich opera under the rubric "Muddle Instead of Music" [*Sumbur vmesto muzyki*].[12] Similarly, beneath the rollicking fun and good-humored banter

Aural Hieroglyphics?

of Aleksandrov's musical *Volga-Volga* (1938) is a sinisterly restrictive cultural model presented in terms of what makes good—and appealing—music. But to understand the centrality of music in film of the 1930s one has to look at its prehistory in debates about revolutionary culture and its practice.

At about the time of the 1917 revolution in Russia, many intellectuals and intellectual movements (most notably in the theater and performing arts, but also to some extent in literature and other branches of the arts) were captivated by the potential of "music" as a formula for cultural regeneration and, often, through it, for societal regeneration as well. Here the notion of "music" should not be taken too literally; what was often intended was some system for the rhythmic orchestration of sound and, where appropriate, bodily movement in *performance*. This was a time when a range of arts was in vogue that foregrounded oral performance, such as oratory and a sense of poetry that emphasized the sound and rhythmic aspects of verse (see, e.g., the work of the Formalists and Futurist "trans-sense" poetry [*zaum*]). In general, orchestration of sound and rhythm was privileged over written texts. In extreme versions, enthusiasts called for replacing the texts of "plays" with eurythmics or pantomime (Znosko-Borovskii, Ashkinazi). One sees a less extreme implementation of these prejudices in the directorial work of Meyerhold both before and after the revolution; in many of his landmark productions, some musical form, such as a casual dance rhythm or a melodic walk, functioned as a sort of *dominanta*, defining individual scenes or characters to the extent that not merely their bodily and vocal gestures, but even the deployment of props and so forth were subordinated to it.[13] One could even see an analog to this trend in the work of Aleksei Gastev, A. A. Ukhtomsky, and others on systematizing bodily movement in the workplace to maximize efficiency.

Here one could talk in terms of the "influence" of theories by figures like Nietzsche and Wagner, although in many instances the Russian theoreticians had transcoded these theories in an idiosyncratic way. Many shared Nietzsche's dream that they might preside again over "The Birth of Tragedy Out of the Spirit of Music." First trying to recapture "the spirit of music" that had been perverted by a "bourgeois" obtuseness and a "petty-bourgeois" commercialism, and then to give back to society that high genre of "tragedy" that must of necessity elude it in an age relentlessly pursuing profit, comfort, amusement, and other such trivial ends, had become the aims of a large segment of Russian intellectuals (their accounts of this "music" were, of course, inevitably various).

This was, then, essentially the agenda of an aesthetic utopianism that sought to recapture a pre-Babelian purity where everyone spoke the same

Katerina Clark

language and there were no differences. As in Nietzsche and Wagner, "music" also provided the formula for regaining a lost *Einheit* and overcoming the alienation that attended the loss of unity among the different branches of the arts.

It is not difficult to see that the dream of a kind of totalizing culture that would be universally applicable dovetailed in some respects with the aims of the Bolsheviks, who were no less bent on driving out "bourgeois" individualism. "Music" was also commonly represented as that aspect of art that is the most authentic. The concomitant prejudices of Nietzsche, Wagner, and others against arid intellectualizing—mere words—also inform a great deal of Bolshevik culture, where the sterile and verbose intellectual is contrasted with the worker-Bolshevik who is "poor in words" but can get to the heart of the matter. The privileging of "music" over words and ratiocination is parodied in Tengiz Abuladze's *Repentance* [*Pokaianie*, 1986]: after the hero is arrested and his wife goes to see her friend in the Party bureaucracy in order that the friend might explain and reverse this miscarriage of justice, the friend begins by trying to rationalize it, but soon shifts to singing the "Ode to Joy" from Beethoven's "Ninth Symphony," whereupon an orchestra and choir take over the rendition and the music swells to a deafening crescendo.

Repentance, through the musical ambitions of its tyrant antihero Varlaam Aravidze, also satirizes Stalin's pretensions to being a connoisseur (and perhaps even performer) of opera.[14] This fact about the "great leader" is, of course, an aspect of his claims to authority in intellectual and cultural areas, to act as arbiter of the worth of many films and novels, and in his "authorship" of the essay on linguistics. Opera was also an important genre for intellectuals, however. As the principal focus of Wagner's theory of the *Gesamtkunstwerk*, opera was not just a genre in which people sing in costumes, but one that was particularly valued because it was able most comprehensively to organize a range of the arts into a single totality. It offered the possibility of a more exalted kind of experience than was to be found in ordinary life. A thirst for this more exalted experience and greater intensity, whether nominated "tragedy" or "opera," led many to join that great joint stock company that was Stalinist culture.

"Music," then, played an important role in the quasi-religious aspects of the Bolshevik cultural experiment. It became, as it were, both a symbolic form and a medium for breaking through beyond the quotidian to something grander, if not transcendent. The movement was also influenced by the dreams of Viacheslav Ivanov and others for achieving "true collectivity" [*sobornost'*] in theatrical rituals. Ivanov (before retreating to Baku), like many others influenced by Nietzsche or Wagner, played a prominent role in formulating early policy for the so-called "people's theater" of revolutionary Russia (Ivanov, "*Doklad*" 4; "*O Vagnere*" 8–9).

The apotheosis of the movement for a "people's theater" was the mass spectacle—to some extent, the paradigmatic expression of early Soviet revolutionary culture. In these spectacles, music also played a pivotal role; revolutionary progress was most often motivated by visual and auditory symbols rather than reasoned dialogue (not entirely practical in a vast, open-air arena) or even by the events represented. The dominant strategy for representing the class war was often as a duel of musics. Thus, among the most famous spectacles of that most utopian of postrevolutionary years, 1920, in *The Mystery of Liberated Labor* [*Misteriia osvobozhdennogo truda*] the signature tune of the oppressed classes was initially Chopin's "Funeral March," while for their oppressors it was the more frivolous and lowbrow gypsy music, but increasingly the oppressed were able to hear the strains of a "heavenly" music issuing from the "Kingdom of Freedom" they sought to attain—music from Wagner's *Lohengrin*—and the measure of their ultimate triumph in the political arena was the way this music drowned out the gypsy completely. Analogously, in *The Storming of the Winter Palace* [*Vziatie zimnego dvortsa*], the duel of musics was between "The Marseillaise" (used to represent the Provisional Government), played progressively more and more out of tune, and "The Internationale," which drowned out "The Marseillaise" in the end. A similar convention was to be found in theatrical productions throughout the 1920s.[15]

The duel of musics was not, of course, per se new to Soviet culture—consider Tchaikovsky's "1812 Overture" and works by Haydn and others before him. The point here is that this convention acquired a particular ideological resonance. An identification was made between *type* of music and worldview, and this kind of identification proved fundamental in Soviet cultural history.

In the 1930s, the practice of representing class and ideological conflicts in a duel of musics had far from disappeared. Consider, for instance, the pointed contrast in Kozintsev and Trauberg's *The Youth of Maksim* [*Iunost' Maksima*, 1934] between the kind of music played in its Prologue to represent the doomed bourgeoisie—a medley composed by Shostakovich that includes the popular dance known as the "Oira-oira" ("the most stupid music on earth" [Kozintsev, "Lektsii" 97]), the music of the cancan, and gypsy music—and the songs from the workers' suburbs and revolutionary movement sung in the rest of the film where, most pointedly, the directors used not composed, orchestral music (as in the Prologue), but authentic songs rendered by unaccompanied voice or accordion (as in *Freeze, Die, Come to Life*). Or consider Aleksandrov's *Volga-Volga*, where much of the plot revolves around a duel of musics between the kind favored by the unspoiled "girl of the people," Liubov' Orlova, and the more Westernized, intellectual, and modernist music of her male opposite number (a duel resolved, predictably, as he sees the light).

Much more significant than these echoes of conventions from the 1920s is the lingering conviction among many of the most famous film directors that the music for a film is in no way auxiliary to its script, but should be the dominant element, to which even the script should be subordinated. This conviction is clear, for instance, in Aleksandrov's later account of how he directed his famous Stalinist musicals of the 1930s and the close involvement of the composer I. O. Dunaevskii in the script itself. In his account of the work on *The Circus*, for example, Aleksandrov states,

> We considered music the most fundamental component in the film and hence subordinated to it not only the dynamic and emotional development of the plot, but the entire rhythm of the new film as well. Long before we began shooting, Dunaevskii and I worked out a detailed musical scenario and partitura for it. The dramatic development of the musical themes often affected the script . . . [which] would be shortened or adjusted to coordinate with the score. . . . Before so much as a single meter of film was shot, we worked out entire scenes with great care, making them accurate to the second. In order to make a truly musical film, we shot our film in accordance with a finished soundtrack. (Aleksandrov 231, see also 192–93, 196–97, 234, 235)

Aleksandrov goes on to claim how ahead of his time he was in giving music such a dominant role, as compared with musical cinema in America.

What in Aleksandrov is represented largely as the key approach to making musical films acquires in Eisenstein's essays of the 1930s and early 1940s the status of a fundamental principle of filmic construction, the equivalent in his theoretical work of that decade to "montage" in his theories of the 1920s. In, for instance, his essay "Vertical Montage" (1940),[16] about the principles that guided his production of *Aleksandr Nevskii* (1938), Eisenstein writes of his main aim of achieving "that mysterious" "*inner synchronicity between picture and music*" (*Selected Works* 2: 334, 330; emphasis in original). His theories here are more subtle and complex than the recipes of Aleksandrov; Eisenstein maintains that it is not material whether the script is adjusted to the film's music or vice versa, because what is important is "not absolute, literal concordance between sound and picture," not a "naive congruence" where the music merely illustrates what is represented on the screen, but other, more complex varieties of compositional and structural congruence, whether graphic, tonal, from "gesture and intonation," or from isomorphy in the trajectories of movement on the screen, both rhythmic and melodic (*Selected Works* 2: 328–77).

Such an inner synchronicity is for Eisenstein not just a formal desideratum, but of fundamental significance. Just as in his earlier account of montage he gave his techniques, simultaneously, both a formal and an ideological dimension,[17] here the inner synchronicity is part of a recuperative project with reverberations well beyond the silver screen. Eisenstein even cites the Greeks, Wagner, and Nietzsche among the predecessors who have sought similar ends. "At all stages, the arts have striven *for single wholeness and a higher unity*," he writes. "It is only in the era of imperialism triumphant and of the beginning of decadence in the arts that *centripetal* movement reverses into one that is *centrifugal*, which flings aside all such tendencies toward unity, tendencies incompatible with the dominance of all-pervasive individuation." Eisenstein then continues immediately, "Let us recall Nietzsche," adducing a long quotation from *The Case of Wagner* about how "the *whole*" is "no longer imbued with life" when the individual word "becomes sovereign" and the work becomes "a collection of parts, calculated, artificial" (Eisenstein, *Selected Works* 2: 377, 344; emphasis in original).

Eisenstein and Aleksandrov might seem to constitute exceptions to the rule that directors of the 1930s gave "music" such a central role in their films. After all, Aleksandrov made musicals, while Eisenstein was a prominent avant-gardist who throughout the decade had problems getting any of his projects passed. Both had worked together on films in the 1920s (generally with Eisenstein as director and Aleksandrov as his assistant); in fact, Aleksandrov had studied American musicals while traveling in the United States with Eisenstein. Yet music also played a central role in the films that essentially launched socialist realism in that medium, Kozintsev and Trauberg's *The Youth of Maksim* and the Vasil'ev "brothers" ' *Chapaev*, both of 1934. In official Soviet histories of film, Kozintsev, Trauberg and the Vasil'ev "brothers" are often singled out as pioneers of socialist realist cinema (*Istoriia* 8, 12), and they together shared first prize (along with Fridrikh Ermler's *The Peasants* [*Krest'iane*, 1935]) at the First International Film Festival in Moscow in 1935.

Both films are typically socialist realist, in that they show the road to consciousness taken by a servant of the revolution; Chapaev was a Civil War commissar; Maksim became a Party activist before the revolution. Both use a general plot structure close to that of the conventional socialist realist novel. *Chapaev* is based on a novel of that name by Dmitrii Furmanov and is one of the canonical exemplars of socialist realism, while *Maksim*, Kozintsev relates, was to convey the "essential qualities of the [proletarian] class"; he and Trauberg consequently decided to structure the film as a "biographical novel," *the* genre of socialist realism (Kozintsev, "Lektsii" 95, 98). Yet in both *Chapaev* and *Maksim*, music and song play a major role.

In both films, some of the motivation for the heroes' political progress is presented through music, rather than events or coherent reasons. In *Chapaev*, revolutionary songs function as the force that bonds the Red Army soldiers and prepares them for battle. The songs also help forge a bond between Chapaev and his young assistant Pet'ka. Indeed, the tragedy of Pet'ka's death in the final battle is at least in part the tragedy of a fine voice that will never see its realization in a career as a singer, an element in the cinematic plot added to the Furmanov original.[18]

The Youth of Maksim, originally to have been called *The Bolshevik*, was in many respects structured according to officially sponsored recipes for socialist realism.[19] As is clear from Kozintsev's published correspondence, Shumiatskii played a close role in determining how the protagonists were to be represented in the film (Kozintsev, "B. E. Shumitskomu [letter of 20 March 1934]," *Sobranie* 5: 382–84). Yet Kozintsev and Trauberg did leave their mark on this film in no uncertain terms, a mark to be found particularly in the central role they gave to music. This was true, not just in the sense that the film included many songs, but that, as in Eisenstein's theories, music was given a *determining* role.

In the account Kozintsev gives of *Maksim*, in a series of lectures he gave to students in 1937–38, he explains that his aim was to convey in the film a "sense of the epoch" [*oshchushchenie èpokhi*], something that is "sometimes hard to convey in words" but can be caught in a kind of "music." Here he was allegedly guided by the poet Aleksandr Blok, who recommended, as a way of giving unity to the disparate facts about a period, finding for it some "single musical thrust [*napor*]" (Blok was, of course, a much more acceptable model politically than Nietzsche or Wagner, though his foregrounding of "music" was influenced by French Symbolists who had in turn been influenced by Wagner). So impressed were Kozintsev and Trauberg by Blok's ideas that they decided to "try not to treat [in the film] any event, protagonist, fact or situation unless it suggests the kind of musical thrust Blok wrote about." Part of the appeal of "music" for them was that it provided a formula for giving the film unity: "One must make not a string of episodes but a coherent film," they concluded, and to this end they rejected the practice of representing the revolutionary movement using the conventions of picaresque or adventure genres (Kozintsev, "Lektsii" 100, 98).

Aural Hieroglyphics?

Music was crucial for achieving this unified picture. It was even deter-mining for the representation of Maksim as the young-worker-impelled-to-become-Bolshevik. In the figure of Maksim, the directors decided, one must find "the best qualities of the [working] class" (Kozintsev, "Lektsii" 99). Yet, in an effort to find a way to "create such a hero," they spent a month not among upstanding young workers, as one might imagine, but listening to songs played by accordion players from Moscow and Leningrad. They were searching for a song that would not be from the village (peasant), or from the operetta or café *chantant* (i.e., the light, commercial repertoire) and that might convey the quintessential Maksim: "And then one day an accor-dion player played 'The Blue Globe Goes Round and Round' and at that moment the image of Maksim cohered [for us] with this wonderful lyrical song" (Kozintsev, "Lektsii" 96).[20] "Wonderful" though the song might be, however, its text is singularly apolitical and largely conveys the exuberance of the singer and his interest in the fair sex.[21]

In this film, Kozintsev and Trauberg eschewed "Hollywood" orchestral accompaniment for the songs in favor of accordion accompaniment or the unaccompanied voice. They also gave a special place to the solo accordion, the instrument of the workers' settlements that had become very popular among avant-garde musical and theatrical groups of the late 1920s. Kozin-tsev wrote later, "We wanted to raise the accordion to the level of tragedy [i.e., inter alia, to elevate it from its usual position associated with banal and low genres]. We used the accordion to pick out the party organizer at the factory. He is constantly walking around with an accordion" (Kozintsev, "Lektsii" 112). Throughout the film, the accordion was used to symbolize revolutionary defiance in the face of oppression; its strains were heard ren-dering revolutionary songs when the authorities tried to close down a work-ers' Saturday school and when they tried to disperse a demonstration. In both cases, who was playing the accordion (in the demonstration, it was played first by someone drunk and then by a random participant) was less significant than the triumphant strains of the music itself. Song was used in a similar way; for instance, in one scene arrested prisoners continue to sing a revolutionary song in prison, even though they are beaten in an effort to silence them.[22] This special role played by music in the film was a sign both of the lingering conventions from the mass spectacle and also of the degree of abstraction in Stalinist culture, where narratives had be-come increasingly depersonalized and deindividualized and music repre-sented an extreme degree of such abstraction.

In their extensive use of the urban song, Kozintsev and Trauberg sub-scribed to an updated version of the cult of the folk song as more authentic than most highbrow varieties of song. They saw the revolutionary song and urban song as the visceral expression of the more authentic subject, the proletarian, whose "straight talk" contrasted favorably with the bookishness of educated speech or mannered "folkism." "We took revolutionary songs . . . and then songs from the workers' settlements," Kozintsev reported. "Songs such as 'The Blue Globe Turns Round and Round' and so forth. Moreover, we set ourselves the task of restoring to these songs their authentic emotion" (Kozintsev, "Lektsii" 112).

More recently, we have seen such lingering prejudices in the enormous popularity of the guitar poetry of Vladimir Vysotskii and others in the 1970s and early 1980s. At that time, Vysotskii was the icon of alternative culture, alternative because it provided an account of "the Russian people" that was the functional antonym of the kind of Folklorico being peddled on television and in the concert hall. Vysotskii, who abjured conventional musical form and expectations to render music, as it were, "from the guts" in a harsh, unmelodic, highly stylized, "authentic" voice, with minimal variation in the strident guitar accompaniment,[23] became a cult figure with a wide following among disparate segments of the population who otherwise found little in common.

In *Maksim*, the use of the unaccompanied voice and accordion has filiations going back to the movement for opera reform that began in the late 1920s. Not coincidentally, Shostakovich worked on the music for all Kozintsev and Trauberg's films, starting with *The New Babylon* [*Novyi Vavilon*, 1927]. This reform movement, which was closely associated with the work of German opera reformers such as Brecht and Weill, arose in reaction against the Wagnerian opera as excessively homogenizing and monumental. Kozintsev saw his direction of *Maksim* as opposed to all such kinds of "monumentalism" (Kozintsev, "Prostranstvo tragedii," *Sobranie* 4: 92). Reform advocates sought a more complex and less harmonious relationship between word and music in opera. (In the 1930s, even Eisenstein sought a more modulated interpretation of "music" than might have been expected of someone who wanted to give it a dominant role, and wrote in "Vertical Montage" of "polyphonic montage" [Eisenstein, *Selected Works* 2: 330].) In the late 1920s, such views were staunchly opposed by members of the Russian Association of Proletarian Music (RAPM) and other such organizations. In these battles over the kind of music to be favored in revolutionary culture, one finds analogues to the debates in linguistics between those who wanted to mandate "a single, unified language" [*edinyi iazyk*] and supporters of what Bakhtin called "heteroglossia."

Thus, music, film, and opera became the sites of some of the great de-

Aural Hieroglyphics?

bates about the shape of revolutionary culture. But, as we know, the position represented by Shostakovich and others was largely bypassed if not persecuted in the 1930s. The prevailing sense of the role of music was one that informed a great deal of state-sponsored cultural endeavor during the cultural revolution of the late 1920s, even as Shostakovich and others were proselytizing for the new opera and a new kind of musical theater; here I have in mind in particular Music for the Masses [*Muzyka massam*], the musical Olympiads where massed choirs and orchestras competed; public spectacles involving orchestration of rhythmic bodily movement on a mass scale (what Siegfried Kracauer has called the "mass ornament"); the ritualization of all of life and the sacralization of the quotidian. This was a fundamental aspect of Stalinist culture and one that informed most of its films, *whether or not* actual music played a dominant role in them.

This trend saw its apotheosis in the parade on Red Square, an event that marks the culmination of Dykhovichnyi's *Moscow Parade*—in this instance, the parade depicted is said to be from 1939.[24] It is to be noted, however, that, while the film's parade proceeds in triumph, many of the protagonists who helped organize it are doomed, and doomed because of what might be called an incongruence with music. At rehearsals the horse chosen to lead the parade, a stallion Rabfak, shies when the military band plays and hence cannot carry the parade's marshall as planned. Those officials from the NKVD responsible for the parade try to extricate themselves from this disaster by using last year's successful leading horse, Marseillaise. Marseillaise is a mare, so they have the props man from the Bol'shoi make her a false penis, in the hope that she can pass for Rabfak, but when this deception is uncovered, heads fall. Since "Rabfak," or "Worker's Faculty," was the acronym for an institution at tertiary schools of the 1920s designed to assist in the "proletarianization" of the ranks of the intellectuals and trained professionals, while "Marseillaise" was the music of the "bourgeois" French Revolution, drowned out by the workers' "Internationale" in pageantry of that decade, both the situation and the names of the horses were obviously intended to have particular resonance.[25]

In other words, the role of sound in recent films is, inter alia, to present a sort of metacommentary on the failed ideals of High Stalinism, ideals to which not just "the regime" but also, if in a different way and somewhat differently conceived, intellectuals themselves also subscribed. The regime insisted that ordinary reality would become as a "fairy tale." Intellectuals, in less crude formulations, looked to find in "music" the recovery of "tragedy," but tragedy regarded not absolutely literally; rather, they looked to more exalted experience than the quotidian could provide. The illusions of such intellectual idealists could be read into the very title of *Freeze, Die, Come to Life*. On one level, the title is the name of an actual children's game and thus alludes to the tragedy of a generation of children who cannot know true childhood. But, on another level, it could be seen as encapsulating the intended trajectory of societal regeneration with religious overtones; "freeze [*zamri*]" standing for the stagnant, bourgeois world; "die [*umri*]," for its death in the scorching fire of revolution; and "come to life [or, more literally, "resurrect"—*voskresni*]" for its regeneration through "music." In the post-Brezhnevo-Chernenkian and immediately (if tenuously) post-Soviet phase, directors have not merely been orchestrating a musical sound track of songs as a sort of "code" or "hieroglyphics," but particularly choreographing the relationship between sound and the visual. What we have, then, is intercoding, rather than just coding.

Although I have focused here on the use of song, there are other ways that this interrelationship has been orchestrated. For example, there has been a return to deliberate use of silence or what might be called zero sound.[26] Mikhail Yampolsky has caught this brilliantly in his analysis of the philosophical underpinnings of the theme of death in recent films and the related use of silence (particularly in the films of Aleksandr Sokurov). There is, however, another aspect to the use of silence that needs mentioning here. The subtlest and most profound effect of silence is to return the message of the images to the film's spectator, a situation analogous to the phenomenon in such group practices as meditation, in which individuals in a group use silence to go into themselves. A film in which there is a long silent scene presents the audience with a space in the performance in which direction from the screen is momentarily less hegemonic. By contrast, the use of song and allied auditory techniques in films (and other forms of revolutionary culture and ritual), entailing the rhythmic orchestration of a verbal text in melodic form, will tend to a more homogenous response, as Plato knew well.

Kira Muratova in her recent films has used different techniques for exploring this aspect of the interrelationship between the sound text and the visual. For instance, in *The Sentimental Cop* [a somewhat inadequate but fairly standard translation of *Chuvstvitel'nyi militsioner*, 1992], Muratova makes extensive use of techniques that might suggest she is returning to the tradition of avant-garde theater and ritual of the 1920s, techniques such as mime scenes without words but sometimes with musical accompaniment; frozen scenes; and gestural and sound leitmotifs and exaggerated movements, at times reminiscent of Chaplin, one of the avant-garde's icons. (The film also contains parodic invocations of such other icons of that avant-garde as the

Aural Hieroglyphics?

Odessa steps, the decorations for the first anniversary of the revolution in 1918, and Malevich's black square.)[27]

Ostensibly, the plot of the film treats the most basic and searing (if potentially "sentimental") human situations such as love, childlessness, and orphanhood. But throughout, Muratova draws attention to its essentially staged nature, its "theatricality." The hero, in recounting his most intense experiences, recurrently uses expressions meaning "as if" [*kak budto, slovno*] and there is a tendency, widely noted by critics, to undermine stable identity with "doubling"—in characters, incidents, and even lines. There are unmotivated vignettes of fatuous declamation with hyperbolically theatrical stylization, gratuitous repetitions, motivated, if at all, by their different inflections, jerky, sudden transitions from one acting style to another, and dialogues that are exercises in noncommunication, some somewhat Pinteresque, others more Gogolian.

One scene is particularly germane to our concerns here. It is the middle of the night, and citizens of a small corner of the seaside town have been awakened by an argument between locals exercising their dogs. Disgruntled and sleepy residents appear on their balconies to sound off in turn about how the militia should be called, how there is not enough to feed children and yet they are feeding dogs, how dog is a friend to man and man is the tsar of nature, and about the evils of the "fascists." These basic statements, essentially clichés of the times shading into schoolroom homilies, are taken up consecutively by the different speakers, some conflating lines or improvising new wording, others giving but a short snatch of the overall text, others again repeating the previous speaker's lines with slight variation or different inflection, or speaking in concert. The effect is that of an opera without music and without costumes (just balconies), an opera of the hackneyed and banal that lacks any ennobling elements or even purpose.

Thus, Muratova has found here her own repertoire of strategies for undermining and parodying "music." One of the more subtle of these used throughout the film is random intrusions of light and sound from somewhere off the screen that, somewhat à la John Cage, become part of the "text." They are intrusions of an otherness that undercuts the ostensible import of the shot, revealing the degree to which metonymy is the master trope of the whole film. This effect is reinforced in the dialogue by an obsession with the chance and contingent [*sluchainost'*]. What in an avant-gardist might have been celebrated as displacement [*sdvig*] or "montage" becomes here mere disjunction. In Muratova's preceding film, *The Aesthenic Syndrome* [*Astenicheskii sindrom*, circa 1989], she frequently used classical music on the sound track as a sort of ironic counterpoint to the Soviet "actu-alities" being shown on the screen.[28] This kind of disjunction between the auditory and the visual, as with the disjunctions between different "tracks" in the auditory, also undermines any projected single perspective. Thus, in *Freeze, Die, Come to Life*, we recurrently hear the hauntingly beautiful songs sung by the Japanese prisoners of war, contrasting with the crude remarks about the Japanese by Galia's father (himself a Tartar) and others, who dismiss them as essentially subhuman creatures.

This trend is especially marked in the film's ending. As Galia's mother runs frenziedly around on her broomstick, she calls out, "Onions, garlic and raspberries." "The picture [*kartina*] is beginning." "No one knows who is fucking whom." Thus, we have here one line that potentially comes from a shamanistic incantation and is hence consistent with the mother's self-presentation as a figure in a pagan ritual (in itself both incongruous with the setting, but also, in a sense, a parody of illusions about returning to a premodern sensibility); *plus* a line that seems to refer to the essential con-structedness of the filmic event; *plus* a line that presents a parodic recoding of the old maxim, "Who [will get] whom" (now "No one knows who . . . whom"), which Lenin and Stalin used as a slogan to rationalize repression as a preemptive strike: Lenin knew, now no one knows.

After Galia's mother has cavorted on her broomstick in the area of the camera, she suddenly darts into the distance. We hear a voice shout, "Where has she gone? Does no one know what to do?" This is a response that seems to refer to the tragic moment, until the voice continues: "Enough of the kids. Get the camera on her [Galia's naked mother]," and we realize it is the film's director speaking. When the mother returns to medium-shot range, he tells her to throw down her broom and walk away. (In Maksim Gor'kii's and Vsevolod Pudovkin's *Mother* [*Mat'*, 1905 and 1926 respectively], the mother picks up the banner of the fallen comrade; here she is to throw down her broom.)

There is no tragedy, only a film that is being constructed. As the screen goes white and then the focus returns again, the camera dollies back while the audience is given a sort of auditory recapitulation of some earlier mo-ments: the haunting song of the Japanese prisoners; the church bells played in an earlier vignette, involving a Moscow Jewish intellectual who has been reduced to madness by his incarceration and yet in some way "hears" a more "heavenly" music in that living hell (a possible reference to the fate of Osip Mandel'shtam, who himself perished in the camp system in the Vladivostok area, where Suchan is located). Finally, a trite waltz tune of the sort that conventional movies are wont to use and that has been played a few times already marks "the end" in an ironic counterpoint to the scene. There are different temporal trajectories and different accounts of reality, but there is no, as Nietzsche might have said, "*whole*." This is the "tragedy" born when the "music" becomes the random notes of a cacophony.

Notes

1. The song was actually composed in 1920 by Iulii Khait and Pavel German, but became a particular hit in the 1930s, when aviation played a major role in the official Imaginary.

2. For more on the question of sound in film, see "*Zvuk v kino*" and Rick Altman.

3. In some films, a major role is played not by songs, but by military band music (e.g., Aleksei German's *My Friend, Ivan Lapshin* [*Moi drug Ivan Lapshin*, 1984]).

4. See, e.g., the climactic fight scene in Vadim Abdrashitov's *Pliumbum, or A Dangerous Game* [*Pliumbum, ili opasnaia igra*, 1986].

5. In several films (such as Pavel Lungin's *Taxi Blues* [*Taksi bliuz*, 1990]), the clash of worldviews is played out as a clash of musical tastes.

6. See, e.g., Sergei Solov'ev's *The Black Rose Stands for Sadness* [*Chernaia roza èmblema pechali*, 1989].

7. See S. Frederick Starr. Note also the recent expostulations about rock by such Russian nationalists as Valentin Rasputin and Vasilii Belov.

8. In *Moscow Parade* [*Prorva*, 1992], for instance, director Ivan Dykhovichnyi presented many songs set to music by the great composer of jazz and popular music in the thirties, A. Tsfasman, but gave them new texts by I. Butsko.

9. This is, however, far from always the case. In Sergei Solov'ev's *House under the Starry Sky* [*Dom pod zvezdnym nebom*, 1991], for instance, the villain sings "The Internationale," no less.

10. See especially Stites, chapters 3 and 4.

11. A case in point would be one of the most popular musicals about the war, S. A. Timoshenko's *Jalopy of the Skies* [*Nebesnyi tikhokhod*, 1946], to which many are sentimentally attached, despite its incredible plot combining Soviet aerial triumphs over the Germans in the early stages of the war and a cream-puff love plot.

12. This was an unsigned and therefore particularly authoritative article (*Pravda* [*Truth*] 28 January 1936).

13. E.g., his productions of Molière's *Don Juan* (1910), Calderon's *The Constant Prince* (1915), and Gogol''s *Inspector General* [*Revizor*, 1926].

14. This theme is also treated in Semen Aranovich's documentary film, *I Served in Stalin's Bodyguard* [*Ia sluzhil v okhrane Stalina*, 1989].

15. E.g., the "duel" in Meyerhold's production of *The Trust D. E.* [*Trest D. E.*, 1924] between Western jazz and the "healthier rhythms" of Soviet Biomechanics.

16. Analogous points were made in other essays of about this time. See, e.g., Sergei Eisenstein, *Nonindifferent Nature* 305.

17. See, e.g., his "A Dialectical Approach to Film Form" (1929).

18. This *topos* is to be found in several films of the 1930s and 1940s. For instance, in Mikhail Chiaureli's *The Fall of Berlin* [*Padenie Berlina*, 1949], one of the heroes who seems

Katerina Clark

destined for a singing career dies even as he climbs the steps of the Reichstag to claim the final victory.

19. This was actually the first film of a trilogy that was to culminate with Maksim's running a state bank after the revolution.

20. Note also how songs, rather than words, establish the essential qualities of the hero in Mikhail Kalatozov's *Valerii Chkalov* (1941).

21. This is amply evident in the text, published in Grigorii Kozintsev, "Glubokii èkran," *Sobranie* 1: 218.

22. In addition to conventional music, the directors made symbolic use of a number of other sounds, such as whistles and sirens.

23. Note also Vysotskii's association with the Taganka Theater, known both for its use of the accordion, guitar, and songs in productions and for its professed links with the tradition of Brecht.

24. The film opens with actual documentary color footage of a parade on Red Square, but it is from 1938.

25. Also involved, of course, is that now somewhat hackneyed point about impotence among agents of Bolshevik power in the Stalin era, a topic I am not treating here.

26. Kozintsev and Eisenstein also discussed this phenomenon in their writings of the 1930s.

27. The work of Meyerhold in, for instance, his 1926 production of Nikolai Gogol"s *The Inspector General* comes to mind particularly, although, as Jane Taubman points out in a recent article, there are biographical reasons for linking Muratova's techniques here with those of the FEKSy (368).

28. Muratova has in these two films made use of classical music in a variety of ways. For example, in the opening, mimed scene of *The Sentimental Cop*, where a militiaman finds a baby in a cabbage patch, Tchaikovsky's "*Les saisons*" [*Vremena goda*] is played throughout, a set piece of the Soviet musical school, also used for broadcasts of weather reports (Shepotinnik 17). In *The Aesthenic Syndrome*, Muratova uses classical music differently in the nude scene to suggest, by her own account, that this scene does not represent "pornography" but "culture" (Muratova 159).

Works Cited

Aleksandrov, G. V. *Èpokha i kino.* 2nd. enlarged ed. Moskva: Politicheskaia literatura, 1983.

Altman, Rick, ed. *Sound/Cinema. Yale French Studies* 60 (1981).

———, ed. *Sound Theory, Sound Practice.* New York: Routledge, 1992.

Ashkinazi, Z. "Teatr Vagnera," *Ezhegodnik imperatorskikh teatrov. Vypusk* 6 (1913): 77–119.

Dobrotvorskaia, Karina. " 'Tsirk' G. V. Aleksandrova," *Iskusstvo kino* 11 (1992): 28–33.

Eisenstein, Sergei. *Nonindifferent Nature.* Tr. Herbert Marshall. Cambridge: Cambridge UP, 1987.

———. *Selected Works.* Vol. 2. *Towards a Theory of Montage.* Ed. Michael Glenny and Richard Taylor. Tr. Richard Taylor. London: BFI, 1991.

Istoriia sovetskogo kino v chetyrekh tomakh. Vol. 2 (1931–1941). Moskva: Iskusstvo, 1973.

Ivanov, Viachelsav. "Doklad ob organizatsii tvorcheskikh sil narodnogo kollektiva v oblasti narodnogo deistva." *Vestnik teatra* 26 (14–16 May 1919).

———. "O Vagnere (Rech' proiznesennaia dlia chlenov s"ezda po vneshkol'nomu obrazovaniiu v Moskovskom Bol'shom teatre pered predstavleniem 'Valkirii' Rikharda Vagnera 17 maia 1919 goda)." *Vestnik teatra* 31 (9–15 June 1919).

Kozintsev, G. M. "Lektsii G. M. Kozintseva chitannye vo VGIKe v 1937/38 uchebnom godu." *Iz istorii Lenfil'ma.* Vypusk 4.

———. *Sobranie sochinenii v piati tomakh.* Leningrad: Iskusstvo, 1982–86.

Kracauer, Siegfried. "Das Ornament der Masse" (1927). *Das Ornament der Masse.* Frankfurt am Main: Suhrkamf, 1965.

Muratova, Kira. "Kira Muratova otvechaet zriteliam." *Kinovedcheskie zapiski* 13 (1992).

Pravda 28 January 1936.

Shepotinnik, Petr. "Opisanie rebenka prilagaetsia." *Iskusstvo kino* 7 (1992): 17–20.

Starr, S. Frederick. *Red and Hot: The Fate of Jazz in the Soviet Union, 1917–1980.* New York: Oxford UP, 1983.

Stites, Richard. *Russian Popular Culture: Entertainment and Society since 1900.* Cambridge: Cambridge UP, 1992.

Taubman, Jane. "The Cinema of Kira Muratova," *The Russian Review* 52 (July 1993): 367–81.

Yampolsky, Mikhail. "Chekhov/Sokurov: Repetition and Recollection." *New Formations* (May 1994).

Znosko-Borovskii, Evgenii. "Teatr bez literatury." *Apollon* 7 (1912): 22–33.

Zorkaia, Neia. "Ot 'Kliatve'—k 'Prorve'." *Iskusstvo kino* 11 (1992): 3–9.

"Zvuk v kino." Kinovedcheskie zapiski 15 (1992).

Two

Televorot
The Role of Television Coverage in Russia's August 1991 Coup

Victoria E. Bonnell and Gregory Freidin

"No seichas idet drugaia drama. . . .
—Boris Pasternak, "Hamlet"

When the State Committee on the State of Emergency (henceforth the Emergency Committee) seized power in the early morning of 19 August 1991, it took steps immediately to assert control over Central Television, radio, and the press. At one o'clock in the morning on 19 August, Gennadii Shishkin, first deputy director of TASS, was awakened by a phone call from Leonid Kravchenko, the conservative director of Gosteleradio (the State Committee on Television and Radio) and asked to come to Central Committee headquarters.[1] By 2:00 A.M., the chief editor of the nightly news program *Vremia* had been awakened. Then, at dawn, military vehicles and paratroopers surrounded the Gosteleradio building at Ostankino.[2]

By 6:00 A.M., arrangements were complete. From that time until the flight of the putschists on Wednesday afternoon, 21 August, regular television programming was suspended, and the central channels became instead vehicles for the transmission of official announcements, news, and press conferences.[3] A similar policy went into effect in radio broadcasting, although several local stations managed to elude official control. In Moscow, all but nine central and local newspapers were silenced by the Emergency Committee.[4]

Since the actions of the plotters were concentrated in Moscow, Leningrad, and the Baltic Republics, most people in the Soviet Union (and even some who lived in these places) acquired information about the events, especially during the first two critical days, primarily through television and, to a much lesser extent, through newspapers and radio.[5] Eventually, television brought into people's homes most of the dramatic moments occasioned by the coup: the tanks rolling into Moscow, the building of barricades, and Yeltsin mounting a tank on 19 August; mass prodemocracy rallies in Moscow and Leningrad on 20 August; the tank incident that led to the death of three civilians defending the White House in the early hours of 21 August; the return of Gorbachev to Moscow twenty-four hours later; the celebration of Freedom Day on 22 August; and the funeral on 24 August. Television provided people with a great deal of information during the coup and by no means all of it proved favorable to the plotters. Predictably, the plotters attempted to use television as a mouthpiece for the Emergency Committee and to suppress information that contradicted the image of a smooth transition to emergency rule. They operated on assumptions that dated from the era before glasnost, when television had been a dependable, cowed propaganda instrument of the regime, promoting the regime's glories and editing out the slurred speech and mispronunciations of its leaders.[6]

Here, as in other respects, members of the Emergency Committee and their supporters underestimated the changes that had taken place in Soviet mass media since 1985. The previous six years had brought far-reaching changes to television, gradually transforming it into a genuine forum for a broad range of ideas.[7] When Kravchenko was appointed the head of Gosteleradio in the autumn of 1990, he took steps to eliminate some of the more outspoken programs, such as the popular *Vzgliad* [*Viewpoint*] which featured controversial reporting and discussions of current affairs.[8] Such repressive measures soon provoked a response from those more sympathetic to the aims of glasnost. The U.S.S.R. Journalists' Union expelled Kravchenko on 12 April 1991, citing his efforts to reintroduce censorship on television. A number of well-known commentators resigned from Central Television in "a dramatic protest" against Kravchenko's policies.[9]

That the spirit of glasnost had made deep inroads into Gosteleradio despite Kravchenko's conservative leadership became evident on 19 August. Faced with an order to return to the pre-1985 style and content of journalism, some reporters, cameramen, editors, and supervisors at Gosteleradio did their best to circumvent the new rules. The situation at Leningrad television—for some years a maverick station in the production of controversial programs—was even more remarkable.[10] Boris Petrov, the president of Leningrad television, cooperated fully with the democratic opposition, led by Mayor Anatolii Sobchak. With a viewing audience of about forty-five million people, extending to Moscow, the Baltic republics, and Belarus, the

Victoria E. Bonnell & Gregory Freidin

Leningrad station exerted considerable influence. On the first day of the coup, Petrov secured a satellite connection to facilitate broadcasting beyond the station's normal range.[11]

From the inception of the crisis, Central and Leningrad television transmitted reports, images, and commentary that conveyed not just one version of the events—the official version promoted by the Emergency Committee—but several other views of what was happening and why. There were, in fact, three major "scripts" that dominated media coverage of the coup. By "script" or "scenario" we do not mean a prepared text that a director or an actor uses in a theatrical performance.[12] Rather, we are suggesting that the leading individuals and groups during the coup had intellectual agendas and political outlooks already well formed before the curtain rose on the putsch (hence, our "script"), and that these, in turn, shaped their responses to the events that unfolded during the crucial three days and thereafter.[13] Furthermore, "script" implies for us a set of symbols, images, and styles that, in accordance with a given situation, signal actors to act or improvise and signal "audiences" to interpret what they see in particular ways. The theatrical metaphor is, of course, an essential ingredient in politics in general and in mass politics in particular, a theme well researched and well documented in cultural and political scholarship.[14] What makes "script" [stsenarii] even more apposite is that it was used by various public figures, along with such related theatrical notions as "plot" [siuzhet], "action" or "performance" [igra], "characters" [personazhi], and "to perform or act according to a script" [razygryvat']. Gorbachev's recollections of the coup offer a telling passage:

> ... during the preceding days, I had actually been working with my assistant Chernyayev on a major article. It dealt with the situation in the country and the possible ways it might evolve. And one of the *scenarios* considered was in fact the introduction of a state of emergency. And now the *characters* from it had turned up here. My reasoning about that *scenario* was that it would be a disaster for our society and a dead end, that it would turn the country back and ruin everything we now have [emphasis added].[15]

The Emergency Committee's script was signalled, first of all, by its "Appeal to the Soviet People," and other decrees and resolutions issued on the morning of 19 August.[16] But the Committee's views were already well known. In the months preceding the coup, conservative groups in the Communist Party of the Russian Republic (RSFSR) and leading members of the KGB, Ministry of Internal Affairs (MVD), and military forces had closed

ranks with ultranationalist writers in opposition to perestroika and the impending Union Treaty. In mid-June, future putschists Valentin Pavlov, Dmitrii Yazov, Boris Pugo, and Vladimir Kriuchkov attempted to carry out a
"constitutional coup d'état" by expanding the power of Prime Minister Pavlov,
an outspoken critic of the Union Treaty that was then being negotiated.
Their efforts failed. On 23 July, twelve Soviet leaders, including high-rank-
ing army officers, published a dramatic appeal in a right-wing paper, *Sovetskaia Rossiia,* calling on Soviet citizens to resist the breakup of the union.[17]

According to the conspirators, the crisis in the Soviet system—a situation they characterized as imminent chaos and anarchy—could only be
resolved by revitalizing the country's links with the past, which for them
meant the Soviet Union before perestroika. This desire to reconnect was
encoded in the very designation of their committee, the GKChP, translat-
ing into the lumbering *Gosudarstvennyi komitet po chrezvychainomu polozheniiu*
[State Committee on the State of Emergency]. These initials implied an
association with the venerable ChK (Cheka), the progenitor of the KGB,
with KP, the Russian initials for the Communist Party, and, of course, with
ChP (an emergency situation), an overused colloquialism over the seventy-
five years of incessant "emergency situations" in the economy, society, and
politics. The continuity thus implied was that of the Communist Party, the
military-industrial complex, the secret police, and, more generally, a unified
state untroubled by the nationalist aspirations of its member republics.

The most important counterpoint to the Emergency Committee's scripting of events from 19 through 21 August came from the democratic resistance, led by Yeltsin. Yeltsin's response to the formation of the GKChP was
swift. By 9:00 A.M., he had issued an appeal, "To the Citizens of Russia."[18]
This was followed by other statements and decrees in the course of the
day.[19] Shortly after noon, he held a press conference in the White House,
and at 1:00 P.M. he mounted tank 110 of the Taman Division near the White
House and appealed to Muscovites and all citizens of Russia to give a worthy
response to those involved in the putsch and to demand the return of the
nation to normal constitutional development.[20]

When the crisis began, the position of Yeltsin and the Russian democrats
was also already widely known. They advocated the creation of a new Russia—a country, a culture, and a polity—that would be, through a miracu-
lous act of will and plenty of wishful thinking, discontinuous with Soviet
and much of pre-Soviet history. Theirs was to be a democratic Russia, one
that had no connection with either Communism or the empire. The barricades were not related to those of the Paris Commune or the 1905 "dress
rehearsal of 1917." They hailed instead from the landmarks of struggle

against Communism: the streets of Budapest in 1956 and Prague in 1968, the Gdansk shipyards, and, most recently, the streets of Vilnius in January 1991, where the old tried-and-true Bolshevik script of "national salvation" was applied on a smaller scale in preparation for the August counterrevolution.[21]

A third script—the perestroika script—remained on the sidelines during the first two days of the crisis, only to emerge with Gorbachev's release from incarceration on 21 August. Unwilling to change his perspective even after the coup, Gorbachev persisted in reading from that script, which portrayed the country's democratic future as flowing out of her cruel and tyrannical Communist past. Socialism, and the Communist Party as the sole surviving pan-Union political institution, could not be omitted from his script. But, if before the putsch a drama revolving around the socialist idea and the Party was attracting fewer and fewer good actors, not to mention an increasingly sparse audience, it became a solo performance in a nearly empty theater after the coup had failed.

In an era of instant replay, major political players and commentators tend to swap rhetoric as much as they swap their primary functions: commentators are a real force in the political game, which in the era of nationalism and democracy revolves around symbols, whereas politicians use their authority and visibility to shape the public discourse in a way that automatically implies a framework of legitimacy for their policies. Having gone through the school of Bolshevism, with its treasury of experience in manipulating public discourse, having graduated from the academy of Gorbachev's glasnost, which introduced into public consciousness the necessity of logical reasoning, open-minded analysis, humanistic values, and, almost, public honesty, the players and commentators of the August days were offered an unprecedented opportunity to deploy their rhetorical and aesthetic skills. It was as if their lives depended on it, and in fact they did.

19 August, Day One: Two Scripts

With the seizure of power in the early morning of 19 August, the eight plotters declared their actions to the world and put forward their claim to legitimacy. Even before the specific formulations in the GKChP's decrees, resolutions, and appeals could be grasped, the style of presentation by television announcers immediately gave a distinctive clue concerning their position: a vintage Soviet script, the absence of the word "Communism" notwithstanding. In fact, the tone of voice and intonations—ponderous and solemn, reminiscent of the days when the Party still had its sacred aura and its pronouncements resonated like the word of God—alerted people to a major change not just of government but of their entire style of life. After six years of glasnost and perestroika, the announcers of 19 August were, discursively and gesturally, herding people back to a time before 1985.[22]

The Emergency Committee's major declaration, the "Appeal to the Soviet People," was read numerous times on television the first day.[23] With its heavy emphasis on the vocabulary of Soviet patriotism and official Russian nationalism, it is reminiscent of the "developed socialism" of the Brezhnev era. The terms "Fatherland" [*Otechestvo*] and "Motherland" [*rodina*] appear numerous times. They are code words, loosely but unmistakably associated with the renascent right-wing Russian nationalism of the imperial variety [*otechestvo*] and traditional Soviet-style patriotism [*rodina*]. The proclamation concludes with a summons to manifest "patriotic readiness" and to restore "age-old friendship in the unified family of fraternal peoples and the revival of the Fatherland."[24]

Apart from regular readings of the Emergency Committee's proclamations and decrees, Central Television broadcast no additional news or information until the late afternoon of 19 August. Ballet, opera, and classical music—all harking back to the good old days when Soviet mass media were dominated by edifying material—replaced the "aerobicized" fare found on Central Television in the twilight years of perestroika.[25] Then a real TV news event took place: the Emergency Committee's press conference was broadcast live, in its entirety, on Central Television.

For their first—and as it turned out, only—press conference, the plotters adopted the format introduced by Gorbachev in 1985, which permitted spontaneous questioning by foreign and Soviet reporters. Considering the care with which the plotters attempted to seize control of the mass media—even to the point of forbidding employees of Gosteleradio to leave with film except by permission of the chief editor—it is certainly puzzling that they submitted to a press conference of that kind, with all its attendant risks. One can only surmise that they felt compelled to do so in an effort to establish their credibility with foreign powers and, perhaps, the Soviet population as well.[26] The press conference cast in sharp relief the style of the conspiracy, leaving little to the imagination with regard to its master script and the ineptitude of its members.[27] Five of the eight plotters participated: conspicuously missing were KGB head Kriuchkov, Defense Min-

Victoria E. Bonnell & Gregory Freidin

ister Yazov, and Prime Minister Pavlov. Since it was a matter of common sense that neither the KGB chief nor the chief officer of the armed forces could have played second fiddle in a conspiracy of this magnitude, their absence diminished the stature and seriousness of the Emergency Committee. Attention was focused on Gennadii Yanaev, the least respected and least powerful member of Gorbachev's entourage and, it turns out, the most reluctant participant in the conspiracy.[28] Yanaev held center stage and answered nearly all the questions, with Interior Minister Pugo participating occasionally. Aleksandr Tiziakov and Oleg Baklanov made only one comment each, and Vasilii Starodubtsev spoke twice.[29] The press conference was, for the most part, Yanaev's show.

In camera work, there are always choices, and the camera lens can be a merciless eye, if so directed. During the press conference, the choice was to focus on Yanaev in such a way that his hands were continuously visible — hands that trembled intermittently, conveying great agitation, in contrast to his authoritative booming voice. Remarkably, the camera returned again and again to that particular framing of Yanaev, though it would have been easy enough to direct the camera's eye elsewhere — perhaps to a close-up of Yanaev's face or a long shot in which the telltale tremors would have been invisible to the television audience. In the control room, a decision had been made to capture the image in a particular way. According to David Remnick, veteran *Vremia* director Elena Pozdniak, who had made a career splicing out Brezhnev's bloopers from videotape, "decided she would do what she could to preserve, at the very least, a marginal sense of honesty. She got a word from Kravchenko and his deputies that, if it was technically possible, she should edit out Yanayev's trembling hands at the press conference, the laughter in the hall, and the scoffing reactions of the correspondents. Although that was very easy to do, Pozdniak thought, 'Let them see it all!' She'd had enough of the lies."[30] Thus, even the officially engineered coverage of the press conference turned out to be a visual humiliation for the plotters.

In the charged atmosphere of an unfolding conspiracy, the desire to understand and to interpret every detail pertaining to it is overwhelming. Yanaev's trembling hands and runny nose (like Nixon's legendary five-o'clock shadow) became for many people a symbol of the plotters' criminality, ineptitude, and inexperience. They evoked the common Russian saying, "trembling hands give away the chicken thief" [*ruki drozhat—kur voroval*], and the usage of *soplivyi*, literally meaning someone with a runny nose, and figuratively meaning a person who is inept, untutored, unskilled, and infantile. The journalist corps contributed to transforming what was planned as a show of political savvy and competence into a chillingly comic farce. One correspondent asked Yanaev about the state of his health, another whether Yanaev had consulted with General Pinochet concerning the plan for the takeover.[31] These questions and others elicited occasional snickers from the assembled correspondents and, in the case of the health question, uproarious laughter at Yanaev's expense. The high point of the press conference came when Tatiana Malkina, a young reporter from *Nezavisimaia Gazeta,* pointedly asked Yanaev, "Could you please say whether or not you understand that last night you carried out a coup d'état [*gosudarstvennyi perevorot*]?" No other correspondent was quite so blunt. Yanaev responded to her question during a prolonged close-up of Malkina, whose face took on an expression of disdain. The camera work, the mocking attitude of the journalists, and the words and gestures of the plotters combined to deprive the Emergency Committee of the appearance of authority and legitimacy it sought to create.

The press conference had a profoundly discouraging effect on potential supporters, such as KGB Major General Aleksandr Korsak and his fellow officers. When Korsak first heard the announcement of the state of emergency at 6:00 A.M., he responded favorably: "The words were the right ones, and the people on the committee carried some weight." The support of KGB officers was indispensable if the coup was to succeed, but the press conference helped to turn them against the conspirators. According to Korsak, "after the press conference by the GKChP, the general impression was created that this was a simple adventure, and the perplexing questions multiplied."[32] Many army and police officers shared Korsak's reservations and refused to cooperate with the Emergency Committee.[33]

In Leningrad, not long after the live broadcast of the press conference, the Leningrad TV news program *Fakt* went on the air. The high point of the program came at 7:20 P.M., when Leningrad Mayor Sobchak made a dramatic live appearance, accompanied by Vice Mayor Viacheslav Shcherbakov, A. N. Beliaev, president of the Leningrad city soviet, and Iurii Iarov, the president of the regional soviet. The plotters had listed both Shcherbakov and Iarov in the local Emergency Committee, without consulting them. The three men repudiated the conspirators and made a moving appeal to the television audience, addressing them as "dear Leningraders," "dear countrymen" [*zemliaki*], and "fellow citizens" [*so-grazhdane*]. Their appearance had a profound effect on Leningraders. According to an interview with Sobchak conducted soon after the coup, the television appeals

Victoria E. Bonnell & Gregory Freidin

helped to dispel "the suffocating atmosphere and disorientation" that people were experiencing and to mobilize in Leningrad popular resistance to the putsch.[34]

19 August, Day One: *Vremia*

At 9:00 P.M. on the nineteenth, millions of television viewers eagerly awaited Central Television's authoritative evening news program, *Vremia*.[35] It began as an archetypal Soviet performance, with incredibly somber, stone-faced announcers—the sexless Adam and Eve of Soviet television—reading the Emergency Committee's first declarations. Time and again, the announcers stressed the dangers of "chaos" and "anarchy" in the country. Reading from the Emergency Committee's "Appeal to the Soviet People," the two announced that "The country is sinking into an abyss of violence and lawlessness." This alarmist language remained central to the plotters' scripting of the events. The tanks, after all, had ostensibly been sent to Moscow in response to the imminent threat of chaos and anarchy. These dangers provided justification for such a massive show of force in Moscow and, more generally, for placing troops on alert in other parts of the country.

But Monday's edition of *Vremia* presented a far more complex and contradictory picture of the situation than the plotters and their supporters at Gosteleradio had intended. Following the lengthy reading of appeals and decrees issued by the Emergency Committee, the announcers introduced reports from Moscow and Leningrad. The first of these is a five-minute segment by Sergei Medvedev, the reporter, and Vladimir Chechel'nitskii, the cameraman. They get off to a good start—visually. The tanks are rolling from across the river and onto Red Square, passing St. Basil's at high speed. As if to provide some link to the overwhelmingly Soviet ambiance of what had preceded this scene, the voice-over of the Soviet announcer comments cheerfully, as though welcoming a shipment of bananas, "Today, on the streets of Moscow, there appeared tanks and armored personnel carriers. They moved quickly toward the center of the city." With these words, the lifeline connecting this report to the Soviet universe is severed. Unlike the preceding voice-over, Medvedev speaks with urgency and animation, each phrase punctuated with a gasp. From the very first line, it is a report from a battlefield. The gasping in the reporter's voice conveys the immediacy of battle, the fright, and also the resolve, with great conviction and force.[36] Held unsteadily, as if by a man elbowing his way through a crowd, the camera pans in all directions, pausing for a moment on the faces of the soldiers, looking confused and apprehensive, smoking, reading a protest leaflet, confronting civilians. The trolleybuses block the tank traffic, and a group of political activists stand atop a speakers' platform in Manège Square, one of them addressing the crowd through a megaphone: "An indefinite political strike has begun, a strike of political protest." More shots of tanks, with children and civilians in the background. Commenting on the shots of small crowds surrounding and haranguing the soldiers, Medvedev resorts to metaphors: "And the human waves kept rolling in, one after another. . . . They were forming eddies. . . . "

Finally, the camera cuts to Yeltsin mounting a tank near the White House to read his first declaration. In a clear and steady voice-over, Medvedev announces that the decree "defines the actions of the Emergency Committee as a coup d'état." With Yeltsin's voice in the background and his towering figure filling the entirety of the frame, Medvedev carefully summarizes the main points of the declaration, down to the very last one, the call for an indefinite political strike. The report concludes with footage of the barricades outside what had become the front line, the immediate surroundings of the White House. Long shots of people building barricades are followed by an interview with a few men who had come to defend the White House, including a worker, an engineer, a student, and an intellectual. Yes, they are planning to stay there all night if need be. "Do you have enough bread to last you?" "Yes, we do," answer some. "We don't need any bread," answers a younger man (a worker, judging by his appearance) with grim determination, "We'll do it without any bread at all." "What made you think that this was the place you should come to?" Medvedev asks them. "It's Vilnius; Vilnius taught us our lesson," answers the intense-looking intellectual with a carefully trimmed beard. One of them, a man in his fifties, most likely a worker, points to his chest and says that his heart told him to be there. He works at the ZIL factory, one of Moscow's biggest industrial employers, and his bosses gave him time off when he informed them of his plans. "We are here because we have something to defend—our legitimate elected representatives, our power," the intellectual cuts in.

Medvedev's interview not only conveyed a great deal of information about developments around the White House, it also presented a symbolic image of the support that Yeltsin enjoyed among a broad cross-section of Muscovites. None of this spectacular theater would have had significant impact had it not been for the framing by the cameramen and the later editing of segments, such as the one by Medvedev on *Vremia*. For example, the image of Yeltsin on the tank, an image reminiscent of Lenin's famous speech on top of an armored car in Petrograd in April 1917, almost immediately became emblematic of the democratic resistance. Yet the crowd around Yeltsin and the tank was quite small, virtually lost in the vast space of the White House driveway and the steps leading down to the embankment; many spectators held umbrellas to shield themselves from a light drizzle. One can easily imagine a long shot through a telephoto lens from atop the high banister. Such an angle and frame could easily have diminished Yeltsin's considerable physical stature to a visually unimpressive human figure flailing impotently on top of a mammoth piece of hardware, surrounded by a sparse crowd of onlookers who were melting away as the drizzle turned into a shower. This memorable symbol of opposition to the conspiracy was carefully scripted, cast, directed, shot, and produced. The team that was present on the spot improvised—it had no time to do anything else—but it improvised from a particular point of view. Thus filtered, most likely through the eye of a CNN cameraman,[37] Yeltsin's rather awkward bulk makes him appear someone "larger than life," his unrefined speaking style the "voice of the people," his rather unkempt appearance a sign, not of the confusion of a politician caught by surprise but of a strong leader, righteously indignant and full of selfless resolve.

Yeltsin's first statement on the morning of the nineteenth was addressed "To the Citizens of Russia," as Medvedev indicated in his report. The plotters' major appeal, by contrast, was directed to "Compatriots, Citizens of the Soviet Union."[38] The language of propaganda encoded two very different ideas about national allegiances and political unity—one was based on a vision of an independent Russia, the other on the tradition of the all-powerful, unitary Soviet state. Visual symbols reinforced these differences: whereas the Soviet flag remained the national emblem of the Emergency Committee, the pro-Yeltsin forces were shown displaying the old Russian tricolor flag, which symbolized Russian national identity.[39]

The circumstances surrounding the filming and the airing of Medvedev's segment disclose a great deal about the situation confronting the plotters at Gosteleradio. Medvedev did not get out into the streets until early in the afternoon. Until then, his main source of information was CNN. Officials at Gosteleradio had attempted to shut off CNN, but the staff had resisted.[40] Medvedev's crew was the only one that applied for permission to film the first afternoon of the coup, and permission was granted. According to Medvedev, he returned to the studio from the White House around 8:00 P.M. The segment was prepared under great time pressure; about five minutes before *Vremia* went on the air at 9:00 P.M., it still had not been completed. Valentin Lazutkin, a deputy to Kravchenko responsible for overseeing the content of the program, looked at the first part of the report and asked what came next. "Well, we'll show the barricades and the people on them,"

Medvedev replied. The footage of Yeltsin on the tank originally ran for four minutes, but Lazutkin told Medvedev to shorten it. "The rest of what [Yeltsin] said I will try to put in my script," said Medvedev. Lazutkin gave his approval.[41] Lazutkin and Medvedev were just two of the Gosteleradio employees who cooperated spontaneously to undermine the plotters' effort to create an illusion of calm and unanimity in the country.

The conspirators and their supporters reacted swiftly to the airing of Medvedev's segment. As Medvedev said, "It was as though the ceiling crashed in on my head. All the telephones began to explode."[42] Calls came from Yurii Prokof'ev, secretary of the Moscow party committee, and Aleksandr Dzasokhov, a member of the Politburo. Interior Minister Pugo phoned Lazutkin and angrily accused him: "The story on Moscow was treacherous! You have given instructions to the people on where to go and what to do. You will answer for this." By contrast, Yanaev, who had not seen *Vremia*, as Lazutkin suspected, congratulated him for a "good, balanced report." "It showed everything from different points of view," concluded the acting president of the U.S.S.R.[43] Apparently, even the plotters could not agree about *Vremia*. Kravchenko subsequently ordered the chief editor to demote Medvedev from commentator to senior editor, with half the salary. Medvedev was also deprived of the right to appear on the air. The chief editor advised him to "go hide somewhere, because I don't know what will happen next. Go take a vacation immediately." Some among the *Vremia* staff were also appalled by Medvedev's uncompromising stance:

> I didn't wait around to see how everything would come out, although before I left, one of the deputy editors began to shout at me, "How could you deceive us? You gave an interview to people in the opposition." He blamed me for a phrase at the end of the report: "If we have the chance, then we will give you additional information later about what is happening in Moscow." Everyone blamed me for this phrase.[44]

But the next day, the obstinate Medvedev took a cameraman and again went to the White House to film. The footage he shot that day did not get on the air until Thursday, when Medvedev himself anchored the first uncensored *Vremia* since the coup began.

Medvedev's segment provided the high point for Monday's *Vremia*. It was followed by a brief report on the situation in Leningrad, showing an antiputsch gathering in Palace Square and many tricolor flags. Juxtaposed to the Moscow and Leningrad reports were a number of short segments designed to show that in provincial cities and other republics—Latvia, Moldova, Estonia, Alma-Ata—life was proceeding as usual, with no disturbances.

The repetitive images in these short segments showed ordinary but mostly well-dressed people (especially women and children) walking down streets, standing in lines, or working at their jobs. Within the framework of the pre-Gorbachev Soviet-style reporting, it was, of course, impossible to present scenes of disorder or popular resistance to the government in any form. In these segments, *Vremia* reporters attempted to follow the old script: everything was peaceful, harmonious, and industrious in the country. The scenes of pedestrians moving smoothly along well-paved streets created precisely the desired imagery of Soviet citizens—imagery that prompted both Elena Bonner and Anatolii Sobchak to comment on Tuesday, "They think we are cattle [*bydlo*]."[45]

By the end of the first day of the coup, the Emergency Committee had made its case to the Soviet people and had applied massive force to ensure its hegemony. Nevertheless, television coverage already revealed major weaknesses in these efforts. Despite strict censorship, the takeover of Gosteleradio and the closure of many newspapers, by Monday evening everyone in the Soviet Union who watched Central or Leningrad television knew that resistance to the Emergency Committee had begun to take form. Viewers saw images of barricades, prodemocracy demonstrations, and tricolor flags.

The Medvedev segment on *Vremia* had a profound impact. As Medvedev told *New York Times* correspondent Bill Keller a few days after the putsch, "Later, I learned that many who defended the White House found out where to go and what to do precisely from this report."[46] His segment turned the image of Yeltsin on a tank into a symbol of resistance, and it brought into millions of homes Yeltsin's memorable words declaring the actions of the Emergency Committee a "right-wing, reactionary, anticonstitutional *perevorot*," spoken from the rostrum of a tank—in a symbolic appropriation of Lenin's famous armored-car speech at the Finland Station—as the minicams were rolling. *Perevorot*—commonly used by Soviet sources to describe the Bolshevik takeover of October 1917[47] and translated into English variously as "coup d'état, revolution, overturn, and cataclysm," was not the only term in the rhetoric of the democratic movement to describe the situation. In Yeltsin's appeal "To the Citizens of Russia," and on the streets of Moscow where chalk-scrawled slogans soon appeared on armored personnel carriers (APCs), tanks, and sidewalks, the events were quickly encapsulated in the word "putsch," the plotters were labeled the "junta." These words of foreign origin, reminiscent of the Nazi takeover and banana republics, made their way onto national television and from there into the national consciousness, before the takeover was even a day old.

20 August, Day Two:
The Struggle of Scripts, Images, and Symbols

The second day of the coup brought an intensification of the struggle in the war of scripts, images, and symbols that had begun on Monday. Central Television remained under the control of the Emergency Committee. The same announcers as the preceding day presented news in the somber and officious Soviet style. But once again, the official news program *Vremia* was far from consistent in its presentation of events. Two very different interpretations could again be inferred from the reports. Tuesday's *Vremia* and its late-night version, *Novosti*, contained a good deal of information to suggest that things were not running smoothly for the Emergency Committee. Viewers learned, for example, that the Moscow Cadets refused to participate in the imposition of martial law; a rally against the coup had taken place in Kishinev; people in Volgograd supported Yeltsin; in Latvia, parliament called the Emergency Committee "illegal"; young soldiers were reading leaflets of Yeltsin's decrees and proclamations; and Estonians, dismayed by the arrival of tanks in Tallinn, appealed to all democratic forces to express solidarity.

Particularly telling were two reports on the situation in Moscow. Both contained similar images: civilians, especially children, sitting and climbing on tanks and APCs with no interference from soldiers or officers. The reports attempted to convey an atmosphere of calm by showing people eating ice cream on tanks, while others posed for pictures in front of them. A bouquet of roses in a gun barrel at the conclusion of the first Moscow report (though the report was obviously cut abruptly at this point) was probably intended to suggest cordial relations between soldiers and civilians, but it also indicated that the fraternization, reported on Monday by Medvedev, was continuing. The implication was that soldiers were refusing to use their guns.[48] A "normalcy" shot focused on a line of people queuing up for vodka. The camera panned to a solitary bottle of Moskovskaya vodka placed on the pavement by an old lady. For several seconds, viewers were treated to a close-up of the bottle, transformed into a visual metaphor of Russia at the crossroads, with vodka as a symbol of the country's future.

The second report on Tuesday's *Vremia*, put together by B. Baryshnikov and A. Gromov, contains a striking visual image. A huge banner is stretched across a street above a tank. The banner announces the premiere of a play whose title is clearly etched in bold letters: *Tsar Ivan the Terrible*. Beneath are teenagers and children romping on the tanks and young soldiers read-

Victoria E. Bonnell & Gregory Freidin

ing Yeltsin leaflets. The juxtaposition between the tyrannical tsar and the Emergency Committee leaps out from the screen. The framing of this image for the television audience—and there can be no doubt that the sequence was deliberately shot and knowingly inserted into the report—sent a powerful message to viewers. The segment also includes an interview with an army major, disclosing that some Muscovites viewed the soldiers and their hardware as "the enemy" and not saviors, as the plotters would have had them believe. A youthful reporter wraps up the report with the statement, "Now everyone understands that the troops are a necessary guarantee of general safety."

Following the first report, *Vremia* abruptly brought to the screen the reporter Vladimir Stefanov. His appearance was pointedly informal: hair slightly ruffled, a casual sports shirt open at the collar. Stefanov reminded viewers that the Emergency Committee consisted of important people, "members of the Government," appointed by even more important people. Although he himself did not like the precise procedure involved in this transfer of power, he did not believe it was worthwhile to risk one's life over the quarrel among top-ranking politicians. "We may not like what has happened," he continued "but life willed it otherwise." With emotion welling in his voice, Stefanov implored his audience, "Anything, anything at all, but please no blood!" [*vse chto ugodno—tol'ko by ne krov'*]. Stefanov's appearance was strikingly different from other *Vremia* announcers and reporters on Monday and Tuesday, with the exception of Medvedev. And, like Medvedev, the camera showed Stefanov speaking with earnestness and informality directly to the television viewer. The decision to put him on the air during Tuesday's *Vremia* emphasizes the importance of style as a component in the battle of the competing scripts: precisely by appropriating the style of their democratic opposition, officials at Gosteleradio expected to make their message more palatable and plausible to the viewing audience or, at least, to some critical portion of it.[49]

On Tuesday, Leningrad television continued its presentation of programs supporting the democratic resistance. The appearance and demeanor of the anchor on *Fakt* immediately suggested a deviation from the straightlaced, Soviet-style announcer favored by the conspirators, a style that dominated Central Television throughout the day. This anchor was a modern-looking, well-dressed young woman who looked straight at the camera and functioned more as a pleasant interlocutor than a mouthpiece for official decrees. *Fakt* included a report of the mass meeting in Palace Square earlier that day, attended, the reporter declared, by 120,000 people. Sobchak was shown addressing the crowd, and many tricolor flags appear in the film footage. Leningrad television also presented a lengthy interview with the Leningrad Party boss, who amiably chatted with the reporter about the impossibility of committing oneself one way or the other regarding the Emergency Committee. A special program on Leningrad television that evening featured Mayor Sobchak, flanked by Vice Mayor of Leningrad Shcherbakov and Rear Admiral E. D. Chernov, commander of the Atomic Flotilla of the Northern Fleet. Shcherbakov minced no words: the junta stands for totalitarianism, he said; they want to make us pay with our bodies for the Communist paradise. Chernov and Sobchak urged people to use their consciences and honor [*sovest'* and *chest'*] to defend the legal government, to assert their human individuality [*chelovecheskaia lichnost'*] in defense of the "great Motherland" [*velikaia rodina*] and "great city" [*velikii gorod*]. The alternative, Sobchak pointed out, was to submit to the junta and be transformed back into cattle [*bydlo*].

Both the Leningrad station and Central Television aired news programs on Tuesday that, in one way or another, alerted viewers to the mounting opposition to the Emergency Committee, not just in Moscow and Leningrad, but in Kishinev, Volgograd, Tallinn, and elsewhere. The mere presence of this information on *Vremia* implied a serious weakness in the Emergency Committee, which had obviously tried and failed to control the one and only news program on Central Television. On this second day of the crisis, the progress of the events could be measured and assessed in terms of television coverage: what began as a *perevorot* had turned into a *televorot*, with television occupying the front line for political struggle over legitimacy and authority.

21–23 August, Days Three, Four, Five: The Victorious Version of the Russian Democratic Script

By Wednesday afternoon, it was clear to all who followed the news that the Emergency Committee was in a full-scale retreat from the democratic forces under Yeltsin's leadership. Seen in retrospect, the victory over the conspirators was, first and foremost, a symbolic one: the conspirators never achieved enough cooperation from the military and the KGB to overwhelm the opposition physically.[50] As it turned out, the really critical struggle was fought not only in the streets but on millions of television screens, where competing scripts, images, and styles offered viewers starkly opposed versions of the past, present, and future. The Emergency Committee suffered defeat in this critical battle over hearts and minds when it failed—whether through oversight or inability—to control Central Television completely

Victoria E. Bonnell & Gregory Freidin

and to deploy rhetoric and symbols in a compelling and credible manner in support of its claim to rule.

While the coup was in progress, *Vremia* functioned as the authoritative news program on Soviet Central Television and also, to a considerable extent, the mouthpiece of those in power. When the conspirators' ship sank, so did their supporters in high places. On the afternoon of 21 August, Yeltsin issued Decree No. 69, "On the Means of Mass Communication in the RSFSR," abrogating the GKChP's measures to reinstate censorship, dismissing Kravchenko from his position as president of Gosteleradio, and placing Gosteleradio under control of the government of the Russian republic.[51] At 5:00 P.M. Central Television began broadcasting live the session of the Russian parliament that was in progress.[52] Gorbachev had not yet returned to Moscow, and what was left of his government was in disarray.

Wednesday's *Vremia* was produced in a power vacuum. The program aired that evening was a hybrid, combining elements from the Russian democratic narrative and some of the style and ambiance of the Soviet script. The announcers were the same dour figures who had presided during the previous two days, but the content of the program was radically different. In a voice that showed little emotion or deviation from the Soviet standard, the announcer began with the dramatic statement that the putsch had been overthrown by the democratic forces. Members of the Emergency Committee were labeled "adventurists" by the same announcers who only twenty-four hours earlier had reported on behalf of the Emergency Committee. Although the plotters had been repudiated, the scripting of Wednesday's *Vremia* did not disengage entirely from the rhetoric and format of the junta days. The key word was still *stabil'nost'*, and the format of the program duplicated that of the previous two evenings; only the political content had changed. After a summary of the major developments, the program showed segments from different parts of the country. As on previous evenings, pictures of urban serenity dominated the newscasts; only now, in such cities as Alma-Ata, Barnaul, and Kuzbass, the proverbial man or woman in the street was implacably opposed to the junta.

Vremia gave extensive coverage on Wednesday evening to public protest in Leningrad. The camera dwelled on the vast crowd that filled Palace Square, many people carrying tricolor flags. Here was the archetype for the victory script of the Russian democratic forces: the finale of the narrative that began with the putschists seizing power in order to reimpose totalitarian rule on the Soviet people. According to this version, ordinary citizens in great numbers and with great courage and conviction defeated the junta. They were inspired by their love of democracy and country, Russia, symbolized by the tricolor flag. A memorable image concluded the report: the Alexander Column archangel blessing the city, and above and around it, Russian tricolor flags. The struggle, according to this scenario, was between good and evil. As Khasbulatov put it to the Russian Supreme Soviet on Wednesday afternoon (in an ironic appropriation of Stalin's wartime slogan), "We won because our cause was right!" Live television and radio coverage of the Supreme Soviet meeting that day made it possible for millions of people to witness this remark and others praising Muscovites, and Russians more generally, for their resistance to the junta.

Only on Thursday did a dramatic change take place in *Vremia*. The day had been proclaimed a national holiday, Freedom Day, by the Russian parliament. Most members of the Emergency Committee had been arrested; one, Pugo, had committed suicide. Yeltsin was at the peak of his popularity. When *Vremia* came on the air, the anchors had been changed: now Sergei Medvedev, the reporter who had put together Monday's prodemocratic segment, presided over the news program. Not only was this a great vindication for Medvedev, but his appearance marked an important shift in the style as well as the content of reporting. Far more casual and direct than his predecessors, he functioned as an anchorman and commentator rather than a mere mouthpiece. Young, energetic and articulate, he spoke in a natural and unformulaic way, without the standard Soviet rhetoric.

The heart of Thursday's *Vremia* was film footage, apparently unedited, of an incident early Wednesday morning that had left three men dead. This clip, shot in semidarkness and accompanied by somber music, had a moving, almost piercing effect: a Moscow street, the barricade of trolleybusses, unarmed people trying to prevent the APCs from passing through the barricades, shots, bodies falling and crushed by tank treads, Molotov cocktails going off, more shots, blood on the pavement, and, later that day, an improvised shrine and grief-stricken Muscovites mourning the "martyrs" who "perished as a result of an unsuccessful attempt to storm the White House." The report helped to create a national surge of feeling for the three young men who lost their lives "defending our freedom."[53] The *Vremia* broadcast was a feast of symbols. The tricolor flag was now the official flag of the Russian Republic, adopted by the Russian parliament the preceding afternoon, and flags were prominently featured in footage shown on the program. The area behind the White House was renamed Freedom Square. And it was the Day of Freedom, a Russian version of the Fourth of July or Bastille Day, complete with fireworks in the evening. The celebratory events of the day, the speeches by Yeltsin and others, the gathering on Dzerzhinsky Square and the subsequent removal of Dzerzhinsky's statue (another highly symbolic moment), were all televised live. Television once again—this time with live uncensored coverage by reporters who had a style and demeanor much like Medvedev's—brought the events and the Russian democratic script to viewers throughout the country.

With the return to television of the feisty program of news and commentary, *Vzgliad*, 253 days after it had been banned by Kravchenko, the Russian democratic script was recast to correspond to the victorious but tragic culmination of events. The Thursday and Friday programs featured documentary films, both called *Perevorot*, that chronicled the preceding three days of political turmoil.

To appreciate the rescripting of the events that was under way, it is helpful to note what the documentary montage did not include in *Perevorot*. Excluded were scenes of the fraternization between Moscow civilians and soldiers, as was the footage of the animated exchanges alongside tanks and APCs, the instances of camaraderie. All of that remained on the cutting room floor. A similar fate befell numerous film clips of civilians who had climbed on tanks and APCs, eaten ice cream atop the tank turrets, scrawled slogans on the armor and used the heavy equipment as so many soapboxes from which to address assembled multitudes. (Yeltsin's was only the most famous among the numerous improvisations in the "Finland Station" style.) The children romping on the tanks—a familiar sight on the nineteenth and the twentieth—were likewise excluded from the documentary. In the version of *Perevorot* shown on Thursday, the ominously rumbling tanks and APCs in Moscow encountered unarmed civilians, who used their own bodies to prevent the tanks and APCs from moving forward (some remarkable footage of this resistance appears in the film). Soldiers, always very youthful, read Yeltsin's decrees. Yeltsin—in person and through his decrees and proclamations—was central to this version and, of course, *Perevorot* included the footage of his appearance on a tank. The democrats' most important symbol, the tricolor flag, found its way into many of the film's segments—a reminder that the resisters owed their primary allegiance to Russia. Brief interviews with such well-known figures as the cellist Mstislav Rostropovich (in the White House on Tuesday evening, sporting a rifle), the film director Sergei Mikhalkov, and the editor of *Moscow News* and newly appointed Gosteleradio president, Egor Iakovlev, were included in the film, juxtaposed to a short segment from the Emergency Committee's press conference, including the famous image of Yanaev's trembling hands.

In *Vzgliad's* scripting of events, the junta and its military hardware now emerged as truly threatening and ominous—no more occasion for child's play! Ordinary citizens were shown as fantastically courageous, to the point of holding back tanks and defending the White House with their bodies; entreaties to soldiers and gifts of sausage and cigarettes did not do justice to this level of heroic resistance. The degree of peril faced by those on the barricades was now fully evident: three had died. But ordinary citizens were not the only heroes. They were helped by soldiers who crossed over to Yeltsin's side, such as Major Sergei Evdokimov's tank battalion from the Taman Division which was shown making the heroic move from one side of the barricade to the other on Monday evening.

Soldiers appeared in the narrative as extremely young and naive but receptive to Yeltsin's decrees. It was Yeltsin whose words and deeds won soldiers over to the Russian democratic cause, instead of middle-aged Russian matrons entreating soldiers not to shoot at their mothers. Yeltsin is the larger-than-life hero of the film, the inspiration and the leader of the democratic resistance. His appearance on the tank now had all the qualities of an iconographic image. The interviews with leading Russian cultural figures during the coup was a novelty; in these segments may be discerned a process of "heroization": tell me what you were doing during the August coup, the film implicitly argues, and I will tell you who you are.

22 August, Day Four: The Perestroika Script

Gorbachev's first public statement following his release from confinement to his Crimean dacha was aired on *Vremia* on Thursday evening. Here Gorbachev spoke of the "attempted coup, foiled as a result of the decisive actions taken by the country's democratic forces. . . . " The term "attempted coup" [*popytka perevorota*] attested to a very different interpretation of the events from the one put forward by Yeltsin and his democratic supporters. Earlier that same day, television had carried a live broadcast of Yeltsin's speech before Russia's Supreme Soviet, where he offered a threefold narrative, reminiscent of Russian folk tales: thrice the right-wing forces tried to stage a coup d'état; twice they failed; the third time, they succeeded:[54]

> [T]he first attempt took place at the beginning of the year, but at that time they were scared off by the statement made by the minister of foreign affairs, Eduard Shevardnadze, and the corresponding reaction of public opinion in Russia, the country, and the world. You all recall the session of the USSR Supreme Soviet, when the same people—Pavlov, Kriuchkov, Yazov—tried to extract for themselves some special powers at the expense of the authority of the president of the country, which virtually amounted to his removal from office, and so forth. But this second attempt also failed: the Supreme Soviet gave them no support. *And*

Victoria E. Bonnell & Gregory Freidin

finally, the third, this time successful, attempt came when the president was vacationing away from Moscow. . . . [emphasis added]

Yeltsin's message in his Thursday speech to parliament was that, while the coup might have failed miserably in Russia, it had succeeded in the U.S.S.R., since no major all-union institution had declared itself squarely against the conspiracy: not the army, nor the KGB, nor the MVD, nor the Supreme Soviet, nor the cabinet, nor the Communist Party. Indeed, the leaders of these institutions were the key conspirators and, now that they had been routed, the U.S.S.R. had only an ephemeral existence. Gorbachev swiftly countered this rhetoric of Russia's supremacy over the Union. Returning to Moscow in the early hours of 22 August, in his first statement before the television cameras, he offered praise, first and foremost, to the *Soviet* people:[55]

> I congratulate the *Soviet* people, who have a sense of responsibility and a sense of dignity, who care, who respect all those whom they have entrusted with power. . . . Some pathetic bunch, using attractive slogans, speculating on the difficulties . . . , wished to divert our people to a road that would have led our entire society to a catastrophe. *It did not work.* This is the greatest achievement of perestroika. . . . I want to express my appreciation to the *Soviet* people, to the citizens of Russia, for their principled position, to Boris Nikolaevich Yeltsin, to the Supreme Soviet of the Russian Federation, to all the deputies, work collectives, which took a decisive stand against this caper. [Emphasis added.]

The scripts offered by the two presidents differed down to the very last detail. Whereas Gorbachev tried to diminish the whole affair by referring to the conspirators as a "pathetic bunch" of treacherous but incompetent men engaged in a "caper" [*avantiura*], Yeltsin portrayed the Emergency Committee as dangerous opponents of epic proportions—powerful men who had presided over the government as part of Gorbachev's latest perestroika team. The stature of the enemy, apparently, conferred stature also on the resisters: the men and women who stood up to tyranny.

In Gorbachev's further statements on Thursday, 22 August, including a press conference broadcast live on Central Television,[56] he appeared chastised but unreformed, still insisting on the role of the Communist Party as a necessary bridge between Soviet totalitarianism and democracy. The scripting of events by the democratic opposition was by then triumphant in the mass media, and his appearance was framed by scenes from the mass celebration of the Day of Freedom in Moscow and elsewhere. Gorbachev's rhetoric and ideas accorded poorly with the images of a courageous people celebrating a heroic victory over a formidable enemy.

24 August, Day Six: The Funeral

On Saturday, 24 August, the live televised broadcast of the funeral for the three who had died on Wednesday morning gave the democratic Russia script its most moving, most fitting coda. The camera followed the progress of the funeral, which began in Manège Square where the mourners were addressed by several prominent political figures including Gorbachev. After the speeches, the funeral procession turned its back on the Kremlin and moved on to the White House. Here Yeltsin, somber, proud, fully in control, spoke the most memorable words of the day, if not of his entire career. Addressing the victims' parents and implicitly the entire nation, expressing traditional humility before the people and implicitly projecting the image of the nation's patriarch, he spoke slowly and clearly: "Forgive me, for I have failed to protect your sons." Now transformed by Yeltsin's speech into a symbol of the entire nation, the procession moved on to the Vagan'kovo Cemetery for the two religious services—Russian Orthodox and Jewish—and finally the interment.[57]

The funeral rally and procession were carefully choreographed media events viewed by millions of people throughout the Soviet Union. The images and rituals served to crystallize some of the major themes developed by the democratic opposition over the preceding week. The main symbolic leitmotif was that of a nation—Russia—committed to common citizenship in civil society. That this commitment was now sealed by the martyrs' blood was of singular ritual importance, especially in view of the long-standing Russian tradition, both secular and religious, of defining the nation around a martyr's ultimate sacrifice.[58] The phrase, "they gave their lives for our freedom," was repeated again and again throughout the broadcast of the funeral. Naturally, the leitmotif of this new social bond found its fullest expression in the television coverage of the two funeral services conducted concurrently for the victims: one in a Russian Orthodox church, the other, a Jewish service, held out-of-doors.

The television coverage moved back and forth between the Jewish and Russian Orthodox services, from the rabbi and cantor to the priests and Patriarch and back again, with an evenhandedness that bespoke deliberate staging for the television audience. In light of the many decades of Soviet antireligious and anti-Semitic policies, the lengthy coverage of both services provided a fascinating spectacle for millions of viewers. But equally remark-

Victoria E. Bonnell & Gregory Freidin

able and politically eloquent was the balanced treatment given to the two religions. That all three should be mourned together was critically important for the victorious democratic resistance. The coverage was scripted to emphasize not only the ecumenical, but also the multiethnic, multiclass citizenship in the new Russia (Dmitrii Komar', an Afghan veteran and a worker, was, judging by his name, Ukrainian; Il'ia Krichevskii, was a Moscow artist of Jewish origin; Vladimir Usov was Russian and an entrepreneur[59]). This important *ecumenical* message was captured in the civic ritual of the heroes' interment. The coffins were covered with a Russian tricolor flag and then lowered into the grave to the accompaniment of the *Russian* national anthem. The TV cameras were positioned high above the graves, figuratively transporting the viewers high into the sky. The image of the flag-draped coffins, with the Russian anthem playing in the background, signalled the fact that this was, above all, a funeral for national heroes, "martyrs," whose deaths were inextricably linked to the forging of a new nation.

The week ended as it had begun: millions of television screens beaming the gripping, real political drama into people's living rooms, bringing the affairs of state and nation building into a close and intimate relationship with every viewer. The funeral served as the culmination of the television coverage of the *perevorot*—coverage that created the first true media event in the history of the Soviet Union. The crisis in high politics had been profoundly and decisively shaped by the electronic eye that transformed, instantly and continuously, elements of a political confrontation into meaningful scripts with their corresponding images, styles, and symbols. The 1991 *televorot* that began at 6:00 A.M. on 19 August with the televised announcement of the formation of the Emergency Committee received a fitting closure on Saturday afternoon, 24 August, with live coverage of a funeral that was as much a memorial to the three men as the consecration of a nation.

Notes

We are grateful to Professor Elliott Mossman for proposing that we write about Russian television coverage of the August 1991 coup. His support and encouragement helped us to complete this project. Joelle Ehre at the Harriman Institute, Columbia University, and Pegge J. Abrams at the Media Center, Duke University, were extremely helpful in providing video tapes of Russian television broadcasts during the week of the coup. We would like to thank George Breslauer, Nancy Condee, Todd Gitlin, Eric Naiman, Ann Nesbet, Vladimir Padunov, Yuri Slezkine, Viktor Zaslavsky, and Reginald Zelnik for their valuable comments and suggestions. A version of this chapter appeared in the *Slavic Review* 52, 4 (winter 1993): 810–38. An earlier draft was presented at the Fourth Meeting of the Working Group on Contemporary Russian Culture, "Russian Culture/Soviet Hieroglyphics," held with the support of the Social Science Research Council, the British Film Institute, and the School for Slavonic and East European Studies at the University of London, 5 through 9 July 1993. In translation, the epigraph to this chapter reads, "A different drama is now playing. . . . "

1. In February 1991, U.S.S.R. Gosteleradio was renamed the All-Union State Company for Television and Radio Broadcasting. On the situation in Gosteleradio before the coup, see Vera Tolz, "The Soviet Media," *RFE/RL Research Report* 1, 1 (3 January 1992): 29–30.

2. For details, see Bill Keller's interview with Sergei Medvedev, "Getting the News on 'Vremia' " and the "Chronology of Events of August 19, 20, 21" in Victoria E. Bonnell, Ann Cooper, and Gregory Freidin, eds., *Russia at the Barricades: Eyewitness Accounts of the August 1991 Coup* (Armonk: M. E. Sharpe, 1994), part 5. Accounts of the coup and its aftermath may be found in the following Russian sources: *Avgust-91* (Moscow: Izdatel'stvo politicheskoi literatury, 1991); . . . *Deviatnadtsatoe, dvadtsatoe, dvadtsat' pervoe . . . : svobodnoe radio dlia svobodnykh liudei* (Moscow: Shakur-Invest, 1991); *Krasnoe ili beloe? Drama Avgusta-91: Fakty, gipotezy, stolknovenie mnenii* (Moscow, 1991); *Korichnevyi putch krasnykh, avgust '91: Khronika, svidetel'stva pressy, fotodokumenty* (Moscow: Tekst, 1991); *Khronika putcha: chas za chasom: Sobytiia 19–22 avgusta 1991 v svodkakh Rossiiskogo Informatsionnogo Agentstva* (Leningrad: Agentstvo 1991); *Putch: Khronika trevozhnykh dnei* (Moscow, 1991); V. Stepankov and E. Lisov, *Kremlevskii zagovor* (Moscow: Progress, 1992). English language sources on the coup include the following: James H. Billington, *Russia Transformed: Breakthrough to Hope: Moscow, August 1991* (New York: Free Press, 1992); Bonnell, Cooper, and Freidin, eds., *Russia at the Barricades: Eyewitness Accounts of the August 1991 Coup;* John B. Dunlop, *The Rise of Russia and the Fall of the Soviet Empire* (Princeton: Princeton University Press, 1993); Mikhail Gorbachev, *The August Coup: The Truth and the Lessons* (New York: Harper Collins, 1991); Amy Knight, "The Coup That Never Was: Gorbachev and the Forces of Reaction," *Problems of Communism* (November/December 1991); Stuart H. Loory and Ann Imse, eds., *Seven Days That Shook the World* (Atlanta: Turner Publishing, 1991); Michael Mandelbaum, "Coup de Grace: The End of the Soviet Union," *Foreign Affairs* 71, 1 (1991–92): 164–83; William E. Odom, "Alternative Perspectives on the August Coup," *Problems of Communism* (November/December 1991): 13–17; David Remnick, *Lenin's Tomb: The Last Days of the Soviet Empire* (New York: Random House, 1993); Lilia Shevtsova, "The August Coup and the Soviet Collapse," *Survival* 34, 1 (Spring 1992); Anatole Shub, "The Fourth Russian Revolution: Historical Perspectives," *Problems of Communism* (November/December 1991): 20–26; Hedrick Smith, *The New Russians* (New York: Random House, 1991); Melor Sturua, "The Real Coup," *Foreign Policy* 85 (Winter 1991).

3. Resolution No. 1, issued by the Emergency Committee on 19 August, decreed that a specially created organ under the GKChP would "establish control over the means of communication." Resolution No. 3, issued on 20 August, gave further details concerning Gosteleradio's control over all Central and local TV and radio broadcasting in the U.S.S.R. The resolution prohibited television and radio broadcasts by the RSFSR channels, especially "Moscow Echo," because they "do not promote the process of stabilization of the situation in the country." The U.S.S.R. KGB and MVD were authorized to take measures to carry out the resolution. *Avgust-91*: 21, 75–76.

4. "Radio Rossiia" and "Ekho Moskvy," both established in 1990, continued to broad-

Victoria E. Bonnell & Gregory Freidin

cast from the White House and other locations during the coup, as did several other stations on short and medium wave frequencies (*Putch: khronika trevozhnykh dnei*, 91–92). The nine newspapers permitted to continue publication were: *Trud, Rabochaia tribuna, Izvestiia, Pravda, Krasnaia zvezda, Sovetskaia Rossiia, Moskovskaia pravda, Leningradskoe znamia, and Sel'skaia zhizn'*. During the coup, Soviet citizens with shortwave radios were able to receive news from foreign stations, most importantly Radio Liberty and the BBC.

5. The following television programs were viewed for this essay (all dates refer to 1991): *Vremia*: 19, 20, 21, 22, 23, 25 August, 19 September; *Vzgliad*: 22, 23, 25 August; *Fakt*: 20 August; *Piatoe koleso*: 20 August; *600 sekund*: 20 August; *Vesti*: 21, 22 August; *Novosti*: 19 September; *Do shestnadtsati i starshe*: 19 September. Televised press conferences: Gennadii Yanaev et al., 19 August; Vladimir Shcherbakov, 21 August; Mikhail Gorbachev, 22 August; Arkadii Vol'skii et al., 21 August. Other coverage: session of the Russian parliament, 21 August; funeral, 24 August; interview with Yeltsin, 25 August.

6. On Soviet television before 1985, see Mark H. Hopkins, *Mass Media in the USSR* (New York: Pegasus, 1970); Ellen Propper Mickiewicz, *Media and the Russian Public* (New York: Praeger, 1981) and *Split Signals: Television and Politics in the Soviet Union* (New York: Oxford University Press, 1988); Kristian Feigelson, *L'U.R.S.S. et sa télévision* (Paris: Institut national de l'audiovisual, 1990). The last years of Brezhnev's regime saw a torrent of jokes about his slurred speech and the official doctoring of recordings. In one of the most popular jokes of this type, audio engineers are trying to puzzle out what Brezhnev had in mind when he offered praise to *sosiski sranye* (crappy hotdogs). They finally realize that what he meant to say was *sotsialisticheskie strany* (socialist countries) and spliced those words into the tape.

7. For a perceptive discussion of the early impact of glasnost on television, see Mickiewicz, *Split Signals*; James Dingley, "Soviet Television and Glasnost'," in Julian Graffy and Geoffrey A. Hosking, eds., *Culture and the Media in the USSR Today* (New York: MacMillan, 1989); Feigelson, *L'U.R.S.S. et sa télévision*; Brian McNair, *Glasnost, Perestroika, and the Soviet Media* (London: Routledge, 1991); Marsha Siefert, ed., *Mass Culture and Perestroika in the Soviet Union* (New York: Oxford University Press, 1991).

8. In addition, Kravchenko interfered with the broadcasts of *TSN*, a news program that provided an alternative to the official news, *Vremia*. His move to suppress *TSN* in March 1991 was a response to the program's coverage of the events in Lithuania and Latvia in January. Under his leadership, Central Television broadcasts "constantly criticized the RSFSR leadership and the democratic forces opposing the Communist Party of the Soviet Union (CPSU)." See Tolz, "The Soviet Media," 29–30 for more details on Kravchenko's efforts to curb glasnost on Central Television.

9. Later in April 1991, the union recalled Kravchenko as its representative to the U.S.S.R. Supreme Soviet, a position to which he had been elected by the union in 1989. Among those who resigned were Vladimir Pozner, Vladimir Tsvetov, Aleksandr Liubimov, and Vladimir Molchanov (Tolz, "The Soviet Media").

10. In the era of glasnost, the Leningrad studio produced some of the most probing and provocative programs on television anywhere in the U.S.S.R., including *600 Seconds, The Fifth Wheel*, and *Alternative* (Sergei Aleksandrovich Muratov, "Soviet Television and the Structure of Broadcasting Authority," in Siefert, ed., *Mass Culture and Perestroika*, 174).

11. See the interview with Anatolii Sobchak, "Breakthrough: The Coup in St. Petersburg," in Bonnell, Cooper, and Freidin, eds., *Russia at the Barricades*, part 3, 218–25.; Fiegelson, 85.

12. "Script," according to *The American Heritage Dictionary*, is, among other things, "a

text of a play, broadcast, or motion picture; especially the copy of a text used by the director or performer."

13. For a pioneering discussion of a similar symbiosis between television and politics in the United States, see Todd Gitlin, *The Whole World Is Watching: Mass Media in the Making and Unmaking of the New Left* (Berkeley: University of California Press, 1980).

14. Kenneth Burke, *A Grammar of Motives* (Berkeley: University of California Press, 1969); Victor Turner, *Dramas, Fields, and Metaphor: Symbolic Action in Human Society* (Ithaca: Cornell University Press, 1974); Karen Hermassi, *Polity and Theater in Historical Perspective* (Berkeley: University of California Press, 1977); Clifford Geertz, "Centers, Kings, and Charisma: Reflections on the Symbolics of Power," in *Local Knowledge: Further Essays in Interpretive Anthropology* (New York: Basic Books, 1983), 121–46, and *Negara: The Theatre State in Nineteenth-Century Bali* (Princeton: Princeton University Press, 1980); Iu. Lotman, "Teatr i teatral'nost' v stroe kul'tury nachala XIX veka," *Stat'i po tipologii kul'tury* (Tartu: Tartuskii gosudarstvennyi universitet, 1973), 42–73; Iu. Lotman and B. Uspenskii, "The Stage and Paintings as Code Mechanisms for Cultural Behavior in the Early Nineteenth Century," in *The Semiotics of Russian Culture, Michigan Slavic Contributions* no. 11, ed. Ann Shukman (Ann Arbor: University of Michigan Department of Slavic Languages and Literatures, 1984). For a study of Bolshevik holiday celebrations as political theater before the era of television, see James von Geldern, *Bolshevik Festivals, 1917–1921* (Berkeley: University of California Press, 1993).

15. Gorbachev, *The August Coup*, 23. Gorbachev echoes here almost verbatim the statements he made in interviews immediately following his return to Moscow on 22 August 1991. In his televised press conference on that day, he also used such terms as *"tiazhelaia drama"* (a heavy drama) and *"fars"* (farce) to describe the coup d'état. In his 25 August interview with Soviet TV, Yeltsin, too, resorted several times to the term "script" in describing the plotters' course of action. Aleksandr Kabakov, a popular writer and the author of the sensational 1991 best-seller *Nevozvrashchenets*, claimed in the TV program *Vzgliad*, aired on 23 August 1991, that his most recent novel, *Sochinitel'*, had *scripted* in advance many of the developments that took place on 19 through 21 August. (We thank Nancy Condee for the reference to *Sochinitel'*.) Characteristically, General Aleksandr Lebed' who, together with his commanding officer General Pavel Grachev, did most to prevent the storming of the White House, entitled his forthcoming memoirs *Spektakl' nazyvalsia putch* (the show was called putsch). The memoir was serialized in *Literaturnaia Rossiia* (the first installment, *Literaturnaia Rossiia* no. 34–35 [24 September 1993]).

16. The following were issued at the inception of the coup: a decree by Gennadii Yanaev announcing his assumption of power because of Gorbachev's ill health; an "Appeal to the Soviet People" from the Emergency Committee; "Resolution No. 1 of the Emergency Committee"; a declaration from Yanaev, Pavlov, and Baklanov; and Yanaev's appeal to foreign nations and the United Nations secretary general. In addition, there was a statement by A. Luk'ianov, president of the U.S.S.R. Supreme Soviet on the Union Treaty.

17. Scott R. McMichael, "Moscow Prelude: Warning Signs Ignored," *Report on the USSR* 3, no. 36 (1991): 8–11.

18. Ivan Silaev, chairman of the RSFSR Council of Ministers, and Ruslan Khasbulatov, acting chairman of the RSFSR Supreme Soviet, were coauthors and signers of the appeal, "To the Citizens of Russia."

19. "Decree of the President of the RSFSR No. 59" (declaring the Emergency Committee unconstitutional, its actions null and void, and those involved subject to criminal penalties); "Appeal of the President of the RSFSR to Soldiers and Officers of the USSR

Victoria E. Bonnell & Gregory Freidin

Armed Forces, KGB, MVD"; and "Decrees of the President of the RSFSR," nos. 60, 61, 62, 63. The texts of all the preceding appear in *Avgust-91*: 34–42, 61–62.

20. "Chronology of Events of August 19, 20, 21," in Bonnell, Cooper, and Freidin, eds., *Russia at the Barricades*, 337–65.

21. Sergei Medvedev's 19 August *Vremia* segment discussed below includes a Moscow intellectual who explicitly drew the connection between the events in Vilnius and the August coup. For A. Akhmedov, a member of the Popular Front of Azerbaijan who went to Moscow during the coup, this association was also self-evident. As he said during the funeral on 24 August, "I came to Moscow as soon as the coup started. . . . It was a continuation of the bloody events in Baku and Vilnius, where I was during the January bloodshed. And the three boys whom we are burying today died for the same cause that people in other republics have given their lives for" (V. Konovalov, E. Maksimova, and L. Savel'eva, "Proshchanie," *Avgust-91*, 217). See also Valerii Zavorotnyi's "Letter from Leningrad," which recounts that the leader of the team building barricades in Leningrad on 19 August had learned barricade construction in Vilnius, where he helped to guard the parliament building as a member of the Leningrad detachment of young volunteers (Bonnell, Cooper, and Freidin, eds., *Russia at the Barricades*, part 2, 147–57).

22. Prior to glasnost, television announcers read their texts "practically by rote, and words like 'I' and 'I think' were excluded." The style of the announcer and anchorperson had been changing under Gorbachev; on the day of the coup, the style of presentation reverted back to the old form. On changes in style under glasnost, see Muratov, "Soviet Television and the Structure of Broadcasting Authority," in Siefert, *Mass Culture and Perestroika in the Soviet Union*, 175.

23. The statement was dated 18 August 1991 and signed "Gosudarstvennyi komitet po chrezvychainomu polozheniiu v SSSR." When the text was published in *Izvestiia* on 20 August, it was given the title "Appeal to the Soviet People."

24. These are the closing words of the "Appeal to the Soviet People." The original Russian text is reprinted in *Avgust-91*, 20–24. A translation can be found in Bonnell, Cooper, and Freidin, eds., *Russia at the Barricades*, part 1, 33–38.

25. In the days before perestroika, Gosteleradio characteristically responded to dramatic official events, such as the death of a leading official, by replacing regular TV programming with classical music and ballet.

26. It is quite possible that the members of the Emergency Committee taking part in the press conference were not aware that the press conference was being broadcast live. The cameras were not turned off right after the press conference drew to a close but lingered for a minute or two, long enough for the viewers to be privy to the following exchange between an enterprising reporter and Yanaev. The reporter: "Gennadii Ivanovich [Yanaev], can you give us assurances that this press conference will be broadcast in its entirety?" Yanaev: "Well, I don't think I am the man to answer this question. You shouldn't really address it to me. . . . " The reporter: "Can you give us assurances that this press conference will be broadcast to the public in its entirety?" Yanaev: "No, really, you should not address this question to me. It is not up to me to decide. . . . "

27. A Russian transcript of the press conference appears in *Avgust-91*, 43–61. An English translation of the press conference appears in Bonnell, Cooper, and Freidin, eds., *Russia at the Barricades*, part 1, 42–54.

28. Stepankov and Lisov, *Kremlevskii zagovor*, 89–91.

29. Aleksandr Tiziakov was president of the Association of State Enterprises and Industrial Construction, Transport, and Communications. Vasilii Starodubtsev was chair-

man of the Peasants Union. Oleg Baklanov was first deputy chairman of the National Defense Council and leader of the military industrial complex.

30. Remnick, *Lenin's Tomb*, 473–74.

31. The question about Yanaev's health was asked by the correspondent from *La Stampa*. It was a double-entendre question, referring not only to the alleged sickness of Gorbachev, but also to the answer Yanaev gave when he was asked about his health at the Supreme Soviet at the time he was being considered for the post of vice-president. "My health is all right," he responded; "My wife ain't complaining." The question about Pinochet was asked by the correspondent from *Corriere della Sera*. Bonnell, Cooper, and Freidin, eds., *Russia at the Barricades*, part 1, 46, 50.

32. These statements appeared in an interview with Korsak, "Nam byl otdan prikaz arestovat' Popova," *Literaturnaia gazeta* (11 September 1991). A translation appears in *Russian Politics and Law: A Journal of Translation* 31, 1: 16–20.

33. See the interview with KGB Major General Viktor Karpukhin and subordinate officers, "Oni otkazalis' shturmovat' Belyi dom," *Literaturnaia gazeta* (28 August 1991): 5, translated in *Russian Politics and Law* 31, 1: 8–15.

34. The interview with Sobchak was conducted by A. Golovkova and A. Chernova and appeared originally in *Moscow News*, 26 August 1991. An English translation of the interview with Anatolii Sobchak, "Breakthrough: The Coup in St. Petersburg," can be found in Bonnell, Cooper, and Freidin, eds., *Russia at the Barricades*, part 3, 218–25.

35. Beginning on 1 January 1968, *Vremia* appeared every evening at 9:00 P.M. The program lasted forty to forty-five minutes, sometimes longer on the occasion of a major policy speech. American research on Soviet television, published in 1987, disclosed that *Vremia* generally covered twenty-two news items, with precedence going to domestic news. In the second half of the 1980s, some modifications took place in *Vremia*, such as the inclusion of more foreign news. On a typical evening around the time of the coup, *Vremia* had an average viewing audience of 150 million people, or over 80 percent of the adult population in the Soviet Union (Mickiewicz, *Split Signals*, 8–9 and chapter 3). See also, Dingley, "Soviet Television and Glasnost'," in Graffy and Hosking, eds., *Culture and the Media*, 8–9.

36. For Medvedev's comments on the circumstances surrounding the preparation of the segment, see his interview with Bill Keller, "Getting the News on 'Vremia' " in Bonnell, Cooper, and Freidin, eds., *Russia at the Barricades*, part 5, 301–5.

37. Whatever the source of the clip of Yeltsin on the tank, it was not acknowledged in the 19 August *Vremia* broadcast.

38. The Russian text has been reprinted in *Avgust-91*, 35–36. For an English translation, see Bonnell, Cooper, and Freidin, eds., *Russia at the Barricades*, part 3, 170–71.

39. The flag has a long history in Russia, dating to 1799 when it was introduced as the country's merchant flag. In 1883 it became an alternative civil flag, and in 1914 Tsar Nicholas II added a double-headed eagle, the symbol of the monarchy. The flag, minus the eagle, served the Provisional Government but was abandoned after the Bolsheviks seized power. Resurrected after 1985 as a symbol of Russian national identity and citizenship, the tricolor flag encapsulated a set of substantive, symbolic, and rhetorical issues that remained central throughout the crisis.

40. This information was conveyed by Aleksandr Petrov, CNN general manager of Soviet sales and liaison with Soviet TV in Moscow. He observed, "We can thank the coup plotters for their ineptitude in underestimating the power of CNN" (Betsy McKay, "From Coup to Champagne," *Advertising Age* 62, 35 [26 August 1991]: 37).

41. Bonnell, Cooper, and Freidin, eds., *Russia at the Barricades*, part 5, 303–4.

42. Ibid., 304.

43. Ibid.; Remnick, *Lenin's Tomb*, 474.

44. Medvedev, "Getting the News on 'Vremia,' " 304.

45. Bonner's remark came at the mass rally held at the White House at midday on Tuesday. Sobchak made the remark that evening on the Leningrad television news program, *Fakt.*

46. Medvedev, "Getting the News on 'Vremia,' " 304.

47. Literary *perevorot* means the turning of things upside down. In modern usage, however, the term has a clear political connotation. The 1939 edition of the Ushakov *Tolkovyi slovar' russkogo iazyka*, vol. 3, ed. B. M. Volin and D. N. Ushakov (107) defines a *perevorot* as a sharp change in the existing social and political order, such as the October *perevorot* of 1917.

48. This segment was put together by R. Oganesov and B. Antsiferov, and concentrated on the Moscow scene in Manège Square.

49. For a provocative discussion of style, see Dick Hebdige, *Subculture: The Meaning of Style* (London: Methuen, 1983).

50. For accounts of the Emergency Committee's failure to persuade military and KGB officers to execute orders against Yeltsin and his democratic supporters, see introduction, in Bonnell, Cooper, and Freidin, eds., *Russia at the Barricades*; Remnik, *Lenin's Tomb*, 482–84; Stepankov and Lisov, *Kremlevskii zagovor*, 171–80 and elsewhere; "They Refused to Storm the White House" and " 'We Were Given the Order to Arrest Popov . . . ' " in *Russian Politics and Law* 31, 1 (Summer 1992): 8–20. (Russian citations of these articles appear above in notes 33 and 34.)

51. For the Russian text of the decree, see *Avgust-91*, 85–86. On 27 August, Kravchenko was replaced by Egor Iakovlev, chief editor of *Moscow News*. Iakovlev reversed some of Kravchevko's key decisions and restored *Vzgliad* as well as *TSN* with its controversial moderators (Tolz, "The Soviet Media," 30).

52. TV programming returned to normal on Thursday morning (McKay, "From Coup to Champagne," 37).

53. Three men perished: Dmitrii A. Komar', Il'ia M. Krichevskii, and Vladimir A. Usov. At the time this report was aired, it was generally believed that the fatalities had occurred during an attack on the White House. Only in the days and weeks following the event did it become clear that, although a military attack on the White House had been planned, it never actually took place. The three deaths occurred when a column of APCs, trapped by the barricades, attempted to extricate themselves by ramming through a row of streetcars blocking an underpass. In the ensuing melee, two of the men were shot, and a third was crushed by an APC.

54. For an English translation of this speech, see Bonnell, Cooper, and Freidin, eds., *Russia at the Barricades*, part 3, 176–80.

55. The text of Gorbachev's remarks was published in *Pravda* 23 August 1991. It is reprinted in *Avgust-91*, 102–3.

56. For the Russian text of Gorbachev's speech, see *Avgust-91*, 109–12. Later that day, he made another extensive statement to introduce his press conference. The Russian text appears in *Avgust-91*, 112–28. A partial English translation may be found in Bonnell, Cooper, and Freidin, eds., *Russia at the Barricades*, part 3, 161–69.

57. The Russian Orthodox funeral service was for Dmitrii Komar' and Vladimir Usov and conducted in the Vagan'kovo Cemetery by the Patriarch; the Jewish service was for Il'ia Krichevskii. Jewish funerals are not held on Saturdays. An exception was made in

this case to coordinate with the two Russian Orthodox funerals, which according to tradition were scheduled for the third day after the deaths. Because the Jewish funeral was held on the Sabbath, the rabbi and cantor (from one of Moscow's two synagogues, both Orthodox) could not offer a regular service in a synagogue.

58. On the political authority of martyrdom in the Russian intelligentsia tradition, see Mikhail Gershenzon, "Tvorcheskoe samosoznanie," and Sergei Bulgakov's "Geroizm i podvizhnichestvo," in M. O. Gershenzon, ed., *Vekhi: sbornik statei o russkoi intelligentsii,* 2nd ed. (Moscow, 1909), 84 and 37, respectively. On the special significance of the institution of martyrdom for eastern Christianity, see Peter Brown, "Parting of the Ways," *Society and the Holy in Late Antiquity* (Berkeley: University of California Press, 1982). On the institution of martyrdom in Russian culture, see Michael Cherniavsky, *Tsar and People: Studies in Russian Myths* (New Haven: Yale University Press, 1961); and D. Obolensky, "Russia's Byzantine Heritage," in *The Structure of Russian History*, ed. M. Cherniavsky (New York: Random House, 1970). Among the more recent works on this subject, see G. Freidin, "By the Walls of the Church and State: On the Authority of Literature in Russia's Modern Tradition," *The Russian Review* 52, 2 (April 1993): 149–63. See also the seminal work on the relationship between violence, martyrdom, and political authority by René Girard, *La violence et le sacré* (Paris: B. Grasset, 1972).

59. In eulogizing the victims in Manège Square, Moscow Mayor Gavriil Popov spoke of them as follows: "Volodia Usov, an employee at a joint venture, an entrepreneur; Dima Komar', a worker and Afghan veteran; and Il'ia Krichevskii, an artist. For six years they had been thwarted [by those who had opposed reform]. They had hindered Usov from being an entrepreneur, Komar' from being a worker, and Krichevskii from being able to create . . . " (cited in Dunlop, *The Rise of Russia,* 230).

Three

Documentary Discipline
Three Interrogations
of Stanislav Govorukhin

Eric Naiman and Anne Nesbet

> Novels, plays, films (their authors should themselves be forced to drink
> the cup of Gulag to the bottom!) depict the types one meets in the
> offices of interrogators as chivalrous guardians of truth and humanitari-
> anism, as our loving fathers.
>
> —Aleksander Solzhenitsyn

Toward the end of *The Sorrow and the Pity,* Marcel Ophuls's 1970 documentary study of Clermont-Ferrand during the Second World War, in the
midst of a serialized interview with a German officer who commanded troops
in France during the occupation, the officer remarks that he just happens
to have with him pictures from those bygone days. He begins to pull the
photographs out of his pocket, and suddenly we see the interviewer's hand
materialize in the foreground and reach across the long table.

We have not seen the filmmaker's body during this interview, but we
have already seen these photographs intercut into the interview. Ophuls
does not now interrupt the session to say triumphantly, "Aha! look what I've
acquired!" Still, that hand straining across the table represents what we
might call documentary desire—a striving for control and understanding
that often substitutes for plot in the making of nonfiction film. Such desire is especially important in films about the past. The past, it would seem,
is already known. To render it unpredictable, to defamiliarize it, *to make it
worth interrogating,* requires work.

It is against this background of documentary desire and interrogation
that we intend to examine the three recent documentary films of Stanislav
Govorukhin. These films, *No Way to Live* [*Tak zhit' nel'zia,* 1990], *The Russia
We Have Lost* [*Rossiia, kotoruiu my poteriali,* 1992] and *Solzhenitsyn* (1992), have
aroused a great deal of interest in Russia and among émigrés in the West,

in large measure because they so insistently claim to examine Russia's current fears, longings, and hopes.[1]

In an age in which "publicistic" writing [*publitsistika*] has dominated over fictions, these movies have provoked as much comment as any "played cinema" [*igrovoe kino*]. For the most part, critics have engaged in a sort of scholarly sniping, pointing out gaps in Govorukhin's knowledge or showing how his imagery and argumentation reproduce the rhetoric of the system he has been criticizing. We want to delve in a different direction, into Govorukhin's poetics, and to investigate their rapport with a double sort of discipline: the discipline of documentary filmmaking and the art of interrogation.

Interrogation, that form of discourse so brilliantly and prophetically elaborated by Dostoevskii, has had a "rich" and terrifying history in Soviet culture. The interrogation has served as an arena for the demonstration both of personal integrity and historical "truth"; even Solzhenitsyn, who describes interrogation as a process of unspeakable brutality, sees in that very brutality the essential nature of the Soviet system. Moreover, for Solzhenitsyn interrogation becomes the metaphysical occasion for a grander, metaphorical investigation of history. The search to document both the fabrication and the commission of crimes becomes the object of Solzhenitsyn's own documentary interrogation of Soviet law and order. We are drawn to Govorukhin's films because they promise insight into changes that may have occurred within this important Soviet chronotope and, more broadly, in Soviet society itself.

Interrogation, of course, has for some time now been central to Govorukhin's films. The brilliant interrogatory technique employed in the defense of law and order by criminal investigator Gleb Zheglov (played by Vladimir Vysotskii) in Govorukhin's television serial *The Meeting Place Can't Be Changed* [*Mesto vstrechi izmenit' nel'zia*, 1979] earned the director an affectionate place in Russian popular culture long before the making of his documentaries.

In his documentaries, Govorukhin's investigatory camera expands its scope to include a wider range of crimes and a broader array of subjects. Govorukhin also tries out new settings, shifting the interrogatory site from the prison to the archive to the editing machine to Vermont, that very special place of virtual solitary confinement. The interrogatory tone modulates along the way, yet this mode of communication continues throughout, from the very first minute of *No Way to Live* to those shots of Govorukhin taking notes as he sits across that long table from Solzhenitsyn in Cavendish. What links these films is a search for a form of interrogation that would not be hollow. Zheglov's mercurial, seductive, and joyous interrogations have been replaced by a sense of investigatory anhedonia, and Govorukhin, suffering from this condition, seems unable to imbue his questioning with the requisite disciplinary desire.

No Way to Live and the Demise of Discipline

No Way to Live opens with crime scenes, a sordid apartment, glimpses of dead bodies, police investigations under way. The first words, heard almost as background noise, belong to the investigator: "What valuables were stolen?" [*A chto vziali iz dragotsennostei?*]—the true (metaphysical) answer to which will be given not in this film, but in the next two films. (It is Russia and Solzhenitsyn, of course, that have been "stolen.") The film thus seems at first to be presenting itself as part of a quest that will unify the filmmaker and his audience in a collective search for value. But there is something missing at the center of this investigation and, more profoundly, at the center of Russian society.

This emptiness is strikingly apparent in Govorukhin's interrogations, interviews that in this film most obviously wear the trappings of criminal procedure. In other movies about historical crimes and tragedies resulting from the ideological perversion of power, dramatic tension arises from watching the filmmaker/interviewer's attempt to move his subjects: they hold some secret that the investigator must ferret out. Whether Claude Lanzmann's subjects are evil or sympathetic, interest in his interviews comes from watching his interlocutors squirm or dissolve into emotion. Lanzmann's questions—in his importunate, tedious foreign accent—reveal a carefully planned strategy that is constantly being adjusted during the interrogation. The camera closely observes the interlocutor's face; it lingers there as the director's questions force mouth, eyes, and skin into motion. In a sense, Lanzmann's approach to the effect of the camera on the face is similar to Dziga Vertov's approach to the camera's effect on the body in *Man with a Movie Camera* [*Chelovek s kinoapparatom*, 1929]. When Vertov's camera moves up and down the legs of a woman lying on a bench, the woman suddenly "realizes" that she is being observed and leaps to her feet, as if stung by the lens.

Govorukhin seems unable to sting the subjects of his observation. His interviews of murderers in *No Way to Live* keep turning into a stagnant draw between his sarcastic barbs and their stony impassivity. The camera, moving over the faces of juvenile rapists, finds only boredom; confessing his crimes, one killer says that he "didn't feel anything" [*ne oshchushchal nichego*]; everything was "in the normal order of things"[*kak v poriadke veshchei*]. The reference to order is significant: the *motions* of discipline remain; the machinery remains; the criminals endlessly and unemotionally reenact their crimes, hesitating only to drag the stand-in policewoman exactly as the murdered girl was dragged, since "the ground is dirty." Order is reduced to numbingly empty etiquette. Where Lanzmann interrogates in order to get the telling twitch that is the sign of internal movement, the hint of a confession, Govorukhin's subjects hide *nothing*—everything is open and stated from the very start. His interlocutors are not, as it turns out, full of secrets, but entirely empty. Thus the task of interviewing loses its interest; it is a chore.

Presumably, Govorukhin's subjects were not always empty. Now they confess their hidden deeds; now they impassively reenact their murders in front of the camera, but they probably did not come to the police and spill their guts of their own accord. The work involved in interviewing, the probing interrogation that produces a response, has already been done by others. Govorukhin is a consumer of other people's interrogations. Those other people are the Russian police with whom Govorukhin has a certain, almost paternalistic, critical intimacy. He looks at them with a mixture of affection and horror. We are reminded of a recent *fait divers* from the California papers: a single mother of two-year-old twins falls dead in the family's little apartment. Ten days pass before friends or family stop by (here one might conclude that even in California *tak zhit' nel'zia!*). Finally the door is kicked open, the corpse of the mother discovered, and—miracle of miracles, still very much alive—the little twins, who have lived off the food they found in the kitchen and even managed, the newspapers noted with admiration, to change their own diapers until the diapers ran out.

In Russia, too, the state's orphaned policemen are heroically going through the motions of the disciplined life, but there in no one left to batter down the door and rescue them. In Govorukhin's television serial, *The Meeting Place Can't Be Changed*, the militia's duties actually encompassed the changing of diapers; now the guardians of order seem as helpless as even the smallest citizens whom they once were so prompt to assist.

Govorukhin travels to New York to make the distinction between orphaned and unorphaned police completely clear. The New York police are well paid, well dressed, and well armed: their state "parent" obviously cares about them very much. If killed in the line of duty, they can at least be comforted in their graves by the thought that their families will receive a handsome pension.

Not so the police-orphans of Russia, who are paid niggardly wages, live in corners of horrible communal apartments, and whose ill-fitting "charity clothes" render them functionally gunless. Even if technically their state parent is still alive at the time of this film's making, they have clearly been profoundly abandoned. And yet, their investigations continue. These interrogations, the film leads us to assume, are conducted by orphaned investigators just barely managing to go through the motions. What these preliminary rituals of power have produced, therefore, are shoddy goods, confessions made in the last few days of the month. Discipline's chronotope, which has been so central to the forging of Russian and Soviet consciousness, is now exhausted and yet still strangely addictive.

In *No Way to Live*, Govorukhin's interviews are conducted from what seems at first like the locus of state power. Seated across a table from a young felon, Govorukhin contemptuously mocks this prisoner by reminding him of his mother and professing astonishment that he does not smoke. How different Govorukhin's stance is from that of his Western counterparts, of those other investigators of historical crimes, Lanzmann (*Shoah*) and Ophuls (*The Sorrow and the Pity, Hotel Terminus*)! Lanzmann and Ophuls tirelessly struggle to get into the castle to determine who is responsible. They struggle to penetrate the individual subject's psychology, convinced that impassivity must always be a ruse. Their work is complicated because their subjects can always get up and leave a frustrated director behind. Their films depict this effort, which becomes a plot [*siuzhet*] quite as compelling as the historical story they seek to uncover.

Govorukhin's first two documentaries are devoid of this methodological pattern. We do not see Govorukhin sweat as he picks the locks of history and power. Even the Berlin Wall is conveniently disarmed before Govorukhin's film reaches it, and all Govorukhin has to do is step over its figurative rubble. Moreover, if Govorukhin is storming the citadel of the existing order, he is doing so from within, occupying the "seat of power." In the three films' sole autobiographical moment, Govorukhin visits the town where he was raised and tells about how his mother always insisted that his father had abandoned the family. "Suddenly I had an idea. I wrote to the KGB and they sent me photographs."

Satisfaction here is virtually instantaneous—no effort seems to have been involved in this personal event. Most bizarre of all, Govorukhin relates this tale while sitting on a bench next to a militia officer, who echoes his words in a barely distinct mumble. No tension exists, either within the related story or in Govorukhin's conversation with this seeming emissary of power.

If Govorukhin is an insider, he is inside the Nothing that has supplanted power. Allied with the police, he continues to function as if what Foucault calls the "dust of events" (the object of police surveillance) amounts to something in the end, and yet the criminals he examines no longer have any secret "souls" to be disciplined: those values/valuables [*dragotsennosti*] have already been plundered, leaving Nothing to be uncovered and Nothing to be confessed. It is enough to drive to despair the unlikely pair of Claude Lanzmann and Catherine the Great, who both believed, along with Dostoevskii and many of Michel Foucault's heroes, that "punishment . . . should strike the soul rather than [although in practice, *along with*] the body" (Foucault 16).

The Russia We Have Lost and the Architecture of History

In his second film about the state of Russia, Govorukhin cannot resist showing us the storming of the Winter Palace. Naturally, he uses footage from Sergei Eisenstein's *October* [*Oktiabr'*, 1928], a pseudo-documentary that now becomes documentary evidence of historical falsification. As the Bolsheviks scale the palace gates, however, Govorukhin freezes Eisenstein's film to note a single concrete, "truthful" detail: the palace was defended only by women, boys, and invalids. His frozen shot is deliberately rude—the ugly head of the woman soldier grimaces from between the legs of the Bolshevik climbing over her into the palace—a hieroglyph of disgust.

There is something obscene in this Winter Palace letting itself be taken so easily, an obscenity that both Eisenstein and Govorukhin recognize and play up, each in his own way: Eisenstein with his attention to royal bidets and toilets, Govorukhin with his emphasis on the grubby immaturity of pillagers who would take such pleasure in their "discovery" that beneath the silk and damask of Their Highnesses lurked merely human bodies. The bidet's illegibility for the sackers of the Winter Palace, Govorukhin hints, just goes to show once again how unhygienic those Bolsheviks really were.

But the real obscenity in this scene is the emptiness of the Winter Palace, an emptiness that the toilets and bidets echo in their ugly physicality: "It's not a revolution but a coup d'état," intones Govorukhin solemnly. Here Eisenstein has to go to all the trouble to create resistance and triumph where there was none; in Govorukhin's terms, by October, "Russia was already completely lost." But Govorukhin's documentary triptych itself testifies to a profound problem, with obscene emptinesses where something should be. The "always already" emptied Winter Palace—reminiscent of the always already emptied criminal souls of *No Way to Live*—is as much an ideological problem for Govorukhin, who needs there to have been a Russia worthy of mourning, as it is for Eisenstein, who must create a Russia worthy of conquering.

When Govorukhin replays Eisenstein's replaying of the impolite Bolshevik violation of the Winter Palace, he once again reminds us of the incommensurability of human flesh with the marble architecture it inhabits. The unmoving persistence of Russia's architecture made Soviet leaders (who quite frequently resorted to dynamite in their attempts to rid themselves of the past's monuments) and Soviet filmmakers very nervous: Vsevolod Pudovkin's 1927 attempt to portray the "End of St. Petersburg" [*Konets Sankt-Peterburga*] was under perpetual threat of sabotage by the insistent physical persistence, in architectural form, of that officially liquidated city.

In Eisenstein's *October*, too, the statues inhabiting the Winter Palace seem to captivate the director despite himself: they are so much more beautiful, so much more deserving of life, that the human actors rustling about the pedestals. It seems almost as if the statues *could* move; indeed, remembering the wild gallop of the Bronze Horseman and the roaring stone lion in *Battleship Potemkin* [*Bronenosets Potemkin*, 1926], we know that they *can* move, that they hold within their silent stone surfaces the secret of true power, but they choose instead to bide their time because they suspect that motion is frequently futile. These statues and the architectural spaces they inhabit become a truly deconstructive force in these early Soviet films, precisely because of their implacable insistence on the futility of action, of change, of *revolution*.

In *The Russia We Have Lost*, architecture is examined again as a *sign* of the life "we" have lost. The Eliseev store—its architecture reminds us—should be overflowing with the bounty of Old Russia, a land where, in images reminiscent of the happy days of Nikolai Gogol"s old-world landowners (before change hits them), food (fish! caviar! etc.!) seems to spring magically, almost effortlessly, onto the Russian plate. The Russia we lost, Govorukhin keeps insisting, was a land of *gloire* and *abondance*. These are the mottos engraved not just on the Bridge of Alexander III in Paris, but hieroglyphically onto every architectural monument and every marble statue that has survived: just as Pudovkin and Eisenstein might have suspected!

That a bridge in Paris should be a key moment in reconstructing a Russia where it would be possible to live [*gde zhit' mozhno bylo by*] is a reminder that Govorukhin's documentary films are also "travelogues," though of a peculiarly static sort. The director journeys to New York, Munich, Paris, Alaska, Vermont. Yet in the first two films, Govorukhin is almost never in motion. He magically materializes in various places—unlimited in his access—and produces evidence like Woland in *The Master and Margarita*. (Are his documents, the spectator may wonder, more reliable that those proffered by Bulgakov's hero?) Govorukhin's ability to move, of course, is a sign of privilege, but, we believe, it is not accidental that in the first two films Govorukhin's movements from place to place are not shown. It is worthwhile pausing on Govorukhin's relative immobility, for it is in its valorization of immobility that Govorukhin's filmmaking is most radical (or most reactionary) and, perhaps, most anti-Soviet.

As so many crucial figures in the early Soviet avant-garde realized, movement and Bolshevism went hand in hand. Aleksei Gastev wrote poems to motion. Andrei Platonov, who in his youth tried to invent a machine for perpetual motion, spent much of his career as a writer in taking that machine apart. Vertov's filmmaking was particularly in the thrall of movement. Not only did Vertov constantly focus on the camera's work and movement, he also made a film about a day in the life of the Soviet people in which movement begins but does not cease—except to illustrate the filmmaker's ability to make things come alive again (in *Man with a Movie Camera*, we see people getting *out* of bed but not getting back in). This identification of Bolshevik ideology with movement is part of what makes cinema an integral part of the early Soviet world and what makes the broader context of early Soviet culture so important to the development of cinema.

One of the most interesting aspects of Govorukhin's kino-poetics consists precisely in his scorn for movement. We see this most evidently on a thematic level. Govorukhin often shows us people engaged in useless or humiliating activity: drunks stumble about; invalids limp; women are shown running one after another as they go about their frenzied shopping, and race for busses to the accompaniment of Patricia Cass singing "*Mademoiselle chante le Blues.*"

This disparagement of movement also occurs on the level of the composition of Govorukhin's shots. We watch a boat move along the Seine, but the boat is completely unimportant; what Govorukhin wants to talk about is the bridge under which the boat is passing. The rails of Govorukhin's trans-Siberian railroad are more powerful than the train that moves along them. The relative immobility of the hemophiliac tsarevich is a sign not only of innocence and suffering, but of nobility. Sometimes there is a certain amount of cliché-breaking humor in Govorukhin's disdain for movement and its ideological connotations. In Simbirsk, "We saw a new church being built" [*My uvideli, kak stroitsia novyi khram*]. But we are not shown workers actually building the church; rather, we visit the church for a service—"being built" [*stroitsia*] is meant in a metaphorical, internal sense. Ultimately, this trend moves in a decidedly uncinematic direction: the victory of the photograph over the moving image.

It should not be surprising that Govorukhin has more photographs than moving pictures to show us from the prerevolutionary and Civil War periods (the few film clips he shows early on are illustrations more of Russian plenitude than of Russian activity). The details of unpleasant, contemporary reality that we see in *The Russia We Have Lost* are all *moving* images, as in the film's final scene, which might be entitled "Sisyphus with Beer," motion equals ugliness. It is the still moments that tend to be pleasing—and the camera swoops in and out, moves up and down as it derives pleasure from the viewed object's lack of motion. The portrait emerges as the privileged art form—a thing of beauty that becomes inextricably linked to its original object—as in the case of Valentin Serov's portrait of the tsar, which, Govorukhin informs us, was torn apart by Bolshevik bayonets. When the subjects of such portraits come into contact with action, the result is ugly and better left off camera: "This boy will be shot in Ekaterinburg. . . . His corpse will be stuck with a bayonet, his killers will divide up his things, they will burn him and bury him nobody knows where" [*tot mal'chishka budet zastrelen v Ekaterinburge . . . trup ego protknut shtukom, ego veshchi razdeliat mezhdu soboi ego ubiitsy, ego sozhgut i zaroiut neizvestno gde*].

Lev Annenskii has noticed the importance of portraiture to this film and suggested that the pathos arises from the question: "With such [bright, good] people, why did Russia fail?" ("Ètot vrednyi . . . "). But we should add that the pathos of the portraits results, too, from the viewer's knowledge of the actions to which the bodies of those represented would later be subjected. Adjectives describing the beauties and talents of the dead become martyrs to the horrifying action of verbs. Where Aleksandr Rodchenko contributed to the glory of Soviet cinema by freeing the photograph from the portrait, Govorukhin attacks the cinema of motion by seeking to reduce it to its constitutive element—the photograph of a single frame—and to the portrait from which Rodchenko had pronounced photography forever liberated (Rodchenko 250–54). By reversing this liberation, Govorukhin seeks to stop the treadmill [*tolkuchka*] on which Russia has been running both before and after perestroika.

Govorukhin's catharsis, then, operates quite literally through paralysis. Profound interior movement is not to be encouraged by scenes of movement, but by the reduction of sensory overload. The filmmaker does not breathe life into frozen figures; rather, he plays the role of the Gorgon or, perhaps, Perseus. Unable to generate much enthusiasm for the dynamic process of interrogation in this "Case of the Murder of Russia"—as Govorukhin calls his film—he abandons all pretense of trying to move the objects of his investigation and instead settles for turning them into stone. We see the most explicit example of Govorukhin's baring his device in the scene in which he freezes the storming of the Winter Palace. Vertov also provided frozen frames, but his *Man with a Movie Camera* stopped action to demonstrate the camera's virtuosity; Govorukhin freezes action to demonstrate what a repulsive tool of historical deceit the cinema has been. Both literally and deliberately, Govorukhin has given us a movie based on the poetics of stagnation [*zastoi*].

There are obvious dangers to Govorukhin's approach. Lack of movement may produce not catharsis but lethargy. The audience may simply become bored by a cinematic interrogation that, on a formal level, floats from one static image to another. By replacing "monologues of movement" with monologues of immobility,[2] Govorukhin risks creating a cinematic Potemkin village.

In *The Russia We Have Lost*, the locus of power shifts from the prison to the archive. The archive is an even more natural place for Govorukhin's kino-poetics, and his relationship to documents is a natural development of his relationship to the subjects of his interviews. The investigatory inertia of Govorukhin's first film has now been transformed into a virtue. Documents do not move; they conceal nothing; all you have to do is read them. Another investigator might have a different, more suspicious, relationship to his material: documents might be contradictory; they might require interrogation. But such an approach is foreign to Govorukhin's ethos.

How did Govorukhin find these documents? Who admitted him to the archives? With archival as with "dialogic" information, it seems, Govorukhin remains a consumer, and for all the film's obvious historical longing, there is still something dissatisfying about its absence of methodological desire. Everything seems to fall into Govorukhin's hands; the information presented to him merely confirms what he already knew.

Only in a single instance does Govorukhin stress the effort it has taken to find some piece of the truth: "attention, antisemites," he says (and we would ask, indeed, for "meta-attention" in this instance): Lenin's grandfather was a Jew. That information, we are to assume, is supposed to neutralize Lenin's position as a statue. In any case, throughout the film Lenin's monuments are disassociated from the rest of Russia's architectural memorabilia: a stone "Lenin in a Fur Hat" at the side of the Siberian tracks looks merely ridiculous, not grand, and the shadow of Govorukhin's helicopter seems to draw a mustache across the abandoned, powerless face.

Eric Naiman & Anne Nesbet

In his book on the birth of the prison, Michel Foucault borrows a scene from Prince Kropotkin. " 'Very good,' Grand Duke Mikhail once remarked of a regiment, after having kept it for one hour presenting arms, 'only *they breathe*' " (Foucault 188, emphasis in original). In a sense, Govorukhin is expressing a similar disciplinary desire about Russia's unruly present and past. The architecture of Russia is always more perfect than its inhabitants. But in Govorukhin's second documentary, the heroes of our lost Russia, those dozens of noble faces enshrined in Govorukhin's stills, have finally achieved the sort of unbreathing and monumental dignity envisioned by the Grand Duke.

Solzhenitsyn and Carceral Charisma

There is an inordinate amount of fuss, in Govorukhin's most recent documentary, over gates and fences. *Solzhenitsyn* begins with a journey, with movement: "We are going to Solzhenitsyn's" [*My edem k Solzhenitsynu*] —in search, it would seem, of lost Russia and lost time. Solzhenitsyn's home, like the Wonderland of Aleksandr Volkov's *Wizard of the Emerald City* and also like the most notorious islands of the Gulag, shows up on no official maps. For the first time in Govorukhin's documentaries, the process of *obtaining* access to an interrogatory site is emphasized. We see Govorukhin consult his charts, ask a local for directions. But, as it soon turns out, this is all a game: a cheerful foray into played cinema. Govorukhin has been here before, knows the password ("Natasha!") that opens the Solzhenitsyn compound's magic gate, and has been merely pointing out the gulf between himself and the ordinary masses ("busloads of Germans, Italians, and Japanese"—a trace, perhaps, of films about the Second World War?) for whom a fence is a fence and to whom the sign on the wall of the local grocery store applies: "No Directions to the Solzhenitsyn Home."

Govorukhin's trip to Solzhenitsyn is a journey to a wonderful self-sufficient land—an island in which all that is wonderful in Russia's past, including, of course, patriarchy, has continued to exist.[3] As in most utopian fiction, the traveler introduces a potentially destabilizing change. Govorukhin more or less brings Solzhenitsyn's advance team—his wife and children—back to Moscow. Chronologically, the movie's last scene occurs in late May 1992, when we see Solzhenitsyn's wife and children arriving in Sheremetevo, where they are picked up by Govorukhin's van, a strange new incarnation of that German armored train.

Like most other utopian spots, however, the Solzhenitsyn home has incorporated into its structure and routines a strong sense of what Foucault calls the "carceral." The Solzhenitsyn family is shown to be living a strictly disciplined existence, in which every hour is correlated with an appropriate activity: buying groceries, practicing the piano, correcting page-proof, greeting the mail truck as it brings Solzhenitsyn books from far-flung American libraries. Govorukhin emphasizes that two great projects are tirelessly, relentlessly pursued here: the production of further volumes of *The Red Wheel* [*Krasnoe koleso*], and the rearing of properly Russian children. Both of these projects seem to be progressing steadily and well. Even young "Stepka" (whom Govorukhin could never address otherwise, he assures us cozily, than with this intimate diminutive) is shown to be respectful of religion and to have read all the right books, especially Gogol'.

It is inconceivable that anyone in this household should stray from the path of proper discipline. As Solzhenitsyn points out so disarmingly, a thinking person is liable to be tripped up on a trail in the actual woods, but here on Solzhenitsyn's little wooden balcony runway, all is smooth. And when the author finally needs to write down a sentence or two—PAF!—down folds a convenient little table, such as Mother Nature could never provide.

Movement is carefully conserved here. As in most utopias, the center is relatively immobile. Solzhenitsyn's mother-in-law, the most marginal of the writer's kin, is "the most mobile member of the family." Solzhenitsyn, himself, works as Conscience should work: through reflection rather than extraneous movement. Solzhenitsyn describes to his interviewer an approach to mobility completely compatible with that of Govorukhin's "Russia": "The greatest governmental wisdom consists in directing all the government's efforts more on internal conditions . . . than on external questions and external actions."

If the great man can sit calmly at his worktable as a wolf passes by, then, unlike Vertov's sleeping woman, he will probably not be too unsettled by a mere film director. Poor Govorukhin! In *Solzhenitsyn* he suddenly becomes all too "visible." We can see too clearly his struggle to be admitted into the Solzhenitsyns' inner circle; we see the anxiety underlying his studied nonchalance. For the first time, Govorukhin shows us himself in motion: we see him in active pursuit of a lost and cherished object. Yet it is worth noting that, in making Solzhenitsyn the object of his desire, Govorukhin cedes to Solzhenitsyn the position of authority that he, the director, has previously occupied. Now Govorukhin is an outsider, desperate to demonstrate to the audience his familiarity with the Solzhenitsyn family. The "familiarity" is so heightened by moments in which Govorukhin flaunts his "freedom" to gaze off into space, to sit on the piano teacher's stool, that members of the audience may join us in wondering just what the Solzhenitsyns say about Govorukhin when he is out of earshot.

Govorukhin has quite consciously made *Solzhenitsyn* a film about his own desire and the ingratiating work that desire makes him perform. It is not surprising, therefore, that Govorukhin looks less robust than he did in the two earlier films. On the way to the Solzhenitsyns, he is short of breath, his eyes puffy. These physical marks could be read as signs that the journey toward truth has exacted a certain cost.

Solzhenitsyn himself, however, demands an even more difficult, internally projected work: meaningful, moving repentance. A particularly tense moment in *Solzhenitsyn* comes when Solzhenitsyn launches into a tirade directed at journalists (and, implicitly, documentary filmmakers?) who criticize others, but do not repent their own sins. Here Govorukhin (has he read the sentence from *The Gulag Archipelago* [*Arkhipelag GULag*, 1973–75] that serves as the epigraph to this chapter?) appears to be looking not at Solzhenitsyn, but straight ahead; when his interlocutor pauses, Govorukhin for the only time disagrees with his subject, referring to Solzhenitsyn's remarks as "idealism." One wonders here just what is going on in Govorukhin's mind, whether Solzhenitsyn's purity will lead him, the interviewer/interrogator, at this moment to purge himself [*ochishchat'sia*].

This is a moment in which the prisoner's ultimate fantasy is nearly realized. Govorukhin, who has carefully been taking notes as he conducts his latest, mildest interrogation, suddenly becomes the object of his subject's moral rage. Here, where Solzhenitsyn threatens to destabilize even further the relationship between interviewer and subject, Govorukhin remains as impassive as his subjects in *No Way to Live*. The first part of this two-part film ends on a somber note of immobility, not internal motion but a dead end. It is the same dead end explored in the first two of Govorukhin's three documentaries: the camera pulls back to reveal the two men facing each other across the table as Solzhenitsyn's voice echoes, "Then we won't save our youth. Then we will be a tree with a rotting hollow." This moment raises the question of the other turns that *Solzhenitsyn* might have taken, had Govorukhin pursued the implications of a film about his own desire for truth.

If Solzhenitsyn's role here can be seen as that of a wise man [*mudrets*], whose words hope to lead an entire nation to a working-through of the past by means of repentance and conscience, then Govorukhin's quiet rejection of such "self-criticism" as an anachronistic practice for Russia (not to mention, his bland face implies, for himself) suggests that, for all the trouble of travel to Solzhenitsyn's kingdom, the "Russia" discovered there would not necessarily find much of a market in contemporary Moscow.

The strange consummation of Govorukhin's documentary desire comes in the second half of the film. Solzhenitsyn has been showing Govorukhin his microfilm reader and library. Here, too, we are made acutely aware of the director's self-inflicted loss of power. If previously Govorukhin was in complete command of his documentary materials, fingering at will the tsar's intimate correspondence and slapping his hand against formerly secret Bolshevik documents, now Solzhenitsyn controls access to history, at one point even stopping Govorukhin and telling him to wait as Govorukhin seeks to pull a book down from the shelf. In what we would like to suggest works as the film's central moment, Govorukhin asks about materials recently returned to Solzhenitsyn by the KGB. Solzhenitsyn agreeably leaves to get the packet. Govorukhin is left "alone" in the inner sanctum. What does he do? He turns to the camera: "Well, lads," he says, "we're in Solzhenitsyn's office. Not everyone has this chance" [*Nu, rebiata, my v kabinete Solzhenitsyna. Ne kazhdomu èto*].

If Govorukhin is going to include this moment of Solzhenitsyn's absence in his film, why doesn't he use it to learn something, to show us something he could not reveal in Solzhenitsyn's presence? Yet the only thing Govorukhin does in defiance of Solzhenitsyn's wishes is to forget for a moment about "the fate of Russia" and to give himself over to self-satisfied inactivity. This humorous and disappointing moment reveals what Govorukhin has been striving for: simple *access* for its own sake, that frisson of proximity to power that has plagued the intelligentsia since the revolution. Or it may be something even more banal and perhaps kinkier: the thrill of being in the place that power has vacated, the same thrill that motivated Eisenstein's sailors in the tsarina's boudoir in the scene from *October* that Govorukhin felt compelled to include in his second documentary. This thrill, which motivates so much work on and about Russia, is itself another form of consumption par excellence. Postmodern and traditional investigators alike take their turns gathering the crumbs of charisma left by those fortunate to recline, for a minute or for a lifetime, in power's still-warm sepulchre.

In this case, though, the tomb traps a bit too much heat. Throughout *Solzhenitsyn*, Govorukhin has seemed distinctly less at ease than in the archives and interrogation rooms of the earlier documentaries. What is it about his subject that makes Govorukhin heave a sigh of relief when Solzhenitsyn finally bounds for a moment out of the room? Perhaps Govorukhin's discomfort has to do with the disconcerting internal energy that propels Solzhenitsyn as he bounces lightly from place to place within the confines

Eric Naiman & Anne Nesbet

of his Vermont refuge. Solzhenitsyn's very immobility—as a Living Classic, as a man in retreat from the vulgarities of capitalism and communism alike, as a person who prefers a twenty-foot wooden walkway to wandering free in the forest—turns out to be filled with energy and movement. In this sense, Solzhenitsyn is as troubling and challenging an object for Govorukhin's kino-gaze as those prerevolutionary statues, ever threatening to stage a coup d'état in Pudovkin's and Eisenstein's work of the 1920s. Unlike the Russia Govorukhin examines in *No Way to Live* and *The Russia We Have Lost*— the Russia of unrepentant criminals and shallow drunkards—here, in the Russia of this man in Vermont, there is not Nothing, but Something. That Something excites Govorukhin, but also makes him nervous. Moreover, that Something leads us to wonder what would happen if these three films were to be melded into one: if Solzhenitsyn were to replace Govorukhin across the interrogation table from the boys with blank faces, for whom assault and murder are "in the normal order of things." Would the interview go differently?

Such a question is somewhat perverse: Solzhenitsyn has always been the Cincinnatus par excellence. Why make him into Porfirii Petrovich? Yet the logic of Govorukhin's three documentaries suggests that it is precisely this expert on terror, violence, and conscience who can pump blood into the director's pale, still world and make Russia worth interrogating again.

Notes

1. *No Way to Live* was even exhibited at a special screening to the 1990 Congress of Peoples' Deputies. According to recently published statistics, in 1992 *The Russia We Have Lost* had the longest run of any Russian film in the capital (Venzher). For reaction to the films in the central press, see Works Cited.

2. The first phrase belongs to Viktor Shklovskii. See his *Za 60 let* 98.

3. In this context, it is worth recalling that one of Govorukhin's first films was *The Life and Surprising Adventures of Robinson Crusoe* [*Zhizn' i udivitel'nye prikliucheniia Robinzona Kruso*, 1973], adapted from Defoe's novel.

Works Cited

Agafonov, V. "Prezident Solzhenitsyn?" *Novoe russkoe slovo* 15 January 1993.
Aleksandrov, Valentin. "Porvat' 'tsep' zla': razmyshleniia posle prosmotra fil'ma 'Tak zhit' nel'zia.' " *Sovetskaia kul'tura* 23 June 1990.
Annenskii, Lev. "Govorukhin u Solzhenitsyna." *Moskovskie novosti* 13 September 1992.

Bulgakov, Mikhail. *The Master and Margarita.* Tr. Michael Glenny. NY: New American Library, 1967.

"Ètot vrednyi vydaiushchiisia fil'm." *Literaturnaia gazeta* 1 July 1992 (roundtable discussion with Lev Annenskii, Leonid Batkin, and Aleksandr Serebnikov).

Ezerskaia, Bella. "Solzhenitsyn i fil'm Govorukhina." *Novoe russkoe slovo* 15 January 1993.

Foucault, Michel. *Discipline and Punish: The Birth of the Prison.* Tr. Alan Sheridan. NY: Vintage, 1979.

Ivanova, Valentina. "Kto na rol' proroka?" *Pravda* 18 July 1990.

Karavaev, A. "V gostiakh u Solzhenitsyna." *Novoe russkoe slovo* 15 January 1993.

Lanzmann, Claude, dir. *Shoah.* France, 1985.

Latynina, Alla. "Sovest' vazhnee vygody." *Moskovskie novosti* 13 September 1992.

Lipkov, A. "Vzgliad v bezdnu." *Iskusstvo kino* 7 (1990): 27–31.

Makarov, Iurii. " 'Tak zhit' nel'zia.' " *Izvestiia* 12 May 1990.

Nemzer, Andrei. "Pod fonarem svetlee: o novom fil'me Stanislava Govorukhina." *Nezavisimaia gazeta* 27 June 1992.

Nitochkina, Anastasiia. "Stanislav Govorukhin: Ot glasnosti k pravde." *Sovetskaia kul'tura* 2 June 1990.

Ophuls, Marcel, dir. *Hotel Terminus.* France, 1988.

————, dir. *The Sorrow and the Pity.* France, 1970.

"Puti Rossii (obsuzhdenie fil'ma Stanislava Govorukhina: 'Rossiia, kotoruiu my poteriali)." *Iskusstvo kino* 9 (1992): 13–26 (roundtable discussion with Valentin Tolstykh, Tat'iana Alekseeva, Viacheslav Glazychev, Andrei Gorodetskii, Georgii Gloveli, Valerii Lebedev, Liliana Mal'kova, Vadim Mezhuev, Sergei Nikol'skii, Vladlen Sirotkin, Vladimir Fedorov, and Vladimir Shevchenko).

Rodchenko, Aleksandr. "Against the Synthetic Portrait, For the Snapshot" [1928]. *Russian Art and the Avant Garde: Theory and Criticism.* Ed. John Bowlt. NY: Thames and Hudson, 1988.

Shklovskii, Viktor. *Za 60 let: raboty o kino.* Moskva: Iskusstvo, 1985.

Solzhenitsyn, Aleksander I. *The Gulag Archipelago, 1918–1956: An Experiment in Literary Investigation.* Tr. Thomas P. Whitney. NY: Harper & Row, 1974.

Titov, A. "S. Govorukhin: 'Period poluraspada zakonchilsia, nachalsia raspad': beseda avtora fil'ma 'Tak zhit' nel'zia' i poèta Igoria Kokhanovskogo." *Iskusstvo kino* 12 (1990): 3–7.

Venzher, Natal'ia. " . . . Vyderzhivaiut tol'ko samye stoikie." *Literaturnaia gazeta* 26 May 1993.

Zorin, Andrei. "Kruche, kruche, kruche . . . Istoriia pobedy: chernukha v kul'ture poslednikh let." *Znamia* 10 (1992): 198–204.

Four

The Gendered Trinity of Russian Cultural Rhetoric Today— or The Glyph of the H[i]eroine

Helena Goscilo

Alas! poor country;
Almost afraid to know itself. It cannot
Be call'd our mother, but our grave.

—Shakespeare, *Macbeth*

"Now here, you see, it takes all the running
you can do, to keep in the same place."

—Lewis Carroll, *Through the Looking Glass*

Indifference to Difference

Anyone examining process or comparing two phenomena or stages may read for sameness or for difference. Journalists and scholars, under the pressure of what Aleksandr Solzhenitsyn peevishly diagnosed as a fatal attraction to novelty, predictably favor difference. Perhaps revelation seems intrinsically to possess more allure than affirmation; it intimates change or progress, the presumed desiderata of the modern technological age. Hence, when people encounter each other again after any temporal lapse, human instinct (trained by social habit and seduced by the promise of narrative) prompts the query, "What's new?" rather than "Hello, what's the same?"

Reading contemporary Russian culture against the current, I contend that, notwithstanding the cataclysmic displacements effected by Russia's incomplete transition to a market economy, one aspect of its present culture demonstrates sameness, subsuming ostensible or incipient difference. That aspect is gender—singled out by recent Western theory, ironically enough, as the locus of difference par excellence. Treatment of gender in Russian culture today suggests that in one respect, at least, post-Soviet culture is more Soviet than post-. Gender-specific Soviet hieroglyphics continue to glyph along, in the sense that if part of what was formerly sacred (Greek *hiero*) now has been declared sacrilegious, the very concept of profanation still engages a "religious" system.

Mother Courage à la russe (or *Matreshki* for Sale)

From time immemorial, the dominant Russian iconography has projected nationhood as female, its ethos and moral identity metaphorized as maternity. Whether the bathetic familial rhetoric of statehood casts the officially empowered ruler who oversees the country's politico-military fate as *tsarbatiushka* or as Stalin—Father of the Peoples, the territory that he disciplines, punishes, or glorifies with his "strong hand" invariably is the motherland.[1]

The pagan divinity of *mat' syra zemlia*—or Mother Moist Earth(!)—venerated by the early Slavs as the fertile maternal body, continued to figure prominently in folk rituals into the twentieth century, the durability of this worship prompting some scholars to postulate the primacy of "a great mother goddess in the early Russian pantheon" (Ivanits 15; Hubbs 52–86). Life-giving soil for cultivation, like the dark continent awaiting discovery and "civilization" (or colonization), was troped as the female body ever ready to be tamed and impregnated.[2]

Accordingly, in Russia's predominantly agrarian and peasant society, mother-land was *rodina-mat'*, *Mat' Rossiia*—land-mother, Mother Russia—, a fecund source of self-perpetuation and nurture. Probably under this pagan influence, Christian Russia likewise perceived the Virgin Mary—*Bogoroditsa* to the peasants—less as virgin than as mother, a compassionate agent of intercession with a higher authority (the male Godhead), attested in such texts as the twelfth-century apocryphal "Descent of the Virgin into Hell" and the seventeenth-century "Tale of Savva Grudtsyn" (Zenkovsky 122–29, 452–74).

As the personification of stoic patience and all-forgiving self-abnegation, Mother Russia embraced her native or prodigal sons and, unlike her counterpart, Germany Pale Mother [*Deutschland Bleiche Mutter*, 1979], glowed with robust color. Such, at least, is the visual image of her emblematic materialization—in the *matreshka*, the national folk symbol of fertility: a brightly (or garishly) painted wooden peasant doll whose rotund body encases another, smaller body, in which nestles a yet smaller one, and so on, in a potentially infinite series of *matreshki* spilling out of a peasant woman's stomach (Hubbs xi-xiii). A memento peddled in every souvenir store frequented by tourists to the Soviet Union, the self-replicating *matreshka*, which originated in the nineteenth century, symbolized the mysterious vitality of Mother Russia.

The gaudy sturdiness of *Matreshka* Multiplex optimistically affirmed the continuity of generations in a culture pathologically committed to tradition. With the disintegration of that Russia, *patreshki*—significantly, not anonymous generic symbols, but individualized as instantly recognizable political *male* leaders—appeared on the market.[3] As Evgenii Evtushenko recently declared, "the nation [*narod*] begins with women" (*Literaturnaia gazeta*), but he neglected to mention that it is misgoverned, hence in constant peril of being ended, by men. If *matreshki* opened optimistic (i.e., unironic) Soviet parentheses, *patreshki* closed them.

Twentieth-century modernization, with its attendant shift to an urban, industrialized culture, only strengthened the maternal metaphor for nationhood, its pagan origins now harnessed to socialist ideology. Such an ostensible paradox becomes demystified if one recalls that, during troubled historical periods, the tendency to a conservative retrenchment of a traditional gender disposition is particularly pronounced. Gor'kii's proto-socialist-realist novel *Mother* [*Mat'*, 1905—a turbulent year by any standards] fashions the definitive archetype of the age in Pelageia Nilovna Vlasova. Refurbished for the new Soviet order, the "soft, melancholy, submissive" Vlasova (11) possesses a "large capacity for motherliness" (126). "Love," we learn, "is the mother of life" (143), a mother who embodies the socialist ethos: "We are all the children of one mother—the great, invincible idea of the brotherhood of the workers of all countries over all the earth" (38). Ultimately, Vlasova as mother, ideologically and anachronistically impregnated by her Christlike son, breeds socialist ideals and nurtures Russian socialist youth.

If, as various commentators have maintained, issues of gender gain greater currency during political or national crises (van Buren 1), in Russia that pattern manifests itself specifically in an intensification of maternal metaphors. Thus the trope of *rodina-mat'* flourished during World War II, as soldiers struggled to protect her and the future she vouchsafed. Aleksandr Tvardovskii's lengthy narrative war poem *House at the Road* [*Dom u dorogi*, 1942–46], for example, which interweaves female images of domesticity with scenes of battle and strife, portrays the birth of a baby boy (the future soldier/citizen) in the midst of war:

And the boy lived. It can't have been
By chance that by nature
He was born of a Russian woman
Who'd grown/increased in freedom. (Zhigul'skaia 42, see also 45)

The Gendered Trinity of Russian Cultural Rhetoric

An anthology titled *Mother: Poems by Russian and Soviet Poets about Mother* [*Mat': Stikhotvoreniia russkikh i sovetskikh poètov o materi*] plays countless variations on the same pseudo-inspiring theme, while revealing that, as Russia's sense of identity grew threatened during the postwar era, the maternal image of nationhood became problematized (Korotaev). Especially the nationalist and chauvinist contingent of literati depicted the mother/motherland as embattled and devalorized. Such a reworking of the metaphor via hagiographical topoi may be seen in Aleksandr Solzhenitsyn's *Matrena's Home* [*Matrenin dvor*, 1963], which in biblical cadences extols the spirituality, capacity for selfless toil, and indifference to material acquisition in the eponymous Matrena, who embodies the quintessential Russian virtues now imperiled by encroaching "modern" (i.e., alien) elements. In the concluding encomium to her memory, Matrena becomes synonymous with the martyred, soul-rich if goods-poor nation: "She was the righteous one without whom, as the proverb says, no village can stand./Nor any city./Nor our whole land" (Blake and Hayward 53).[4]

Thirteen years later, Valentin Rasputin premonitorily expanded the element of martyrdom within the maternal metaphor in his elegiac *Farewell to Matera* [*Proshchanie s Materoi*, 1976], which, as Barbara Heldt has correctly noted, portrays the squandering of a female ecology by guilt-ridden males (Buckley 167). Or, to phrase it differently, Rasputin laments the violence wrought by contemporary trends on old Mother Russia, with her rituals, traditions, and self-validating hierarchies. In an apocalyptic scenario that anticipates much of glasnost cultural production, the text predicts the extinction of Russia's sacrosanct heritage, the obliteration of nature through a dubious culture, as a consequence of which Russia's inhabitants lose their spiritual moorings and flounder helplessly in the darkness of nonbeing: "Only water and fog around them. Nothing but water and fog" (Rasputin 224).

It is no coincidence that Rasputin's story appeared during the purported demographic crisis of the 1970s in the Soviet Union—in actuality, little more than the culmination of racist fears on the government's part that the population in the Asian republics, with their traditionally higher birthrates, would eventually outnumber that of the European sections of the empire. Those misgivings prompted a campaign for larger families that urged women's return to the home, especially within the Russian republic. Ironically, that blueprint for the nation's moral deliverance, mutatis mutandis, resurfaced during perestroika, when Gorbachev vowed to liberate women by enabling their retreat into their proper domestic domain, where they could fulfill their preordained roles as mothers (117).

Today, articles, essays, and letters to editors echo these very sentiments at a time when unemployment has become a gendered problem in both Moscow and Petersburg, where women constitute more than 75 percent of those laid off from work. According to a voluble faction of post-Communist Russian society, the solution to the country's anomie rests in mothers' tender hands. Crime would decrease, men would recover their masculine dignity (not to mention sobriety and sexual potency), disaffected adolescents would buckle down to meaningful activities, and the breakdown of the family would fade to a memory—were women to reprise their predetermined function in the maternal metaphor of nationhood. Women's magazines, including not only the institutionally endorsed *Rabotnitsa* [*Woman Worker*] and *Sovetskaia zhenshchina* [*Soviet Woman*], but also newer post-perestroika publications (e.g., *Sudarushka* [*Little Lady*] and *Delovaia zhenshchina* [*Business Woman*]) assert that "motherhood is woman's fundamental function and her chief predestination" (*Rabotnitsa* 7).[5] Anxious that men not suffer identity crises through joblessness, proponents of women's unemployment cum domestication in Russia may even outnumber health zealots proselytizing against smoking in the United States.

The Bad Mother: Revamped and Retroversed

Post-glasnost literature and film have tackled this moth-eaten gendered rhetoric of national identity in a number of ways. Several works elaborate the metaphor, only to reorient it, extending its vertical implications by troping Russian social history as multigenerational families of women in an environment that relegates men to the periphery (e.g., Goscilo, "Petrushevskaia's Vision" 5, 14). Viacheslav Krishtofovich's signally titled film *Adam's Rib* [*Rebro Adama*, 1991], Liudmila Petrushevskaia's story *Night Time* [*Vremia noch'*, 1992], and Galina Shcherbakova's *The Ubiquists* [*Ubikvisty*, 1992] all operate on the principles of "time forward" [*vremia vpered*] and "time back" [*vremia nazad*] in the interests of synchronization, whereby maternity absorbs both past and future, collapsing them into a paradoxically timeless image of stasis in the "present" of the viewer's and reader's experience.

These works belong, in a sense, to a more general tendency ushered in by glasnost—that of pinpointing the origins of and deviations in what Russians perceive, somewhat linearly, as the developmental course of their history. From the mid-1980s on, articles by historians, journalists, and philosophers (e.g., Vladimir Seliunin, Aleksandr Tsipko, Vladimir Kozlov), as well as belles lettres, took up with a vengeance Trifonov's earlier quest for roots and causes of the catastrophic present—unfailingly characterized as a consequence of earlier decisions, policies, events, and personalities. Crediting

The Gendered Trinity of Russian Cultural Rhetoric

the past with enormous explanatory power, these publications tacitly embraced a pre-Tolstoian view of history and a mechanical concept of temporality.

In this respect, Mikhail Kuraev swam against the tireless tide, inasmuch as his atypical *Captain Dikshtein* [*Kapitan Dikshtein*, 1989] denarrativized "history as master plot" into random components, not only alinear but also ultimately unknowable (with both story [*fabula*] and plot [*siuzhet*] eluding certitude). Replacing causality with fortuitous sequentiality, blurring lines between fact and fiction, Kuraev interrogated the primacy of "big events" and the unitary concept of history that shaped the treatment of historical topics in the scholarship, journalism, and literature of the period. Glasnost "fiction" and drama by Dudintsev, Grossman, Shatrov, and others intent on recuperating an officially withheld past not only sustained the fictional pretence poorly, but reduced history to the transparency of fully accessible facts inertly awaiting incorporation into a comprehensive Truth. By contrast, perhaps the most fascinating aspect of the pertinent works by Krishtofovich, Shcherbakova, and especially Petrushevskaia is the complex, paradoxical way in which they trope temporality as female physicality to produce an ambiguous, dispiriting view of Russian history that merits analysis.

The Feminization of History

An appropriate subtitle for all three works might be "Mothers and Daughters" [*Materi i deti* or *Materi i docheri*][6]: in each work, women are reproducers and survivors, those who outlive men and enable other women's continued existence. Mothers all double as daughters (hence are figures simultaneously representing the past and future), and family genealogy defines itself in female terms (in some cases paternity is not even conclusively established). Yet where generations in Aksakov and Tolstoi, for instance, figure continuity, in these works the ceaseless conflicts between mothers and daughters that might elsewhere connote development, change, or progress, become meaningless, in a sense, robbed of significance by the realization (on the part of the reader/viewer—and in Shcherbakova's case, a character) that the daughter, despite her too-visible rebellion, actually replicates her mother. Daughters seem less future bearers of the torch than imperfect Xeroxes of the past. Their life plot duplicates their mothers'; their weaknesses and desires pull them back into the protofemale pattern of their forebearers' existence (in Krishtofovich, physical or fleshly frailty, whether it be sexual susceptibility or incontinence). Hence the peculiar end effect of stasis, of a *perpetuum mobile* within the temporal space that produces "history"—conceived as rote repetition without significant change or momentum.

Imagery contesting generational development emerges strongly in Krishtofovich's film in the grandmother's (i.e., "first" mother's) paralysis and the centrality of her bed (a coffin of sorts, where she "tolls the bell" and wordlessly releases bodily fluids); in the almost complete overlap that Petrushevskaia's novella [*povest'*] installs between key aspects of Anna Adrianovna's character and biography and those of her mother and daughter; and in Nina's total identification with her mother Niura in Shcherbakova's *The Ubiquists*, in specific psychophysical terms that grammatically denote not affinity, but sameness ("in that pose on the little bench in front of the open stove, scooping out the ashes, she suddenly felt that she was Niura. Even her knees were placed just the way her mother's used to be during that task. . . . And she broke up the chips just as her mother used to . . . " [55]). In kindred fashion, Nina's daughter Lizon'ka unexpectedly perceives the sameness between her mother and Lelia, the sister who superficially seems Nina's polar opposite. ("And at that moment Lizon'ka suddenly noticed how alike they were, after all. Sisters through and through. . . . The fact that one was a housewife and the other a Party worker made no difference, it turned out" [63].)

Immobility, repetition, and the centrality of a fixed site where rituals are enacted (the bathroom and the grandmother's bed in Krishtofovich, Anna Adrianovna's apartment in Petrushevskaia, and Niura's kitchen in Shcherbakova) all spotlight the adynamic nature of history—defined à la Pushkin and Tolstoi not as extraordinary battles, but as everyday prosaics,[7] and troped as successive generations of women.

One might conceivably bracket these works within Russia's sweeping tendency today to reinstate the past into its future, and not only among the predictably regressive supporters of what used to be called Village Prose. Essaying new beginnings by recouping former traditions seems the current way of life in Russia (its "re"- era), most apparent in the political groups advocating a modern tsardom, the rebirth of religious "faith," the revival of cossack activities, the reissuing of early works formerly prohibited by Soviet ideology, and the restoration of prerevolutionary names to towns, streets, and organizations (the return of Leningrad to St. Petersburg, Gor'kii Street to Tverskaia, Frunzenskaia Street to Znamenka)—transformations that not only confuse visitors, inhabitants, and even experienced taxidrivers[8] but also normalize such flagrantly contradictory terms as "new old," "former future," and so forth. By moving forward into the past, Russians intent on replacing recent orthodoxy with distant Orthodoxy have profoundly histor-icized their present moment.[9]

Of the three works that entropize history, only Krishtofovich's offers relief from a pervasive aura of degrading struggle and gloom by occasional injections of humor. Yet the visual image of a mute, paralyzed matriarch as an incontinent but despotic "animal," the ringing bell (a relic of the past) that at any moment may summon her daughter Nina Elizarovna and grand-daughters Lida and Nastia, the persistent pull of all dramatis personae to the matriarchal vortex that unremittingly demands service, yet produces solely excrement—all these not only reduce the daughter and granddaugh-ters to the status of appendage, but simultaneously infantilize the grand-mother, proleptically equating her with the baby that Nastia is expecting. Moreover, by associating all of the women with such motifs as crime (crip-pling/robbing), sexual betrayal, and physical need, the film collapses them into a single Womanhood. Their interchangeability is emphasized visually in scenes of role reversal (e.g., when Nina Elizarovna docilely obeys her daughter Nastia's order to switch on the TV for the motionless grandmother) and doubling (e.g., when Nina Elizarovna tries on Lida's new bikini as both women, standing first one behind the other, then side by side, study their reflections in a mirror).[10]

If the title of *Adam's Rib* automatically conjures up misogynistic bibli-cal dicta about women's derivative status vis-à-vis malehood, the film actu-ally subverts that stereotype.[11] It is men whom Krishtofovich relegates to secondariness, to the status of incidental (or accidental) figures. Having served their purpose of impregnation, they maintain little contact with their biological offspring and are merely invited to "play father" when fes-tive occasions demand their presence at the apartment that Kurchatkin, in the novella from which the film derives, pointedly dubbed "*women's* home" [*babii dom*].[12] Since "*dom*" for all intents and purposes defines the sphere of human activities in the film, those outside that sphere fall outside life pro-cesses. Choices and decisions, moreover, reside in the hands of women: Nastia resolves to have her child, even as she permanently dismisses the half-witted Misha who fathered it; Lida does not join her philandering mar-ried boss at a resort for the romantic interlude they planned mainly because of her encounter with the man's wife; Nina Elizarovna's mother, we learn, persuaded Nina Elizarovna to shed her first husband. Plans regarding the addition of a new member to the household receive serious attention only after the drunken, rowdy men leave Nina's nameday party.

The film's closing scenes, wherein a freak accident restores speech and mobility to the grandmother in a veritable "recovery ex machina," may be interpreted as heralding an abrupt, unmotivated (and unconvincing) opportunity for radical change—a change that the remainder of the film has removed from the realm of probability.[13] If Nastia's pregnancy and the expected baby point to a future generation that finally will "mobilize" Russian history in a spirit of "free speech" (post-post-glasnost society) then the last-minute resurrection of the matriarch makes sense. For the promise of such a development should at the very least qualify the historicized metaphor of muteness and paralysis or eliminate it altogether.[14] But perhaps this interpretation assumes too much about the grandmother's condition, the true nature of which Krishtofovich leaves weightily enigmatic at film's end. Until that juncture, history assumes the form of a changeless configuration through which generations pass in meaningless succession.

Petrushevskaia also depicts three generations of women, focusing, as does Krishtofovich, on the middle-aged protagonist/narrator who likewise must attend to an incontinent, bedridden mother (hospitalized) and a daughter given to extramarital pregnancies. Furthermore, *Night Time* also ultimately elides three females into a single persona by a duplication of familial scenarios, biographical patterns, and mother/daughter dynamics.[15] All of Anna Adrianovna's narrative stratagems calculated to enshrine her "difference" serve only to expose her ineradicable kinship with her mother Sima and daughter Alena. Moreover, Petrushevskaia's complicated scrambling of time sequence privileges uniformity over distinctions. Like *Adam's Rib*, the narrative ends on a highly ambiguous note susceptible to several readings. In consigning her mother to a psychiatric home, Anna Adrianovna gains a "freedom" of sorts, just as Alena does by escaping with her offspring from the psychic prison of the maternal apartment. Yet by synchronizing these moments, Petrushevskaia reinscribes sameness and neurotic pattern even as she hints at their potential termination. Alena's seeming liberation from the disabling family blueprint is orchestrated with the kind of cryptic qualifications that Petrushevskaia habitually employs to arouse readers' skepticism.

Shcherbakova's text, while more openly concerned with history in its traditional (undomestic) mode, filters "historical" events (collectivization, war, Stalin's reign of terror and repression) through the experiences of a multigenerational family, presented chiefly through its female members. The novel's title, which Shcherbakova explains in a footnote, alerts the reader to what precisely the family ultimately achieves. That achievement, as in Krishtofovich and Petrushevskaia, is survival.[16] Yet, as the terms of Shcherbakova's own definition of "ubiquists" imply, that capacity to endure comes at the price of humanity: "Ubiquists are plants and animals that may be found everywhere, capable of living in the most diverse conditions. For example, the reed and the wolf" (11).

Shcherbakova entertains no illusions about the endless cycle of reproduction, which she presents as no more *than* re-production. In the novel's cheerless conclusion, which parallels that of *Night Time*, An'ka leaves her mother and country for Canada, on a visit that undoubtedly will become emigration. Although her escape may intimate the possibility of individual fulfillment, the novel strongly suggests that the millions who remain "at home" will continue to experience life as "survival" amidst an infinite series of pointless repetitions. The last paragraphs of the novel record her mother Lizon'ka's visit to the cemetery where Lizon'ka's grandparents are buried. Significantly, her final dialogue takes place with their imagined voices projecting from the youthful photographs adorning their graves in Soviet fashion.[17] Losing all sense of place and time, Lizon'ka in a moment of existential despair poses the un-Soviet, Karamazovian question, If human existence is the random chaos she and her family have known, why live? ("For what? For what?" [*Zachem? Zachem?*] 88.)

One might reasonably object that these works, rather than offering a fresh perspective, actually perpetuate the dusty habit of equating women with body, reproduction, domesticity, and conservative attitudes. Indeed, to some extent they do. Moreover, in troping history along gendered lines, they implicitly supply to the imperishable question, "Who Is to Blame?" [*Kto vinovat?*] an ominous answer that attributed moral responsibility to Russian womanhood. The originality of these works, therefore, consists less in their representation of gender than in their refurbishment of the maternal trope—now an inimical and destructive force—and above all in their concept of Russian history. All three works erase the commonplace Soviet separation between the private and the public, between the everyday and the historical. If read as narratives of national history (and they encourage such a reading), the works propose a disturbingly somber view of Russian history at odds with the glasnost phase of cultural commentary. That view originates in the conviction that Soviet Russian history has had no "course," but has merely undergone a fundamentally static replaying of the same elements, even as its propaganda trumpeted the revolutionary change that its surface appearance sometimes confirmed.

In that sense, Soviet Russia has been not the optimistic nurturer, but the bad or incapacitated mother, giving birth but also blighting one's life. Through this bleak, revisionist image of motherhood, the works document, as Krishtofovich remarked in an interview, "not how we lived . . . [but] how

Helena Goscilo

we survived" (Fein 22). By extending the conventionally vertical trope of motherhood, the works posit Soviet history as a gruelling, mechanical reenactment of a limited set of paradigms—paradigms that turn experience upon itself with a pleonastic futility that diminishes life into mere prolongation.[18]

Whore as Homeland

In another recent complication of the maternal metaphor, artists have conflated motherhood with another hackneyed female trope—that of the prostitute. Contrasted to the mother metaphor on account of its horizontal qualities (in all senses), the image of the prostitute normally conjures up antifamilial values, social degeneration, and the readiness to sell for money what (presumably) should be freely yet selectively given. It stands to reason, then, that the trope would proliferate during the transition to market, when, indeed, the myth of boundless Russian generosity has collapsed under the grim reality of the huckster, the *valiuta*-hungry bargainer.

Nikolai Shmelev's "Visit" [*Vizit*, 1988], Galina Shcherbakova's "The Three 'Loves' of Masha Peredreeva" [*Tri "liubvi" Mashi Peredreevoi*, 1990], and Viktor Erofeev's *Russian Beauty* [*Russkaia krasavitsa*, wr. 1980–82, pub. 1990] reflect this trend, as does Tofik Shakhverdiev's semidocumentary video *To Die of Love* [*Umeret' ot liubvi*, 1990] and Razika Merganbaiba's twenty-minute Uzbek film *Dignity* [*Dostoinstvo*] on prostitution in Tashkent (Buckley 164).

In Erofeev's pointedly titled *Russian Beauty*, the pregnant heroine, prostitute Irina Tarakanova (Cockroach), represents the new Russia ("two fates were to be decided: Russia's and mine" [227]) and voluntarily (if only temporarily) assumes responsibility for the country's moral salvation via a self-sacrificial Joan-of-Arc death (236). The novel, while parodying a host of Russian myths, nonetheless enthusiastically resorts to the malestream rhetoric that tropes nationhood as mother, and, more recently, prostitute. As Irina elegantly formulates it, "My beaver is bigger than my brainbox, and that, you must admit, is as it should be for a woman" (300). Ultimately, Erofeev's *Russian Beauty* proves a pretentious-existentialist *Intergirl* in reverse: tropologically speaking, the solution to Russia's travails potentially lies in Irina the Cockroach's "beaver," the repository of Leonarchik's life-giving seed. Or, to unpack the lightweight metaphor, the re/birth of Russia necessitates its vastly belated recuperation of a Renaissance that bypassed it, but that now, in the overdetermined figure of old Leonardo (da Vinci), may inject new life into a semibarbaric culture finally open, so to speak, to congress with invigorating foreign elements.

The Gendered Trinity of Russian Cultural Rhetoric

1. *Intergirl (Interdevochka)*, 1989. Director, Petr Todorovskii.

A key metatext in this regard is Vladimir Kunin's novella *Intergirl* [*Inter-devochka*, 1989], which Petr Todorovskii transformed into a huge cinematic box-office success the following year.[19] The double image of womanhood (see Fig. 1) fashioned by current Russian cultural rhetoric is personified in Tania, a hard-currency hooker, and her mother, a schoolteacher. The tropes interact simultaneously along sequential and relational planes: both icons of the modern Russian ethos are erased in a scenario of mathematically calculated formulas, the Mother committing a symbolic suicide to restore violated honor (Kunin 158), while the prostitute daughter perishes, appro-priately, in the spoils of her profession (a foreign car—a Volvo) as she be-latedly races to rejoin saintly mother and sacred motherland (with a peni-tential death cry of "Mama, Mama, Mama!" [153]).[20]

In their choice of whore as organizing trope, these works respond simul-taneously to the new permissiveness, which allows the portrayal of Russian prostitution, and to the dislocation of national mythologies (Russians nowa-days pragmatically charge for what under the "kinder," "gentler" conditions of tsardom and pseudo-Communism the "great Russian soul" disbursed gratis). As both Florence Nightingale and trick-turner, Tania emerges as the "perfect imperfect" transitional synthesis: her role of nurse and loving daughter, as well as her verbatim recall of High Culture poetry and her affection for animals, are inherited from her mother (old Russia); her eco-

2. "Hospitable Democracy" ("*Gostepriimnaia Demokratiia*").
Cartoon in 4 December 1992 issue of *Literaturnaia Rossiia.*

nomically motivated sexual services are symptomatic of the new capitalis-
tic drives overrunning a nation seduced by evil foreign influences.[21] Her
corrupt aspect recalls the iconography from a recent issue of *Literaturnaia
Rossiia* [*Literary Russia*], which boasts a cover portraying "Hospitable Democracy" [*Gostepriimnaia demokratiia*] (a Western import) in a sexualized
sadomasochistic image—as a woman (shown only from the waist down)
with transparent gauzy gloves, lacy-gartered stockings on legs exposed by
a waist-high slit in her dress, holding a whip in one hand, and opening an
animal cage with the other (see Fig. 2).

Apart from unprecedented explicitness in physiological detail, then, the
troping of nationhood along feminine lines as mother and whore—Body,
Nature, Reproduction—has not undergone revolutionary change. Modifications exist primarily in the details.

All Things to All Men: Troping Pushkin

But what of the rhetorical representation of Russian culture itself, traditionally viewed as the supremely male arena of artistic activity? Unsurpris-
ingly, it likewise continues to rely on its hardiest metatrope: the metonym

that is Aleksandr Sergeevich Pushkin. Whereas maternity (biology/body) ensures historical continuity and safeguards (or neglects) national morality (praxis), creativity (aesthetics) and governance remain inherently masculine talents (intellect and imagination; activity and theory). Biological utility constitutes women's principal asset, whereas men's expertise encompasses multiple spheres: art, philosophy, administration. Women procreate—produce babies; men create—generate art and ideas. Accordingly, flanked by the metaphors of mother and prostitute, the metonym for high art that still reigns supreme is Pushkin, the protean Prometheus. These strange bedfellows constitute the gendered trinity of current cultural rhetoric, not unlike Mary and Magdalene alongside Christ.[22] As Mary Ellman ironically notes in her witty *Thinking about Women*:

> Christ honored only the mother who conceived without intercourse and
> the prostitute who resigned from it. So they [Mary and Magdelene]
> were alike, after all, and both at fault in the sexual form which God the
> Father had presumably designed for them. (179)

To the question "Why Pushkin?" my answer is threefold: (1) Russia's peculiar penchant for ideological legitimation through "high" art—and no artist in Russia is "higher" than Pushkin[23]; (2) the specific demands of any cult formation, for which Pushkin's relatively brief biography is eminently suited[24]; and (3) Pushkin's reluctance to foreclose a text or an issue, which renders him a multidextrous image (to modify and transpose Gerald Graff's term [Graff 603]) inviting multiple, even mutually exclusive, extrapolations. In possibly the most stunning appropriation, Black Americans adopted Pushkin as one of *their* glorious native sons (see Fig. 3), popularizing a highly selective version of his biography (as "man of color") in a series of comics documenting great men in black history ("The Life").[25]

For Russians, not idolizing Pushkin is tantamount to betraying Russia, abrogating all human values, or involuntarily revealing crass imperviousness to aesthetics. The process of the poet's canonization, launched by the Pushkin Celebration of 1880, was consolidated in the ensuing 100-odd years by official campaigns orchestrated to capitalize economically and politically on Pushkin's name and its totem powers (Levitt especially 154–75). Despite appropriative gestures by Valerii Briusov and Marina Tsvetaeva (both named their *professions de foi My Pushkin* [*Moi Pushkin,* 1929 and 1937, respectively], the state ensured that the poet became and remained *our* Pushkin—a national treasure, not only the fountainhead and acme of Russian art, but the slippery signifier invoked to legitimate whatever ideology dominates at a given moment.

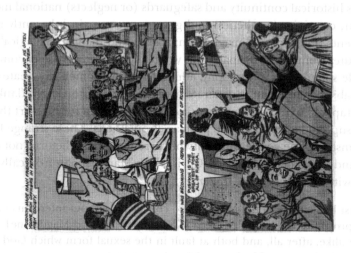

3a and 3b. Issue of *Golden Legacy* magazine depicting "The Life of Alexander Pushkin."

The Gendered Trinity of Russian Cultural Rhetoric

Pace Solzhenitsyn's somewhat quixotic claim that, in Russia, literature functions as an alternative government,[26] Pushkin's case vividly illustrates the state's preemption of literature and its producers for the purposes of forced unification via pseudo-artistic self-vindication. Pushkin's aesthetic attitude to ideas made him the ideal candidate for cooptation by radically divergent interest groups. Hence the liberal press hoped to use the Pushkin Celebration of 1880, which unveiled the Opekushin monument in Moscow, as an argument for constitutional reform (Levitt 120), while conservative nationalists (Dostoevskii) used the occasion to stimulate nationalist pride by eulogizing the writer's universality and messianism.

During the 1880 Celebration, Dostoevskii's apotheosis of Pushkin as "pan-human" and yet quintessentially Russian, as well as the political rivalry that accompanied the festivities, set the course for future Pushkin rituals and marketing strategies.[27] The year 1887, the fiftieth anniversary of Pushkin's death (when the copyright to his works expired), witnessed the sale of approximately two million copies of Pushkin's works, amounting to 12 percent to 18 percent of books published that year nationwide (Levitt 155). The 1899 Pushkin jubilee and subsequent rituals unleashed a Pushkinomania that reached its apogee under Stalin in 1937—not insignificantly, coinciding with the height of the purges. At the Party's behest, publishers printed nineteen million copies of Pushkin's writings; the president of the Academy of Sciences declared that interest in Pushkin among soldiers in the Red Army surpassed that of the pre-Soviet bourgeoisie; and the poet was officially pronounced *the* model for "the new Soviet man" (Levitt 164–65). The cult of Pushkin in belles lettres, in short, mirrored Stalin's "cult of personality."

Since then, the wave of memorials, monuments, museums, "Pushkin places," postcards, and reissues of his works has swelled to tidal proportions. Recognizing the hyperbole and near-hysteria of this canonization, fascinatingly, does not curb the wild excesses of Pushkin worshippers. At the peak of perestroika (1987), Sergei Zalygin announced that Pushkinology is synonymous with "Russianology," "humanology," "history," and "futurology," while the Petersburg poet Aleksandr Kushner resorted to Christological analogy by calling Pushkin "the bread we eat, the wine we drink" (Levitt 173). While one divinity after another has toppled in the last decade, Pushkin as cultural metonym has withstood all the vicissitudes of glasnost, to emerge intact.[28]

Not only literati, but literature itself has enthusiastically colluded in the Pushkinization of whatever political, moral, and aesthetic values a given text espouses. In Evgenii Zamiatin's *We* [*My*, 1920], Pushkin is synecdochically equated with free, imperishable art, in diametrical opposition to the mechanical, state-serving oratory disgorged on demand by poets of the Single State. Boris Pasternak's *Doctor Zhivago* [*Doktor Zhivago*, 1954] glorifies Pushkin as the genius of unpretentious simplicity. Mikhail Bulgakov's *Master and Margarita* [*Master i Margarita*, 1928–40] implicitly makes Pushkin synonymous with an Art that accesses transcendent Truth, while Solzhenitsyn's *First Circle* [*V kruge pervom*, wr. 1955–64, pub. 1968] figures Pushkin as the ultimate criterion for art and the exemplar of a timeless universal ethics. Andrei Bitov's *Pushkin House* [*Pushkinskii Dom*, 1978] (the cradle of Russia's cultural-artistic heritage, as opposed to the humble domesticity of *Matrena's Home*) deconstructs the Pushkin myth, but in the process of dismantling the "artifact," reinstalls the Pushkin who transcends all categorization by his "divine right of genius." (The Christ analogy recurs in Bitov's reference to the locale of Pushkin's duel as "the sacred place, watered by *his* blood" [338]—a return of sorts to Lermontov's earlier outrage at d'Anthès's spilling of "the blood of the righteous" [*pravednuiu krov'*, Lermontov, I: 9].)[29]

And now? Even amidst the post-Communist general disavowal of Soviet sacred cows, Pushkin remains the saintly steer. Glasnost and post-glasnost texts whose links with postmodernism elicit expectations of partial debunking, though they ironize myths, tellingly opt for Pushkin as the myth of choice: the most colorful examples include Bitov's story "Pushkin's Photograph (1799–2099)" [*Fotografiia Pushkina (1799–2099)*, 1987], Valeriia Narbikova's "Running through the Run" [*Probeg-pro beg*, 1990], Dmitrii Prigov's "The Captivating Star of Russian Poetry" [*Zvezda plenitel'naia russkoi poèzii*, 1991], and Tat'iana Tolstaia's "Night" [*Noch'*, 1987] and "Plot" [*Siuzhet*, 1992].

The impulse shared by all of these texts to contest or demythologize, while inevitably also reinscribing (Hutcheon 129), is exemplified in Iurii Mamin's film *Sideburns* [*Bakenbardy*, 1990]—whose domestic circulation, significantly, was blocked, presumably because of an organized boycott cum payoff by ultraconservative factions of precisely the sort satirized by Mamin (Lawton 220). A carnivalesque dystopia that explores how totalitarian institutions appropriate art (metonymized as Pushkin) for their coercive aims, the film cleverly exposes the perils of cultism and single-minded politicization.[30] By simultaneously portraying Pushkin fanatics as advocates of phallic power (they tread unsoftly and carry a big stick), Mamin, whether intentionally or not, underscores the masculinist roots of the Pushkin trope (see Fig. 4). Likewise Andrei Siniavskii's idiosyncratic but often commonsensical *Strolls with Pushkin* [*Progulki s Pushkinym*, wr. 1966–68, pub. 1975], which enraged Russians by its deconstruction of their cultural icon, detropes Pushkin

The Gendered Trinity of Russian Cultural Rhetoric

4. *Sideburns (Bakenbardy)*, 1990. Director, Iurii Mamin.

in the interests of humanization, yet manages to retain its own brand of idolatry. Not unlike the corpse of Stalin/Varlam in Tengiz Abuladze's film *Repentance* [*Pokaianie*, 1984/1986], Pushkin as trope cannot be laid to rest, his ubiquity cutting across political lines, generations, and national borders.

Russians who may agree about nothing else become united in proclaiming Pushkin their "all," their Genius, their divinity, the "soul" or "spirit" of Russia, and Art incarnate. The only element powerful enough to dethrone Pushkin, after sharing cultural space with him, is the American hamburger—aka McDonald's. The selection of Pushkin Square (with its revered monument of the Great Poet) for Russia's first McDonald's symbolically captures a defining aspect of Russia's present moment: the rivalrous and sometimes rancorously debated coexistence of High Cultural traditions and pragmatic entrepreneurial innovation.[31] In short, as long as Culture retains its lofty perch, Pushkin reigns supreme. When Culture slips irrevocably to the lower case, Pushkin's status will be lowered accordingly.

What does all of the above suggest? If cultural rhetoric offers eloquent clues to the mores of a given society—and I believe it does—then anyone seeking a reconceptualization of gender roles in post-Communist Russia will enjoy more success if she looks for snow in Africa. For the last few years have not noticeably modified, let alone overturned, the misogynistic mental habits shaping and shaped by the ironclad cultural rhetoric I have outlined. Attempts by Russians to revise notions of gender—such as the formation of women's groups and clubs, feminist publications, conferences on gender, and the establishment of the Gender Center in Moscow, as well as the introduction of Women's Advanced Studies at the Russian State Humanities University (RGGU)—represent isolated, minuscule islands of activity and change in a sea of sameness (Goscilo, "Domostroika"). Familiarity with the work of the Gender Center scarcely extends beyond the narrow circle of its members (i.e., a handful of scholars); communication and exchange between the Center and faculty or students involved in gender/feminist studies at RGGU verge on nil; unsystematic or delayed distribution of announcements about conferences on gender results in erratic attendance; publications addressing gender issues appear in insignificant runs, tend to depend on Western financial support,[32] and are vastly outnumbered by the infinitely more popular pornography, mysteries, adventures, and romances disseminated throughout the capitals[33]; and some of the unscholarly "women's publications" themselves are code-affirming—i.e., they reinforce all-too-familiar sexist binary oppositions.

A case in point is the Petersburg publication *Natali*, named, grotesquely, after Pushkin's wife, presumably the uxorial ideal whose fame derives from the country's chief Cultural icon.[34] The two issues of *Natali* I have perused focus on cosmetics, gossip, babies, and ads for beauty contests and nursing jobs.

In the sphere of gender, then, analysts of post-Communist Russian society discover copious evidence of continuity rather than rupture. Perhaps that explains why the tiny minority of feminists active in Moscow and Petersburg have turned increasingly to their Western counterparts in hopes of finding moral and financial support, learning from precedents, and elaborating some program that eventually will trigger a genuine perestroika not only in women's lives, but in the dominant cultural rhetoric of their country.[35]

Notes

My thanks to Bozenna Goscilo for her critical response to this chapter, to the Center for Cultural Studies at the University of California (Santa Cruz) for hosting the conference on "Postcommunism: Rethinking the Second World," at which I delivered an earlier version of the essay, and to Greta Slobin, the conference organizer.

1. Numerous scholars have commented on Russia's emotional attraction to leaders with a penchant for brutality and mass murder, exemplified by Ivan the Terrible and

The Gendered Trinity of Russian Cultural Rhetoric

Joseph Stalin. The cult of Stalin especially has been the subject of recent films, including Semen Aranovich's *I Served in Stalin's Guard* [*Ia sluzhil v okhrane Stalina,* 1989] and Tofik Shakhverdiev's *Is Stalin with Us?* [*Stalin s nami?,* 1989], both of which examine contemporary Russians' fond attachment to Stalin's memory and utter obliviousness to his inhuman methods. See Lawton 143–45. Nostalgia for a "strong hand" has captured segments of post-glasnost society partly because of the chaos and perceived lack of united leadership in the country.

2. Mikhail Yampolsky, an astute critic indifferent, at best, to gender issues, has acknowledged, nonetheless, that women's bodies in early Russian films such as Dovzhenko's *Earth* [*Zemlia,* 1930], for instance, function exclusively as metaphors. See video by Yampolsky.

3. With only isolated exceptions, the "male dolls," dubbed *patreshki* by Vladimir Padunov and Nancy Condee, represent the country's leaders from Lenin to Yeltsin. Recognizable historical referents confer an individual identity upon the male figures, whereas their female counterparts continue to dwell in universalized anonymity.

4. On the national-religious elements in Matrena's portrait, see Jackson, especially 69–70.

5. Susan Larsen at Yale University has also noted the persistence of dusty misogynistic stereotypes in both recent film and the current press. My appreciation to her for our various exchanges on the topic and for her generosity in pointing me to several sources.

6. Both Petrushevskaia's and Shcherbakova's interest in mother-daughter relations is evident in other works of theirs: e.g., Petrushevskaia's "Kseniia's Daughter" [*Doch' Ksenii*], "Land" [*Strana*], "Medea" [*Medeia*]; Shcherbakova's "The Three 'Loves' of Masha Peredreeva" [*Tri 'liubvi' Mashi Peredreevoi*] in *Chistye prudy* [*Clear Ponds*] (1990) 214–53; "Daughters, Mothers, Birds, and Islands" [*Dochki, materi, ptitsy i ostrova*] in *Soglasie* [*Concordance*] 6 (1991): 82–89; *Anatomy of a Divorce* [*Anatomiia razvoda*] (Moskva: Molodaia gvardiia, 1990).

7. I borrow the term "prosaics" from Saul Morson, who elucidates usage of the word in a historical context at considerable length in his study of Tolstoi's *War and Peace* (Morson).

8. During a recent stay in Moscow, my efforts to locate a bookstore on Znamenka (formerly Frunzenskaia) were complicated by the "aid" of a driver whom I had flagged down. An official driver for the police, neither he nor the six policemen whom he asked for directions had any notion where Znamenka was located. When I happened to spot a road sign bearing the street name on it as the driver was racing past it, he sheepishly confessed his ignorance of most of the "new" "old" names—i.e., of "today's history."

9. That moment shows Russia poised to embark on its "real" history, whose unfolding presumably was thwarted by the perverse imposition of Sovietization.

10. The backward rhythm that finds expression in the grandmother's hold on the younger generations is reinforced by numerous details in the film—the *Vorgeschichte* that elides World War II, sexual infidelity, the maternal bed, and mother-daughter relations; Nina Elizarovna's employment in a museum; and the retrospective cast to the nameday party, at which Nina's two exhusbands "go back over old territory." Retrogression is buttressed by the repetition of actions and situations: Nastia's constant appropriation of others' possessions (Lida's gloves, Lida's scarf, some tongue for the party) and the appropriation of Lida's lover by her "friend" Marina—a lover whom Lida has appropriated from his wife (in an echo of the *Vorgeschichte*); Nastia's dismissal of her child's father, which resonates with Nina's "throwing out" Lida's father Viktor (at her mother's reported urging).

11. Krishtofovich originally opposed naming the film *Adam's Rib* because he considered the biblical connotations too recondite (!) and pretentious, but with time grew enamored of the title. Fein 22.

12. The title of Anatolii Kurchatkin's novella, published in *Oktiabr'* [*October*] 6 (1986): 3–54, underscores the link between women and home that Krishtofovich's film can establish directly by the simple visual expedient of confining the film's action almost exclusively to the "closed space" of the women's apartment.

13. It is characteristic of the film's passion for paradoxes and generation reversals that Nastia's implicit reference to the grandmother's anticipated death ("But surely this will end some time?") coincides with the moment of the old woman's "rebirth."

14. Interestingly, Krishtofovich in an interview reportedly disclaims interest in "politics" and "big" topics, choosing to focus on "ordinary lives and minds." That the issue of generations fascinates him may be deduced from the material he has used in his films, e.g., the 1984 TV film he based on Lev Tolstoi's story "Two Hussars." Fein 13.

15. As in *Adam's Rib*, parallels between generations emerge most vividly in sexual matters: Both Sima and Anna Adrianovna engage in shouting matches with their daughters, whom they suspect of usurpation (Petrushevskaia 101); both make life unendurable for their sons-in-law, whom they denigrate as "*darmoed*" and "*krovopiets*," and unfit to shoulder responsibilities as head of the family (100–101); both lock themselves in their room when they feel threatened (102); both terrorize everyone in their orbit so as to assert their rightness (99). Anna Adrianovna similarly shares with her daughter a desire to punish her mother, a checkered sexual history and an association with the sexually loaded motif of stallions.

For a more detailed analysis of the story, see Woll; Goscilo, "Petrushevskaia's Vision."

16. The notion of survival as a significant achievement, of course, belongs to the genre of war and camp literature and current Western feminist writing on such subjects as abuse, rape, and battering. That the discourse of heroic survival may be unproblematically invoked for women's "private" suffering indicates the West's greater progress, perhaps, in validating women's experience. (I am grateful to Bozenna for drawing my attention to this point.)

17. Like Krishtofovich and Petrushevskaia, Shcherbakova both emphasizes time's passage and negates or problematizes it, here through the paradox of Lizon'ka's speaking with the dead (shades of Lucian and Menippean satire in general), whose decrepitude, moreover, is belied by their visual representation in snapshots taken of them in their youth (Shcherbakova 88).

18. Curiously enough, contemporary American therapy increasingly approaches a number of psychological problems manifested in physical disorders (especially those diagnosed as gender-specific, e.g., bulimia and anorexia) from a multigenerational perspective that addresses such issues as fusion or replication, transmission of obsessive patterns, and individuation. On this topic, see Root, Fallon, and Friedrich, especially chapter 5, entitled "Multigenerational Issues."

The perception that "plus ça change, plus c'est la même chose" animates a recently published poem by Vladimir Kornilov, which evokes the fairy tale of the golden fish to dismiss the likelihood of a free market in Russia:

Khren s toboi, zolotaia rybka!
Plavniki svoi unosi . . .
Nikakogo ne budet rynka
Na ogryzkakh vseia Rusi.

Bylo khudo i stanet khudo.
Ubiraisia, i Bog s toboi . . .
Zhdali chuda i netu chuda—
Snova nevod s morskoi travoi.
(*Konets veka* 146)

19. It is, of course, no coincidence that Vladimir Kunin wrote the filmscript for *Adam's Rib*.

20. For additional analysis of the film from the standpoint of gender and pornographic values, see Helena Goscilo, "New Organs and Members: The Politics of Porn," *Carl Beck Papers* (1993), REES, University of Pittsburgh.

21. To what extent prostitute is presumed to be woman, and Western market practices signal the sale of sex, is illustrated by such post-glasnost phenomena as the sexual peddling of boys dressed and made up as girls. One journalist reports the lucrative business of a Muscovite who sells the sexual favors of three boys, aged eight and nine, to foreign and domestic clients. The boys, "transformed" into girls by dresses, skirts, and cosmetics, readily service customers for $20 a day or more. On this, see Serrill.

22. Lev Tolstoi in his later renunciation of "pure" art's value in *What Is Art?* [*Chto takoe iskusstvo?* 164] implies Russian culture's paralleling of Pushkin and Christ. For instances of such homological thinking and for an overview of the early phases of mythmaking around Pushkin, see Debreczeny 270 and passim.

23. Inspired by Madame Tussaud's, a group of theatrical artists under the leadership of Nikolai Zelenetskii established the Theatrical Museum—a wax museum in Moscow's Sokol'niki Park. Among the various tableaux of fifteen historical figures, an orthodox yet peculiarly eloquent juxtaposition links Stalin with Ivan the Terrible, who holds in his arms not the son he killed (as depicted in Repin's famous painting), but the culturally overdetermined figure (in both senses—body and metonym) of Pushkin! See Freeman and Berton 63–64.

24. Marcus Levitt correctly observes that the comparative brevity of Pushkin's life conveniently enabled "a relatively close succession of 'large' ('All-Union') jubilee dates" (168). The frequency with which the Soviet establishment could organize Pushkin anniversaries manifestly benefitted its program of ideological reinforcement.

25. My gratitude to Nancy Condee and Volodia Padunov for acquainting me with this fascinating publication.

26. In *The First Circle*, where Pushkin's verses serve as a moral *ur*-text.

27. Pushkin's purportedly "purely Russian" nature had already been stressed by Nikolai Gogol"s article, "A Few Words about Pushkin" [*Neskol'ko slov o Pushkine*, 1834], by Mikhail Lermontov's "Death of a Poet" [*Smert' poèta*, 1837], excoriating the foreigner who had killed him, and by practically all subsequent votaries at the Pushkin altar. See Debreczeny 272–73, 276.

28. For more examples of pre-glasnost Pushkin idolatry among such literati as Tiutchev, Platonov, and Kaverin, and for commentary on the 1987 special January issue of *Novyi mir* [*Novyi mir*], see Debreczeny 283–90.

29. The preoccupation with Pushkin's blood (e.g., aristocratic, African, pure, Russian, spilled) reflects its boundless potential for figurative purposes, whereby Pushkin's blood becomes a martyr's sacramental "essence."

30. The commonality between cults of the poet and the political leader is illustrated with witty economy in a scene in which a few strokes by a sculptor suffice to transform a statue of Lenin into Pushkin's likeness. The process of petrification is identical.

31. Were the monumental Pushkin to glance over his shoulder, he could conceivably peer into McDonald's. In fact, whenever the crowds of hungry hopefuls patiently waiting in line to eat at McDonalds become large enough, they snake around the block, winding up at the Pushkin monument.

32. Of the several studies by scholars from the Gender Center published in 1992, *Zhenshchina v meniaiushchemsia mire* (Nauka) had a run of 1,100 copies; *Zhenshchina i sotsial'naia politika*, ed. Z. Khotkina, of 500 copies; and *Feminizm: Perspektivy sotsial'nogo znaniia*, ed. O. A. Voronina, 500 copies. The last two were in-house publications. At least two other projects, including translations from Western feminism, were funded in part by Katrina vanden Heuvel.

33. At the same time, pornography itself seems to have lost the broad popularity it enjoyed a year ago. The numerous porn publications that randomly overran stands in 1991 and 1992 either have found a more specialized audience (i.e., one motivated by more than a general curiosity) and therefore a genre-specific sales-space, or have lost their appeal and diminished in number. For the most recent dramatic shifts in sales patterns of printed material in Moscow, see chapter 7 of this volume, by Condee and Padunov.

While few would deny that popular culture is ousting Culture from the contemporary Russian market, that revolution should not blind one to the strong link between high and low culture: namely, the misogyny that reduces women to physiology, irrationalism, and mother/whore troping in the first, and to cat (cunt-ass-tit) in the second.

34. No spouse of any writer in Russian (or possibly world) history has inspired such impassioned interest as Natal'ia Goncharova. Despised as the ball-obsessed philistine incapable of appreciating Pushkin's verse and as the empty-headed cause of Pushkin's demise or defended as the innocent, honorable wife of a Great Man, Goncharova in her lifetime elicited comments above all about her shapely figure.

35. The new women's prose (fiction by Svetlana Vasilenko, Marina Palei, Larisa Vaneeva, Nina Sadur, and Elena Tarasova, among others), which sundry Russian commentators have berated for its unwomanliness (see Goscilo, *Skirted Issues*), represents the first revisionist step in literature. Such publications as the bilingual issue of *Heresies* entitled *Idioma* fulfill a kindred function in art. For that reason their appearance marks a significant moment in Russia's cultural development.

Works Cited

Bitov, Andrei. *Pushkin House.* Ann Arbor: Ardis, 1987/1990.

Blake, Patricia, and Max Hayward. *Half-way to the Moon: New Writing in Russia.* Garden City, NY: Anchor/Doubleday 1965.

Buckley, Mary, ed. *Perestroika and Soviet Women.* Cambridge, MA: Cambridge UP, 1992.

Condee, Nancy, and Vladimir Padunov. "*Makulakul'tura:* Reprocessing Culture." *October* 59 (Summer 1991): 79–103.

Debreczeny, Paul. "'*Zhitie Aleksandra Boldinskogo*': Pushkin's Elevation to Sainthood in Soviet Culture." *South Atlantic Quarterly* 90 (Spring 1991) 2: 269–92.

Ellman, Mary. *Thinking about Women.* San Diego: Harcourt Brace Jovanovich, 1968.

Erofeyev, Victor. *Russian Beauty.* London: Hamish Hamilton, 1992.

Evtushenko, Evgenii. *Literaturnaia gazeta* 3 May 1989.

The Gendered Trinity of Russian Cultural Rhetoric

Fein, Esther B. " 'Adam's Rib' Finds Hope amid Pain." *New York Times* 3 May 1992.

Freeman, John, and Kathleen Berton. *Moscow Revealed.* New York: Abbeville Press, 1991.

Gorbachev, Mikhail. *Perestroika. New Thinking for the Country and the World.* New York: Harper & Row, 1987.

Gorky, Maxim. *Mother.* Secaucus, NJ: Citadel, 1947/1974.

Goscilo, Helena. "Domostroika or Perestroika?: The Construction of Womanhood under Glasnost'." *Late Soviet Culture: From Perestroika to Novostroika.* Ed. Thomas Lahusen. Durham, NC: Duke UP, 1993, 133–55.

———. "Petrushevskaia's Vision: No Ray of Light in the Kingdom of Darkness." Unpublished paper delivered at AAASS Conference in Tucson, AZ 1992.

———, ed. *Skirted Issues: The Discreteness and Indiscretions of Russian Women's Prose. Russian Studies in Literature* 28 (Spring 1992): 2.

"Gostepriimnaia demokratiia" (cartoon). *Literaturnaia Rossiia* 4 December 1992.

Graff, Gerald. "The Pseudo-Politics of Interpretation." *Critical Inquiry* 9, 3: 597–610.

Hubbs, Joanna. *Mother Russia.* Bloomington: Indiana UP, 1988.

Hutcheon, Linda. *A Poetics of Postmodernism: History, Theory, Fiction.* New York: Routledge, 1988.

Ivanits, Linda J. *Russian Folk Belief.* Armonk, NY: M. E. Sharpe, 1989.

Jackson, Robert Louis. " 'Matryona's Home': The Making of a Russian Icon." *Solzhenitsyn.* Ed. Kathryn Feuer. Englewood Cliffs, NJ: Prentice-Hall, 1976, 60–70.

Konets veka 4 (1992): 146–48.

Korotaev, V., ed. *Mat': stikhtvoreniia russkikh i sovetskikh poètov o materi.* Moskva: n.p., 1979.

Kunin, Vladimir. *Intergirl: A Hard Currency Hooker.* New York: Bergh, 1991.

Lawton, Anna. *Kinoglasnost: Soviet Cinema in Our Time.* Cambridge, MA: Cambridge UP, 1992.

Lermontov, Mikhail Iu. *Sobranie sochinenii v 4-i tt.* Moskva: Khudozhestvennaia literatura, 1957.

Levitt, Marcus C. *Russian Literary Politics and the Pushkin Celebration of 1880.* Ithaca: Cornell UP, 1989.

"The Life of Alexander Pushkin." *Golden Legacy* Illustrated History Magazine, Vol. 14. Dix Hills, NY: Fitzgerald, 1972.

Literaturnaia gazeta 20 December 1989.

Morson, Gary Saul. *Hidden in Plain View. Narrative and Creative Potentials in "War and Peace."* Stanford: Stanford UP, 1987.

Natali 3, 4 (1991).

Petrushevskaia, Ludmila. "Vremia noch'," *Novyi mir* 2 (1992): 65–110.

Rabotnitsa 3 (1990).

Rasputin, Valentin. *Farewell to Matera.* Evanston, IL: Northwestern UP, 1991.

Root, Maria P. P., Patricia Fallon, and William N. Friedrich. *Bulimia: A Systems Approach to Treatment.* New York: W. W. Norton, 1986.

Serrill, Michael S. "Defiling the Children." *Time* (21 June 1993): 53–55.

Shcherbakova, Galina. *Ubikvisty. Soglasie* 2 (1992): 11–88.

Solzhenitsyn, Alexander. "The Relentless Cult of Novelty and How It Wrecked the Century." *The New York Times Book Review* 7 February 1993.

Tolstoy, Leo N. *What Is Art?* Indianapolis: Bobbs-Merrill, 1960.

van Buren, Jane Silverman. *The Modern Madonna: Semiotics of the Maternal Metaphor.* Bloomington: Indiana UP, 1989.

Woll, Josephine. "The Minotaur in the Maze: On Lyudmila Petrushevskaya." *World Literature Today* 67.1 (Winter 1993): 125–30.

Helena Goscilo

Yampolsky, Mikhail. "V poiskakh utrachennogo naslazhdeniia" (Èrotika v russkom kino). Video supplement to *Ogonek* 5 (1990).

Zenkovsky, Serge A., ed. *Medieval Russia's Epics, Chronicles, and Tales*. New York: E. P. Dutton, 1963.

Zhigul'skaia, A. F., ed. *Poèmy pobedy*. Voronezh: Tsentr.-Chernozemn. kh. izd., 1976.

Five

In the Shadow of Monuments
Notes on Iconoclasm and Time

Mikhail Yampolsky
Translated by John Kachur

In Walter Benjamin's *Moscow Diary*, there is an entry concerning the topography and architecture of the Kremlin:

> It is easy to overlook one of the basic conditions of its beauty: none of
> its broad expanses contains a monument. By contrast, there is hardly a
> square in Europe whose secret structure was not profaned and impaired
> over the course of the nineteenth century by the introduction of a
> monument. (65)

It is true that within the space of the Kremlin there is something that runs counter to the idea of the anthropomorphic monument, whose place was taken long ago by the Tsar Bell and the Tsar Cannon. Even in the Brezhnev era, no one risked defiling the Kremlin by introducing a real monument. The seated figure of Lenin, purposely small and intimate, was placed so as both to observe decorum and not be particularly striking.

In my view, any monument would be superfluous within these walls literally because of the walls themselves. Traditionally, monuments are erected in areas that are maximally open and accessible to view (important exceptions, of course, are gravestones), most often in the squares formed by street intersections, or on an elevated spot. Pragmatically, this is motivated by the fact that, by its very nature, a monument is intended to be admired, contemplated, and worshipped. In reality, however, monuments rarely become objects of a genuine cult or even of admiration. In the urban landscape, as a rule, their perception is automatized and they virtually disappear from the field of vision. Moreover, their positioning often violates the golden rule of the street's visual text: the obligatory placement of the object at—or slightly above—the passerby's eye level, a rule that advertisements invariably follow. The high pedestals that long dominated the architecture of monuments render the memorials almost indiscernible from up close. Easily visible from afar, they appear to fade from the field of vision as one approaches them.

Such a structure of perception makes the monument a rather distinctive cult object: it keeps the worshipper at a distance. This distance is inscribed into its function, and therefore approaching the monument is always a sort of transgression of a sacral zone. A number of monuments in Moscow, for example, were consciously erected in this field of inaccessibility. Dzerzhinskii, to whom it was physically impossible to get close, stands out among these aloof monuments.

The attribute of distance is closely connected with the height of the monument. The lower the monument, the easier getting close to it is, though a certain feeling of transgression accompanies even this "permitted" approach. This impassable zone in its own way resembles the "personal reserve" spoken about by Ervin Goffman, or the zone of bodily self-manifestation described by Merleau-Ponty. But these personal protective zones surrounding the body are situated around living beings and not images carved out of stone. Nevertheless, when we look upon workers installing or dismantling a monument, their physical contact with the object subconsciously shocks us.

Meanwhile, the ritual transgression of these protective zones enters into the very functioning of the monuments. Significantly, one of the most famous Soviet monumental attractions, Vuchetich's sculpture of Mamai's burial mound in Stalingrad, was wholly built so as to immerse the human being gradually into the world of cyclopean monuments, among which the visitor was intended to move about, attaining a traumatic proximity with these immense idols. Precisely the immensity of the monument, so keenly felt in close proximity, lends the monument the quality of the colossal, the incommensurable, and ascribes to it the fiction of infinite height and unconquerable strength.

Jacques Derrida has shown that colossal proportions are nothing other than the expression of the figure's incongruity with whatever concept it is ostensibly called upon to represent (136–38). The monument's immensity is a sign of the unrepresentability so important for the monument's functioning. Unrepresentability, to a certain extent, forces the monument beyond the boundaries of human semiotics, imbuing it, like anything colossal, with an elemental, innate quality. Being, of course, the fruit of man's labors, it aspires to transcend its human nature. Hence, the traditional striving of monumental forms toward coarse, "innate" styles and the open rejection of a naturalistic resemblance with the prototype.

After all, while laying claim to figurativeness and the qualities of portraiture, the monument usually corresponds only weakly to any concrete human personality. It is simply a colossus, a huge magic mound, existing in complete contrast to the laws of mimesis, similitude, and imitation. Any similarity to a portrait is purely a concealment of the monument's true function.

The existence of a sacral zone around the monument has, in my view, several causes. One of them, which I will mention only in passing, is the monument's duality and its correlation, therefore, to Freud's *Unheimlich*. This aspect is well elaborated in the "sculptural myth," to use Roman Jakobson's expression (the relationships between Don Juan and the Stone Guest or Evgenii and the Bronze Horseman address, in part, precisely this topic). This cause, however, does not seem to me to be the main one.

A second cause can be described in terms of proxemics. According to Edward Hall, the "public distance" between two bodies supposes the significant remoteness of one body from the other, such that the figure removed to a "public distance" occupies in the field of vision only the very center of the retina (fovea) (124–25).[1] Because of this, the dimensions of the monument dictate a large expanse between itself and the viewer. The higher the monument, the larger is its protective zone.

But there is yet another cause, the one that most interests me here. I have in mind the monument's absolutely unique influence on the structure of time. In actuality, the main reason for raising a monument is the desire in some kind of magical way to affect the course of time, either to change it or to avoid its influence.

In his classic work *The Modern Cult of Monuments*, Alois Riegl proposed a classification of monuments according to the temporal value contained in them (21–51). Foremost are those that contain "age-value," most often ancient structures and ruins. They are significant because they carry the imprint of elapsing time and affirm its all-conquering power over the creations of human hands. Ruins are an ironic memento mori that unmasks the laughable pretensions of human artifacts, the expression in stone of the victory of nature over history. The all-conquering time of ruins is extrahistorical, corresponding to eternity to the extent that nature transcends human temporality. In a strange way, certain structures (such as, for example, the Egyptian pyramids or the Coliseum) may also emerge as carriers of age-values, ironically emphasizing the transitoriness of human pretensions.

The opposite category consists of monuments possessing an "intentional commemorative value," that is, originally and consciously conceived as monuments. These memorials are called upon forever to cement the memory of a certain event or individual, and therefore they also in their own way transcend history. Their task is to preserve unchanged a given moment. "Intentional" monuments, thus, negate the march of time and oppose to it the permanence of human action. They are not meant to be subject to traces left by time and therefore are objects of constant renovation and restoration.

In the real urban landscape, intentional monuments, of course, interact with those that bear age-value. This interaction is far from neutral. These two types of monuments contradict each other too openly to coexist in peace. As a result, the erection of certain intentional monuments demands the reconstruction of the entire urban environment. The installation of the gigantic figure of Lenin on Moscow's October Square, conceived as the country's main Lenin memorial, demanded the complete reconstruction of the square. A special milieu was created for the monument, the distinguishing feature of which was its absolute ahistoricity. The memorial, destined for eternity, should not have to compete with a single historical building. The ahistoricity of the monument demanded the complete ahistoricity of the surroundings.

All this allows us, if only partially, to answer the question of why the Kremlin has not had to endure any contemporary monuments within its grounds. This may be connected with the fact that its cathedrals have absorbed such a concentration of history that a monument, which denies history's progression, could not withstand the powerful weight of historical evidence. By their historical gravity, the cathedrals would destroy the pathos of any anthropomorphic monument.

One could also suppose that any monument creates around itself a kind of special temporal expanse in which time moves differently than in other places, a sort of mystical protective zone that surrounds the monument and is apparently connected with the experience of temporal metamorphosis. Approaching the monument, one seems to enter the context of a different time, simply to fall out of the temporal context and step into a zone where the eternal present reigns, where time, in Shchedrin's words, has ceased its movement.

The innate quality, one way or another present in large Soviet memorials, is to a certain extent also responsible for that special ahistorical time that is connected with monuments. In this connection, the process itself of the slow approach to the monument may be described as the gradual transformation of the temporal flow. While a person is far away, the monument retains its anthropomorphicity and only weakly affects the sensation of time. The nearer one approaches, the more the monument's features gradually lose their ties to figurativeness. In many cases, the sculpture seemingly shields itself with its high pedestal—the stone mound, mainly connected with the idea of innate, nonlinear time, with the idea of nature as eternity.

Now I can explain why it appears to me that, apart from anything else, the surrounding Kremlin walls render a monument superfluous. In the contemporary urban structure, the Kremlin is a glaring anachronism—a fortress whose gigantic walls were erected in the seventeenth century, that is, precisely at the time when, throughout all of Europe, fortress walls were being dismantled as unnecessary. The liquidation of the fortress walls' historic inner city was a sign of urbanistic modernism. Vienna was one of the last European capitals to tear down its fortress walls, replacing them with the construction of the famous Ringstrasse, itself a symbol of modernism (Schorske 24–115). Above all, modernism was expressed in the opening up of space and, consequently, in the unification of time, which in its own way filtered into the various zones of the city. In Moscow, the rejection of European modernism was expressed spatially in the preservation of the Kremlin as a completely autonomous historical zone, one not subject to changes or the passage of time. In this sense, the Kremlin as a spatial structure fulfilled the same functions as a monument: it paralyzed time with its cyclopean walls.

The transfer of the capital to Moscow and the concentration of political power in the Kremlin have their own symbolic aspects. This is, of course, a transfer of power from the periphery to the spatial center, but it is also the placement of power inside walls, as into a core protected by a shell. Power becomes its own monument, symbolically moving beyond the boundaries of time. Michel Foucault has observed that "at the end of the eighteenth century architecture begins to deal with questions of population, health, and building in urban areas. Previously, architecture was concerned only with the necessity to make visible power, divinity, and might" (148). In Russia, this task is addressed by space much more than in Europe. The Kremlin, of course, was captivating to rulers because of its exceptional suitability to the symbolic manifestation of power.

The significance of monuments for the semiotics of Soviet power is not completely clear. It seems to me that their function as signs—to organize certain islets of eternity in the movement of time—is considerable. But it was precisely toward achronistic space of this type that the whole ideology of the Soviet regime gravitated, its aim being the immediate achievement of an ahistorical condition (Communism) that originally was supposed to arise as atemporal islets in the social space, gradually spreading and seizing the whole country. The construction of tall buildings, which became the favorite décor of official films, was oriented precisely toward the creation of some sort of utopian preserve of the future where time would not flow. Sculpture has an especially intensive existence in just such preserves.

The urban space of the 1930s through 1950s (a schema also followed in the urban utopias built under Khrushchev) is based on the opposition between (on the one hand) streets and avenues along which there is ceaseless movement of people and cars, and (on the other) squares adorned with monuments. Here movement is dried up into an immovable atemporality. In such a structure, the monument has an utterly unique function. It does not so much portray someone as it serves as a sort of vertical centering axis that spatially organizes the hierarchy of social signs. In monuments of the Soviet epoch, as I have already noted, it is not the similarity to a model or the mark of workmanship that is essential, but rather two qualities: a fundamental solidity and dimensions. A monument is not so much meant to imitate one or another person as it is to express the idea of not being subject to time, of extrahuman temporality, of ahistoricity.[2] Thus, the monument finds itself literally at the center of the totalitarian project, which, according to Hannah Arendt, is constructed as endless movement centered around an unattainable core.

A social structure of this type, reflected in the urban utopia, demands a monument for its completion. Moscow's uniqueness stems from its uncommonly wide arterial roads, along which transportation is organized according to a strange sort of logic. Left turns are prohibited almost everywhere, and even right turns are often not possible. City authorities have diligently replaced above-ground pedestrian crossings with underground ones, and prohibited not only parking, but even stopping along such major roads as, for example, Tverskaia. As a result of these diligent measures, traffic on Moscow's main streets ideally should not stop for even a minute or change its direction. This astonishing movement—ceaseless and only forward— transforms Moscow's "traffic" into a sort of social utopia. It is noteworthy that Walter Benjamin, discussing Moscow of the 1920s, observed revealingly, "Thus, even the traffic in Moscow is, to a large extent, a mass phenomenon" (*Reflections* 112).

Moscow's streets were built for the potential movement from place to place of huge masses of the population. But in such a stream the masses also remain their own type of potential phenomenon. The people's movement condenses into a *mass* only when it stops and when the people composing that mass are concentrated in a particular space—on a kind of symbolic square, or agora.

Elias Canetti proposed that a pile of stones might be considered one of the symbols of the masses: "Such heaps are made of stone precisely because it is difficult to take them to pieces. They are meant to endure for a long time, for their own brand of eternity, and to never shrink, but to remain always as they are" (*Crowds and Power* 88). By their contours, Soviet monuments mostly resembled precisely piles of stones rather than the works of sculptors. But, by the same token, they also absorbed the symbolism of the masses. The masses form themselves around a monument; its solidity (and the solidity of the Communist future is first of all the solidity of the masses and of the authority that commands them) is supported by that atemporal expanse that crystallizes around the monument. This expanse is as difficult to penetrate as it is to abandon.

That every monument is only a substitute for a pile of stones appears to me to be extremely important. The commemorative function of the totalitarian monument is always gradually yielding room to age-value, essentially to the symbolism of eternity as such. Commemorativeness is only the initial motivation for the emergence of monuments. Therefore, even a new monument seems to incorporate a sense of unseen future ruins. In 1938, Hitler's sculptor, Albert Speer, elaborated his "Theory on the Significance of Ruins," in which he praised ruins as the unshakable signs of a heroic past. In the opinion of Paul Virilio, Speer's own architecture was constructed precisely with future ruins in mind: "In the end, to construct a building is first of all to foresee how it will be demolished so that, as a result, you will have the kind of ruins that a millennium later 'will inspire thoughts just as heroic as did their ancient prototypes' " (101).

In some sense, ruins are the ideal condition of any totalitarian monument, just as the pile of stones is the fullest symbol of the masses. It is impossible not to observe, however, that whole complexes of monuments in the Soviet Union seemed to incorporate into themselves ruins, made transparent through the novelty of the construction. The complex on Mamai's burial mound, with figures standing out from imitation ruins, is a good example of this. The ruins are the final state beyond which any evolution, any movement of time, is already impossible. Communist society, in this sense, is a world of ruins.

Public squares with monuments in the center are the utopian component of the urban totalitarian space. Of course, no plan for monumental propaganda could provide for monuments at every intersection of the existing main streets. Their surrogates, however, structured the urban space in the form of gigantic, inscribed figures of Lenin, workers, and collective farmers staring out from walls and huge panels. Erik Bulatov's famous picture *Krasikov Street* (1976) well reflects the work of such monumental simulacra.

Mikhail Yampolsky

And, finally, there is another important property of monuments in the context of social time. It is well known that Lenin's plan for monumental propaganda emphasized mass production. Of course, this was accompanied by unprecedented iconoclasm, the destruction of old monuments. The point was to replace some monuments with others quickly, as if the emptiness created by the broken idols possessed some sort of destructive force that had to be subdued.

The fact that the new (and, as a rule, temporary and short-lived) monuments were constructed on the locations of the old, demolished monuments is far from accidental. Destruction and construction can be understood, in a certain context, as two equally valid procedures of immortalization. Destruction affirms the power of the victor to the same extent as the erection of a monument to victory. A tradition has developed historically to build a new monument precisely on the site of the old one, as though accumulating in one place two commemorative gestures: vandalism and the erection of a new idol. Hitler's hesitation, analyzed by Canetti, is curious: either to destroy Paris, or to let it be, both gestures to an equal extent connected with the strategy of immortalizing the victor. Canetti describes Hitler's indecision as "the twofold delight in permanence and destruction, characteristic of the paranoiac . . . " (*The Conscience of Words* 163).

This "paranoid" enjoyment is expressed especially graphically in the last one hundred years in cinema, which has felt a particular weakness for the fixation (potentially for eternity) of various kinds of destruction, including that of monuments. Film in a sense immortalizes the moment of destruction, transforming it into its own brand of monument. The immortalization of destruction as something eternal, or eternally recurring, was fully apparent in Sergei Eisenstein's *October* [*Oktiabr'*, 1928], which shows the destruction of the monument to Alexander III repeatedly, from various angles. At some point this ceaseless destruction is transformed into its opposite; by the reverse motion of the film, the monument "assembles itself" out of ruins. This eternally protracted moment of destruction resembles the sadistic Freudian compulsion to repeat, in which iconoclasm imperceptibly turns into a new fetishism. This is particularly evident in Eisenstein's film, with its obsessive attachment to the theme of monuments.

The new monument erected on the place of the old one becomes, in some sense, this kind of memorial to eternal destruction. It paradoxically turns out to be also a vestige of what is absent, its substitute. Such a "monument-successor" is the signifier of two signifieds: itself and what is absent, its demolished predecessor.

Such a double semiotics can be readily traced in the history of the Cathedral of Christ the Savior. This cathedral was demolished. In accordance with Canetti's principle of "twofold delight," a new cathedral, the Palace of Soviets, was supposed to have appeared in its place. This huge building was never erected. On the site of the Cathedral of Christ the Savior, a large swimming pool was constructed. The pool, which, as it were, is a minus-cathedral (a foundation pit instead of a pyramid), is interesting in that, for a long time now, it has been a sign of two nonexistent buildings: the Cathedral of Christ the Savior and the Palace of Soviets. One of them existed and was demolished; the other never was and never will be built. But both of these phantom structures in their own way are inscribed into the pool, which is transformed into a sign of memory. Mnemonic traces of this type are scattered all over Moscow, all over many Russian cities.

In the case of the Cathedral of Christ the Savior, the principal role in its phantom existence was played by the cinema.[3] The destruction of the cathedral was filmed. In the last few years, this small newsreel fragment has been shown in theaters and on television hundreds of times. One could say without exaggeration that this fragment today is the most shown piece of the Soviet chronicle. In a significant number of films, the precise moment of the collapse of the cathedral, of the explosion that smashes it to pieces, is shown in slow motion or repeated over and over. The directors/producers of the interesting documentary film *Disgraced Monuments* (1992), Mark Lewis and Laura Mulvey, did not escape this temptation.[4] Twofold delight from immortalized destruction, which is so fully manifested in cinema, transforms the Cathedral of Christ the Savior into a sort of supermonument of totalitarian culture, a monument to never-ending destruction, the dual will of vandals, which both does away with the huge stone structure and does not allow it to collapse once and for all (see Fig. 5).

This perpetual destruction (similar to *perpetual return*) contains within itself a deep tie with the principle of pageantry as such. It instantly makes supersignificant a monument that is usually effaced in the urban landscape. The moment of explosion is, from the point of view of spectacle, undoubtedly the most significant in the whole biography of the monument. Destruction increases space (in this sense, every wide main street in contemporary Moscow carries within it the bleeding mark of mass destructions, somehow symbolically analogous to Stalinist terror). An empty expanse is the unending potential for new spectacles, but it is also a sort of higher moment in the "creative" utopia of destruction. Walter Benjamin remarked that such emptiness "is a sight that affords the destructive character a spectacle of deepest harmony" (*Reflections* 301).

The connection that arises between new and old monuments by preserv-

Mikhail Yampolsky

5. *Disgraced Monuments,* 1992. Directors, Mark Lewis and Laura Mulvey.

ing unchanged the location of the monuments, reflects through their memory the contradictoriness of *time* as they represented it. Such an early orientation toward new monuments is intimately connected with the concept of revolutionary time, by its nature standing out as something *new,* something that breaks with the uninterrupted flow of preceding history. In the context of the radical regeneration of time, however, the monument by itself looks, of course, paradoxical. It instantly creates the illusion of continuity, organizes a genealogy, and introduces into the consciousness the very concept of a father-founder, so indispensable for the legitimization of any new regime. Not accidentally, for example, the monument to Lenin in the Kremlin stands on the exact same spot where earlier was situated the monument to Alexander II. By the same token, Lenin is symbolically transformed into the tsar's "legitimate" successor. At the same time, the idea of *founding* is extraordinarily strong in Russia. The founding of Moscow and the creation of a new city on the Neva were the most important facts in the national mythology, which, by the way, acted within the boundaries of a traditional paradigm that saw every founding as a renewal (Rome as the new Troy, Moscow or Petersburg as the new Rome). Every founding within such a paradigm paradoxically demands a forerunner.[5]

   It is interesting that, within the confines of imperial mythology, every new imperial capital—Rome, Constantinople, Moscow—arises as though on the ruins of one that has been destroyed. The ruins enter the complex of each new imperial capital in the capacity of source. The destruction of the predecessor allows for the realization of founding in the form of Freudian repetition. Ruins become a mnemonic sign on which there appears a likeness that both cancels and repeats it. Destruction and memory have so solidly entered into the basis of empires that, as Elisabeth Bellamy has noted, "the association between the fall of Troy and the faculty of memory has become so conventional throughout cultural history that it is almost as if Troy existed only to the extent to which it was remembered" (56).[6]

If we look at the films of destruction of monuments or the cathedral of Christ the Savior from this point of view, then we see before us, in essence, the mystical act of *founding*, naturally manifested in the form of destruction, obliteration, negation[7] (in Freudian terms, repression). This is the unceasingly contested "primal scene" of Soviet power.

There is probably still another cause for the obtrusive necessity of repetitiveness in the representation (particularly in cinema and on television) of scenes of the destruction of monuments. The capital-forerunner always appears in the form of ruins also because the unconsciousness of the "successors" calls into question the very fact of inheritance. Troy and Rome are repressed, so to speak, as ideological fictions, not having any connection at all to the new capital. They undergo what Freud called "de-realization."[8] De-realization takes the form of obliteration. Troy *must* by destroyed because, in reality, it is not a predecessor of Rome. Ruins, thus, become the product of the self-proclaimed empire's political unconscious.

The destruction of symbols of the Russian Empire after the revolution expresses the "homelessness" of the new leaders, that is to say, the unconscious of pretenders who settle on the tsar's throne while simultaneously blowing it up, or de-realizing it.

The need for a predecessor, apart from these "psychological" causes, is connected with the destruction of the old state system and its structures in a more pragmatic way. It is well known that, in pregovernmental social formations, the cult of ancestors played a fundamental role in structuring society. Only gradually among the Greeks was the cult of ancestors replaced by the cult of hearth and its god Zeus Herkeios, and also the cult of heroes. The historical tie between the cult of ancestors and the cult of heroes was established by Erwin Rohde in 1893.[9] Societies with unconstituted state systems often attempt to organize themselves according to an archaic type. Totalitarian society, with its underdeveloped civil institutions, attempts to preserve the archaic stage of "family" organization (the leader as father).

Thus, monuments of predecessors are organizers of continuity, fictitious indicators of the uninterruptedness of time and, simultaneously, the presence of an origin (the very act of foundation, the first model, the primordial act of creation). The masses organized by these monuments are a metaphorical family, whose time, of course, is nonhistorical. It may be mythological or private, but in any case it is excluded from historical chronology.

Red Square in Moscow, which since the twenties has gradually been transformed into a public square cum cemetery, becomes the symbolic point of concentration for such a mass-family. The central grave of the necropolis that unexpectedly arises here is, of course, Lenin's mausoleum. But a genuine cemetery soon springs up around it. The penetration of graves into the very heart of the symbolic social sphere is less surprising than it seems to some observers. In the Middle Ages, the cemetery was usually the site of basic social manifestations, including commerce, carnivalistic celebrations, and so on. Philippe Ariès has shown that such an interpenetration of what seem to be functionally diverse social spaces is connected exactly with the presence of the dead and the special sacral status of consecrated burial grounds. The cemetery is the kingdom of the dead and, because of this, is extraterritorial (62–71). The "return" of corpses to the central square merely marks, in its own archaic manner, the special sacralization of space here, a transformation of the world from profane to "other-worldly."

The exclusion from historical time marked by such spaces is one of the fundamental traits of socialist culture, which, although it also cultivates an ideology of progress, is wholly oriented toward a stable atemporality. The individual in socialist society sometimes experiences stability and the absence of change as something oppressive, but most often this atemporality creates the psychological basis for stabilizing inner conflicts.

Of course, human beings exist as though in two temporalities: the cyclical time of everyday life and myth, and the chronological time that brings them closer to death. Chronological time is always painted in dramatic tones. It is quite possible that the greatest achievement of Soviet culture was the maximal suppression of chronological time and the creation of the illusion of stability and stasis indispensable for the functioning of the masses.

This static time most clearly manifests itself in the space surrounding monuments. It is as though the monument were guarding with its weight the clot of stagnant time that is so soothing to the human psyche. Every monument seems to contain a sign of the cemetery, a sign projected onto the surrounding space. It is here that every memorial reveals its genealogy from graveside sculpture, from ancient Greek colossus.

The disintegration of the masses and of the utopia cementing them is

In the Shadow of Monuments

inevitably expressed in the transgression of the zone that surrounds the monument and in the aggression directed against the monument itself. Attacks on monuments, characteristic for certain stages of change in Russia, cannot, in my opinion, be described in terms of pure iconoclasm. Rather, they express the deep dependence of the masses on the monument they are attacking. The transfiguration of the masses, their transformation, often symbolically takes place around the monument.

Naturally, monuments acquired a special significance during the August coup. The very direction of the coup fully depended on the complexly organized mass mise-en-scène on the streets of Moscow. On the side of the coup plotters, the main operation became the filling of the capital's streets with masses of soldiers and armored equipment. As for the opposition, resistance chiefly amounted to the formation on the streets of large masses of the population, who did not abandon their "posts" day or night. With this in mind, the coup plotters steadfastly attempted not to allow the accumulation of people on the streets during the night. Little by little, the coup assumed the form of a clash between two masses. It is well known, however, that a mass of people, being a dynamic formation, cannot remain for long in a state of immobility. The downfall of the coup plotters became more or less obvious when the slow decomposition of the mass of soldiers began, as though they were breaking up and becoming bogged down in the crowd of Muscovites. In general, I can say as an eyewitness that the military columns in Moscow were symbolically effective only on the march, that is, when the columns of tanks moved, rolling the streets with an unbelievable roar. Such movement was, of course, the embodiment of indestructibility. At the moment the armored vehicles parked in the back streets, they lost their potential to frighten, as though they'd been sucked into the urban mass.

As far as the coup symbolically took place through the theatricalized clash of the masses, through their organization, preservation, and disintegration, the urban expanse during the coup acquired a dramatic significance. As during any revolution (and the coup was such a microrevolution), events shifted entirely onto the streets, where the fearsome and the laughable were combined in an openly carnivalistic structure. And, as the carnival prescribes, it ended with the destruction of some kind of symbolic figure (the scarecrow tsar, Shrovetide, and so on).

It is well known that the monument to Dzerzhinskii on Lubianka Square became the main object of aggression after the collapse of the August coup. Its choice is seemingly easy to explain by Dzerzhinskii's specific role as founder of the ChK, the embryonic form of the KGB.[10] Other factors, however, also played a role in the enactment of its defeat: above all, its location in the very center of the square. The roadway here fenced in the monument, so to speak, by means of the repressive authority of the traffic police. This spatially least accessible monument symbolized the complete inaccessibility of the KGB itself, in whose honor, essentially, the monument had been erected. But at a certain moment, not far from Dzerzhinskii, another monument unexpectedly appeared—a stone in honor of the victims of KGB repression, installed with the participation of the KGB itself. This situation in and of itself was, of course, extremely paradoxical. By that I mean the proximity of the memorial in honor of the founder of the secret police to the monument in honor of its victims. The second monument signified that the organization founded by Dzerzhinskii was criminal, which, of course, irrevocably compromised the founder himself.

Dzerzhinskii's monument escaped the traditional vandalism of revolutionary times. On the order of Moscow's mayor, Gavriil Popov, it was carefully dismounted, hoisted by a crane, placed on a platform that had been pushed up next to it, and driven away. The next day, attempts were undertaken to erect a cross on the monument's pedestal (in memory of the KGB's victims, which would finally have turned the pedestal into the likeness of a grave), but the authorities systematically hampered these attempts. They decided, however, to preserve the pedestal because, as it was announced, it had belonged to a prerevolutionary monument (to General Skobelev) and therefore was of historical value. The pedestal's preservation recalls the dictum of Polish writer Stanislav Lec, "Destroy the monuments, but keep the pedestals!"

In reality, the semiotic situation of Dzerzhinskii's monument is more complicated than it seems at first glance. A monument was detached from a pedestal that was recognized to be historically more valuable than the monument itself! The pedestal remains and is even preserved by the authorities, while the monument is carted away. The question arises: to what is the pedestal a monument, if there is no figure on top of it? The answer is, apparently, the stability of time, a stability completely autonomous of any hero or any event, simply stability as such. The pedestal without Dzerzhinskii is unique in that it continues by itself to designate a place of the accumulation of time as pure abstraction.

Dzerzhinskii's monument in Moscow was taken down during the night of 21–22 August 1991. The next day, the Lenin monument in Tallin was taken down, also by order of authorities, and also with a crane. The empty pedestal instantly became a place of pilgrimage for the residents of Tallin.

In the Shadow of Monuments

The emptiness above the pedestal begins to radiate time; the pedestal itself becomes a monument.

But that is not the only point. The preservation of a pedestal as the carrier of special historical value is maximally, if it can be expressed this way, humiliating to the monument itself. The usual value relationships are turned upside down. The heightened value of the base only emphasizes the complete depreciation of the figure. It is essential that the statue itself was not destroyed. The first gesture of iconoclasm for a long period of Russian history was wholly inscribed into a situation of variable temporality.

The movement of the crane that separated the Iron Felix from its pedestal tore the monument out of the zone of sacred, immovable time and transferred it into the space of "ordinary" temporality. Today this statue, along with several others, is installed alongside the House of the Artist on Krymskii Val, and has thus been inserted into a chronology. If, earlier, it was guarded by the government, restored, and symbolically excluded from the written text of time, now people can go up and touch it, even scratch it a little. From now on, the statue is just as subject to the influence of time as all the objects that surround it. Thus, the iconoclastic gesture became only a gesture indicating the change of status: the intentional commemorative value was in an instant exchanged for the value of historical antiquity. The monument was transformed from a symbol of intransigence into a symbol of vanity and the inevitability of destruction. I would define this gesture as *temporalization*.

It seems to me that this temporalization reflects a certain fundamental and highly traumatic moment in the recent evolution of Russian lived experience: the engaging of a chronometer that seems as if it had been stopped for a long time. The most important words in recent accounts of Russian actuality are "rapid changes." Common passages in today's descriptions go something like this: "in the past three (four, five) months everything has changed so much that you can't recognize anything."

Curiously, the pronouncement of these changes rarely is accompanied by anything convincingly concrete. A friend of mine, a Slavist with a good knowledge of Russia, recently spoke of his impressions of Moscow after a year's absence: "Everything has changed so much in the last year that it's not even easy to put it into words. . . . "

"What exactly?"

"There are fewer outdoor stands in the streets and more kiosks. The sense of danger on the streets is greater, but the salespeople in the kiosks are very polite . . . " and so on.

Mikhail Yampolsky

I could feel that my friend was having difficulty formulating the essence of the changes until he had found a precise sign of their head-spinning velocity: money, inflation, the insane price increases.

Of course, money and prices are the basic motif of today's stories about Russia. This fact is connected not only with their fundamental significance, but also precisely with the fact that they are namely the most effective metaphor for the sudden lurch and forward rush of time.

I will quote another entry from Benjamin's diary:

> I don't think there's another city with as many watchmakers as Moscow. This is all the more peculiar since people here are not particularly worried about time. But there must be historical reasons for this. When you watch people on the street you rarely see anybody rushing, unless, of course, it happens to be very cold. They have gotten into the habit of walking in zigzags. (It is quite significant that in some club or another, as Reich was telling me, there is a poster on the wall with the exhortation: Lenin said, "Time is Money." Just to express this banality the highest authority had to be invoked.) (47)

The connection between money and time, as Benjamin justly observed, is, of course, a banality. Russian time to some degree reflected the oddity of Russian money. This money existed, but it was impossible to buy anything with it. Being an exact equivalent, money was practically never exchanged for anything. Russian watches ran, but time stood in place. The Kremlin's chimes were one of the central symbols of the country, even providing a title for Pogodin's play, but their function mainly was to mark the cyclical stability of static time.

Money and time are mobile, circulatory, and intimately connected with the human body. Inflation sharply alters the sense of time. The future now does not accumulate in the form of money, but passes by with unbelievable speed. Sharp jumps in prices and the impossibility of saving money psychologically plunge the individual into a stream of time almost physically flowing away from him. This situation is particularly unpleasant, since people try to structure their time on the principle of repetition, cyclicality, and recurrent rhythms. Inflation, for instance, forces a person to experience time as an irrepressible and traumatic linearity. Benjamin writes, "When a currency is in use, a few million units of which are insignificant, life will have to be counted in seconds, rather than years, if it is to appear a respectable sum" (*Reflections* 87). Indeed, in Russia today there reigns the ubiquitous sense of life's depreciation, particularly in the persistent theme of dreadful crime, of gangsters who kill innocent citizens without reason on the street in the middle of the day.

In my view, money in Russia in the past, however much it provided the semblance of normal existence, was to a greater degree a clear sign of stability (hence the important ideological emphasis in the past on the reliability of the ruble, though everyone understood that as hard currency it was a sham). The coinciding of inflation with the crash of both stable prices and the consciousness of a guaranteed future is not at all accidental. Money has started to work in Russia today as a symbolic equivalent, but only in order to reflect the disappearance of all equivalents in society. The stability of the ruble previously was guaranteed by the will of god, the church—in other words, the state. The state is destroyed, its symbols turned into dust. Inflation, while having dramatically intensified the feeling of instability, has also incarnated in itself the catastrophic alteration of temporality.

The disappearance of the stable ruble is somehow connected with the disappearance of monuments. Money, like monuments, originally was manufactured from metals resistant to corrosion and doomed to eternity. Coins were decorated with sculptured depictions of monarchs and therefore had a commemorative value. The middle ground between coins and monuments was the medal, which possessed a specific value potential. During the reign of Louis XIV the difference between a medal and a coin was far from clear and even the object of special deliberations; in 1702 the abbé Tallemant determined that the only difference between medals and coins was that the medal commemorated a specific event.[11]

Curiously, the disappearance of monuments coincides with inflation. Inflation, meanwhile, causes the phasing out of metallic money, that is, precisely the kind that is meant to last. Incidentally, it might seem paradoxical that the least valuable money is minted in eternal metal while large denominations are manufactured out of paper. There are several reasons for this, the first of which is historical. Banknotes were substituted for mass quantities of metal coins that were inconvenient to transport, and as a result they began to take the place of *masses* of money. The second reason is a semiotic one and, for us, the more interesting. Paper money, being an expression of pure fiction, had to be supported by an element with at least some nominal value. The value of paper money was to a certain degree guaranteed by the aggregate value of the metal in the coins, the sum of which was represented by the banknote.

The symbolic disappearance, therefore, of metallic money from everyday life is a sign of an inflationary avalanche. Paper notes lose that fictitious

Mikhail Yampolsky

foundation of guarantee that is created by the customary presence of coins. The disappearance of coins—those micromonuments for personal use— like the disappearance of monuments on the public squares, marks both the destruction of cocoons of temporal stability and cyclical recurrence, and the switching on of a swift, linear time.

Preserved only in paper form, money sheds its last connection with reality and genuine value. A sign of this phantasmagoric fiction was the retention on the money (right up to 1993) of the symbols of the extinct Soviet Union. Significantly, the Soviet emblems have also remained on passports, lending these two important "texts" what seemed to be an intentionally fraudulent character. The two texts that most guarantee in society a broad identity and equivalence have, for an extended time now, referred symbolically to nonexistent realities as the main signs of legitimization.

This preservation of what no longer exists imposes itself on the renaming of what is unchangeable, cities and streets. The total replacement of names disorients a person and also contributes to the feeling of swift changes. After all, names and naming are basic means for the stabilization and organization of chaos.

Canetti has made note of the intimate tie between inflation and the behavior of the masses. In his opinion, someone accustomed to relying on the value of money cannot help but experience a feeling of personal degradation when this value falls: "the *individual* feels depreciated because the unit on which he relied and with which he had equated himself starts sliding . . . " (*Crowds and Power* 186).

The special phenomenon of the inflationary crowd has appeared, consisting of masses of depreciated individuals. The inflationary crowd is precisely the crowd in Hannah Arendt's understanding, that is, the totality of the "refuse" from all groups and classes (*Origins* 155). Its emergence is closely connected with alterations in temporality. Such "refuse" appears precisely as a result of the *passage* of time, which discards certain elements as outdated and anachronistic. It is not hard to observe that, for the first time in all the years of Soviet power, perhaps since the 1920s, an image has entered peoples' consciousness of a part of the population as being left behind, thrown by the wayside, and doomed. The accumulation of inflationary crowds, of course, is a very dangerous phenomenon, fraught with, among other things, the possibility of fascism. It is also for the first time, however, that this new mass formation arises precisely when an excited group of people crosses the invisible boundaries of the sacral zone surrounding monuments, switching on the chronometer of history, and, by this very act, condemning themselves to be left behind.

In the Shadow of Monuments

Notes

1. That the tenets of proxemics extend to monuments follows if only from the accepted norms of photography. In the absolute majority of cases, monuments are photographed at their full height. The visual articulation of the monument always presupposes some aesthetic or ideological higher task. The human body, in this sense, is much less protected from any visual manipulations.

2. In this sense, the totalitarian monument is close to the ancient Greek colossus that, in the opinion of Jean Pierre Vernant, "while substituting for the corpse in the depths of the grave, does not strive to reproduce the characteristics of the deceased, or to create the illusion of its physical appearance. It embodies and immortalizes not the dead, but life beyond death" (67). Like the Greek colossus, the Soviet monument only embodies atemporal existence, "life beyond death." Both of them are located somehow between naturalistic figurativeness and the abstractness of stone or ruins. On the history of the worship of nonanthropomorphic stones, see Donohue 219–30.

3. The same could be said also about the Palace of Soviets, the design and model for which were shown repeatedly on television. As a result, the real, demolished cathedral possesses the very same phantom reality as does the palace that never existed.

4. It is extremely interesting to what extent "twofold delight" is present in Lewis and Mulvey's film, two artful masters given to complex reflection on the problems of revolutionary iconoclasm. In spite of this, the film, a significant portion of which is devoted to shots of collapsing statues of Lenin and Stalin, cannot completely avoid the melancholy tone that is inescapably connected with allegories of vanity and perishability. In spite of the directors' wishes, something different appears in the film: a fixation with what is departing, the immortalization of what is disappearing. The film itself, thus, falls within the semiotic sphere of monuments.

5. On the paradoxes of this paradigm within the boundaries of "revolutionary" consciousness, see Arendt, *On Revolution* 179–214. Among other things, Arendt shows the presence of an intimate tie between the ideology of "foundation," the mythology of the child, and the Christian cult of birth and the infant (211). It seems to me that the cult of the "happy childhood" and the abundance of children in Soviet iconography may also be compared with this complex.

6. Bellamy provides an interesting analysis of the connection between the destruction of Troy, the displacement of its memory in Aeneas, and the founding of Rome.

7. Walter Benjamin described such destructive creativity through the cabalistic metaphor of angels created by God and instantly disappearing or perishing (Scholem 213). In "Theses on the Philosophy of History," Benjamin proposes another metaphor. He describes an angel who has turned its back to the future, is looking into the past, and appears in the form of a constantly growing "pile of debris" (*Illuminations* 260). In such a context, destruction is the equivalent of historical creation. The demolition of the Cathedral of Christ the Savior makes history before the faces, seized with horror, of the angels. And like any creative act, it *must* be immortalized and endlessly repeated.

8. Freud links, for example, the gap in memory (repression) that he experienced on the Acropolis with the fact that as a child he did not believe in the Acropolis's reality (317).

9. Finley gives a contemporary account of this problem (47–49).

10. This stone openly resembles a cemetery gravestone and was its own kind of debris

or ruin. The constant intrusion of the thematics of cemeteries and ruins into those city spaces that are subject to intensified sacralization seems significant to me.

   11. On the semiotics of medals and coins, see Marin 156–57.

Works Cited

Arendt, Hannah. *On Revolution.* Harmondsworth: Penguin Books, 1977.

———. *The Origins of Totalitarianism.* New York: Harcourt Brace Jovanovich, 1979.

Ariès, Philippe. *The Hour of Our Death.* New York: Vintage Books, 1982.

Bellamy, Elisabeth J. *Translations of Power: Narcissism and the Unconscious in Epic History.* Ithaca: Cornell UP, 1992.

Benjamin, Walter. *Illuminations.* Ed. Hannah Arendt. London: Fontana, 1973.

———. *Moscow Diary. October* 35 (Winter 1985): 9–121.

———. *Reflections.* Ed. Peter Demetz. New York: Schoken Books, 1986.

Canetti, Elias. *The Conscience of Words.* New York: Seabury P, 1979.

———. *Crowds and Power.* New York: Ferrar, Straus, Giroux, 1984.

Derrida, Jacques. *La vérité en peinture.* Paris: Flammarion, 1978.

Donohue, A. A. *Xoana and the Origins of Greek Sculpture.* Atlanta: Scholars P, 1988.

Finley, M. I. *Use and Abuse of History.* Harmondsworth: Penguin Books, 1987.

Foucault, Michel. *Power/Knowledge: Selected Interviews and Other Writings 1972–1977.* New York: Pantheon Books, 1980.

Freud, Sigmund. "A Disturbance of Memory on the Acropolis." *Character and Culture.* Ed. Philip Rieff. New York: Macmillan, 1963.

Hall, Edward Twitchell. *The Hidden Dimension.* New York: Doubleday, 1982.

Marin, Louis. *Le portrait du roi.* Paris: Ed. de Minuit, 1981.

Riegl, Alois. "The Modern Cult of Monuments: Its Character and Its Origin." *Oppositions* 25 (Fall 1982): 21–51.

Scholem, Gershom. "Walter Benjamin and His Angel." *On Jews and Judaism in Crisis.* New York: Schoken Books, 1976.

Schorske, Carl E. *Fin-de-siecle Vienna: Politics and Culture.* New York: Vintage Books, 1981.

Vernant, Jean Pierre. "Figuration de l'invisible et catégorie psychologique du double: le colossos." *Mythe et pensée chez les Grecs, II.* Paris: Maspero, 1971.

Virilio, Paul. *Guerre et cinéma I: Logistique de la perception.* Paris: Cahiers du cinéma-Ed. de l'Etoile, 1984.

Six

Encoding Difference
Figuring Gender and Ethnicity in
Kira Muratova's *A Change of Fate*

Susan Larsen

Kira Muratova's 1987 film, *A Change of Fate* [*Peremena uchasti*], opens with a woman's voice telling a story: "And then, awakened by a daring kiss . . . ," only to trail off. The screen is blank (black) during this first voice-over, then dissolves to the face of a white woman wearing a red sweater and a black half-mask—no fairy-tale Sleeping Beauty she. In the background, a distant howling—like that of wolves—commences and continues throughout this opening scene. The masked woman's lips do not move, but her voice is heard again, "And then, awakened by a daring kiss. . . . " Behind the mask the woman's eyes flicker open as a male voice is heard off-screen, "You wanted my advice about a present." "I don't want [it] now." The camera remains focused on the woman's still face as the voice-over continues, "You wanted to give your husband a gun." As the woman's voice replies, "I don't want [to] now," the film cuts away to a thicket of palm trees and boulders inside an enormous arboretum. Now the man, also white, comes into view, leading the woman by the hand through the trees. He wears a white suit that contrasts sharply with the woman's red sweater and black skirt as they pursue each other through the arboretum, tripping over exotic foliage and their own words:

—You wanted my advice about a present.
—I don't want [it] now.
—You wanted to give your husband a gun.
—I don't want [to] now.
—You don't want advice?
—I don't want [it].
—My advice or to give the present?
—My husband left me a revolver. If you touch me, I can kill you, if you don't go away.[1]

The couple repeats this dialogue four times—speaking sometimes in a furious whisper, at others, in a weary monotone—as the film cuts back and forth between close-ups of the masked woman, sitting motionlessly in a grotto, and long shots of the couple as they pursue and flee each other, embrace, and struggle. It is never clear whether they are struggling in earnest or in play. It is also possible that the scenes in the arboretum are simply a product of the masked woman's imagination, framed as they are by shots of her masked, silent self.[2] As if to point up the cognitive problem, the camera constantly films the couple from a distance, often through a screen of tropical plants, boulders, and plant-filled shelves that further obscure the spectator's view.

At one point the man approaches the woman silently from behind her chair, removes her mask and tosses it away. One might, following Laura Mulvey, interpret this as an assertion of the man's role as "bearer of the look," yet these opening scenes provide no "satisfying sense of omnipotence" to either character or spectator (62–63). As the man repeatedly complains to the woman in this scene, "You understand everything, you like to pretend, you like to torment me." *A Change of Fate* problematizes the "to-be-looked-at-ness" of this female figure, foregrounding the male gaze in order to frustrate it—and with it, the spectator's "visual pleasure" (Mulvey 62–63).[3] Unmasked, the woman remains unmoved, staring silently off-screen as the man stoops to embrace her from behind, curling down and around her still frame. From this upside-down, semi-fetal position, the man returns to their script, "You wanted to ask my advice about a present. . . . "

This opening scene immediately confronts the viewer with one of the film's central issues—the problematic origin and consequences of this woman's desire. The opening line sounds like a citation from a pulp romance; the blank screen suggests that it is a "daring kiss" that brings the woman to cinematic "life"; yet she resists both the kisses and "advice" offered by the man in white. Throughout the tangled dialogue and tortured embraces, the woman's constant refrain is the phrase, "I don't want [it/to]" [*ne khochu*]. Her insistent negation of desire ends in silence, as she stares defiantly back at the man, shouting "I don't want [to]." "To give the present or to take advice?" Silence.

Cut to a cavernous underground chamber with bare stone walls. A person of indeterminate sex helps the woman bathe from a basin and pitcher. This underground room is a prison cell where the woman is confined, awaiting trial, as it turns out, for murder. The prison warden enters and sounds another of the film's leitmotifs:

Encoding Difference

We are all civilized people, *white* people; we should be friends, united in solidarity. I can't endure native women—only a white woman is a woman. That is, they are—strictly speaking—also white, but sort of yellowish. You are a real treat for us. It's been a long time since there was a white woman in this prison. . . . We all have to stick together here. We have a murderer here, a real murderer, but he's white. That's the main thing, isn't it? We must all help one another. . . . We are people, we have to keep up appearances [*oblik*], stick together. I could never have dreamed that I would see a white woman so close—a noble, innocent, pure lady. You can lose your appearance [*oblik*] here—habits save us.[4]

Later, when the warden introduces his replacement, these lines are revealed as the prison house refrain, for the new guard intones, in a markedly different accent, the very same speech: "We are all civilized people, *white* people; we should be friends; we should be united. I can't endure native women, only a white woman is a woman. . . . " Andrei Plakhov has criticized these lines as unsubstantiated by other evidence in the film, arguing that "the 'race problem' is wedged in artificially, in words only, it misses the target" (46). He misses the point—the stylized quality of this speech, which points to its *ritual* function as incantation rather than "realistic" critique of the "race problem."

In "The Other Question: The Stereotype and Colonial Discourse," Homi Bhabha writes:

An important feature of colonial discourse is its dependence on the concept of "fixity" in the ideological construction of otherness. Fixity, as the sign of cultural/historical/racial difference in the discourse of colonialism, is a paradoxical mode of representation: it connotes rigidity and an unchanging order as well as disorder, degeneracy and daemonic repetition. Likewise the stereotype, which is its major discursive strategy, is a form of knowledge and identification that vacillates between what is always 'in place,' already known, and something that must be anxiously repeated . . . as if the essential duplicity of the Asiatic or the bestial sexual license of the African that needs no proof, can never really, in discourse, be proved. (312)

The jailers' repetition of the formula "only a white woman is a woman" [*tol'ko belaia zhenshchina—zhenshchina*] exemplifies precisely such "fixity." Jailers are figures par excellence of "fixity," holders of keys and arbiters of separation/difference—usually of criminal from innocent, but here—of "white" from "native," of "woman" from "not-woman." Muratova's oft-noted penchant for repetition, moreover, works in this film to reveal the rigid social order the jailer is sworn to uphold as simultaneously—in Bhabha's terms—disordered, degenerate and daemonic.[5]

The film thus moves in its opening scenes from one white woman's "awakening" to desire and subsequent negation of "wanting" [ne khochu] to the jailer's assertion that only white women are desirable. The juxtaposition of the jailer's formulaic statements ("we are all civilized people, white people") with his denial of the "native woman's" womanliness ("only a white woman is a woman") places the intersection of gender and ethnicity at the heart of Muratova's film. While the jailer defines "womanhood" as a phenomenon exclusive to "civilization," the exotic setting and "wild" howling in the background of the film's first scenes suggest that this white woman—however "noble, innocent, and pure" may constitute an exception to his rule.

A Change of Fate—But Whose?

Based on W. Somerset Maugham's 1927 story "The Letter," *A Change of Fate* is only one—albeit the most recent—of many stage and screen adaptations of Maugham's story. "The Letter" was revised for the stage in 1927 by Maugham himself and subsequently filmed in at least four different versions—a 1929 Paramount film starring Jeanne Engels; a 1940 version directed by William Wyler and starring Bette Davis; a 1947 version titled *The Unfaithful*; and a 1974 made-for-television movie starring Lee Remick.[6] Muratova's film follows the general outline of the Maugham story, but differs in several significant details.

The common plot is as follows: a white woman is in jail for murder—she claims to have killed a distant acquaintance (also white) when he tried to rape her while her husband was away. Her lawyer is puzzled by the fact that "such a quiet and well-bred woman" could have shot anyone six times, even when provoked, but is nevertheless certain that she will be instantly acquitted. "Public opinion," he tells her husband, has been decisively on her side since it became known that the deceased man had for some time had a "native" mistress. The lawyer soon learns of the existence of a letter written by the white woman to the dead man, whom she claims not to have seen for several months, inviting him to her house on the night of the murder, specifically because her husband was away. When confronted, the white woman initially denies having written the letter, but subsequently acknowledges it as her own. She then claims unpersuasively that she had intended simply to ask for advice about the purchase of a gun for her husband's upcoming birthday. The letter is in the possession of the dead man's "native" mistress, who has reluctantly agreed to sell it—but only for a sum that will require all the resources of the accused woman's husband. The letter is purchased and the husband takes possession of it. After the white woman is, as expected, acquitted and applauded by the court, the woman realizes that her husband knows she is guilty of both adultery and murder. The woman tells her lawyer "the truth" only after her husband has left the party celebrating her acquittal: the man she killed had been her lover for many years. She shot him because he wanted to break off their affair. In both story and film, a central factor in the white woman's fury at her lover is the fact that he has not only taken a "native" mistress, but that the "native" woman's "look" reveals her knowledge that the white woman is also the man's lover.

Here the similarities between story and film end. Maugham's story has a specific setting—British colonial Singapore sometime between 1911 and 1926—and his characters have names that mark them as British. The murdered man is Geoffrey Hammond; the lawyer, Howard Joyce; the married couple, Leslie and Robert Crosbie. The only Chinese character in Maugham's story with a proper name is the lawyer's clerk, Ong Chi Seng. All the other non-European characters are named exclusively in terms of their race and gender: the "Chinese woman," the "fat Chinaman," the "Chinese head-boy."

Muratova's film is, by contrast, deliberately vague about its cultural and historical referents. The location is never named, but is clearly not Singapore. The film was shot in Tadzhikistan (around Isfara), but the "native" costumes and behaviors resist ethnographic designation (of which, more below). Even the time period seems unclear—the "white" characters' costumes suggest the 1920s, but the ambience is emphatically *not* Soviet. In keeping with this tendency to abstraction, only three characters in the film have proper names, but these names indicate only the characters' generic "non-native" origin. The Leslie Crosbie character in Muratova's film is "Maria," her husband "Philip," and her lover "Alexander." All the other characters are identified, if at all, by occupation: "clerk," "lawyer," "jailer."

Racial difference is named equally generically as either "white" or "native." The Russian term I have translated as "native" [*tuzemnyi*] literally means "of the other land." In contrast to the "white" characters, the "native" clerk never describes Alexander's nonwhite lover as "a native female" [*tuzemka*], but always as "a woman of local origin" [*zhenshchina mestnogo proiskhozhdeniia*]. She may be, as the clerk asserts, "a very ignorant woman" [*ochen' nevezhestvennaia zhenshchina*], but she is in his eyes, nevertheless, a "woman," despite the jailer's assertion that "only a white woman is a woman."

These generic identifications of the characters invite the spectator to "read" the film as a general statement about any and all colonial relationships. Muratova herself has described her choice of the Maugham story as motivated by her fondness for "the situation with the note" and her desire for "a kind of eclecticism—some undefined Eastern country, a colony, a colonial, without any particular national identity—just natives and colonials, as a sign" (Taubman 377).[7] The question arises, a sign of what? Or, rather, in which—or whose—sign system?

What fascinates me in the film is its coding of racial difference in terms of gender. Maria's jailers insist that only "white women" are appropriate objects of desire—and, on one level, the plots of both film and story uphold their argument. The female protagonist (Maria) murders her lover (Alexander) because he has taken a "native woman" as his mistress. Knowledge of this fact turns public opinion in Maria's favor. Maria's European peers condone her murder of Alexander as much because of his sexual involvement with the "native" woman as because of Maria's charge that he had tried to rape her—itself a lie. The real crime of which Alexander is guilty in the eyes of "public opinion" is his violation of racial, rather than sexual, purity. The film further develops the theme of miscegenation in its silent depiction of the "native woman" with an unidentified, but very blonde infant. This infant's only toy is a large silver pocket watch that dangles over his "primitive" cradle. The never-articulated implication is that this is a child of "mixed race"—to whom, perhaps, "time" now belongs.[8]

On another level, however, the film constantly undermines the distinctions it asserts between "white" women and "native" cultures. The story has already set up a potential equivalence between the two women—"white" and "native"—in that both are lovers of the same man, and the incriminating "letter" of the one is in the possession of the other.[9] Muratova's film elaborates the role of "woman" and "native" as similarly—if not, perhaps, equally—"to-be-looked-at" (Mulvey 62). The "looking relations" that the film sets up, however, are constantly disrupted and questioned as sources of either comfort or knowledge for both "white" people, in general, and "white" men, in particular.[10]

The hothouse atmosphere of the opening scenes establishes the realm of the female protagonist, Maria, as one both exotic and enclosed. In the subsequent prison scene, Maria is equally confined and equally "exotic"— the jail warder brings in a group of three eccentrics to "perform" for her, warning her that "they stare like that because it's interesting for them to look at you." Yet, strictly speaking, it is the three male prisoners who are displayed for Maria's "visual pleasure" rather than the reverse. One demonstrates "cosmetic" exercises, "especially beneficial for women," while a second performs card tricks, and a third bites into and chews up a drinking glass.[11]

Although Maria nominally "bears the look" here, the craziness of these convicts' performance—and the fact that it takes place in prison—remind the spectator of the rarity and the precariousness of such reversals of stereotypical "looking relations." At the conclusion of this "brief entertainment for the lady," Maria herself performs for the gathered eccentrics, as she sings a wordless tune, looking directly at the eccentrics (and the camera) for their approval only at her song's conclusion. It is her most demure moment in the film—and clearly marked as self-conscious "play." As the jailer embarks on yet another monologue, Maria laughs and exclaims—with apparent sincerity—"What fun it is in prison!" [*Kak veselo v tiur'me!*].

Her gaiety is in marked contrast to the following scene, which opens with her husband Philip's exclamation, "This is mockery!" [*Èto izdevatel'stvo!*]. Philip is a far more delicate creature than Maugham's burly Robert Crosbie. Philip is seen almost exclusively in furs, speaks in high-pitched, often hysterical tones, and is of a markedly "soft" character. (He also has a gun fetish—of which more later.)

This scene establishes the husband's faulty vision, as he insists on the "inhumanity" of holding his wife prisoner for having shot the man whom she accuses of having attempted to rape her. Philip repeatedly describes Maria as having shot Alexander "as if he were a mad dog." As the film's final scenes reveal, however, it is Maria who is "mad." "I was mad with fury," she tells the lawyer in her final confession at the end of the film.[12] Philip fails to realize his wife's capacity for rage, however, exclaiming in near ecstasy, "She has everything, and it's all so balanced, so well-proportioned, have you noticed? She is neither tall, nor short, but precisely average in height!" The lawyer's repeated queries about the six shots Maria fired into Alexander's body suggest, however, that she is not as perfectly "balanced" as her husband insists. The camera provides an ironic counterpoint to Philip's speech in this scene as it focuses on the neoclassical statue of a nude female torso (headless and armless, but not the Venus de Milo) that stands on the lawyer's desk.

Philip's insistence on Maria's "average height" implies her general "averageness." She stands in for all women, however "decent," in whom, as the lawyer ultimately concludes, "it is apparently impossible to tell what barbaric instincts lie concealed." Maria is thus representative of all so-called "decent women," who, the film's visual logic implies, are moral "dwarfs," in contrast to their idealized role in "civilized" society. I use the word "dwarf" deliberately, as Maria has a young "ward," played by the female dwarf Ok-

Susan Larsen

sana Shlapak. There is no precedent for this oddly adult "child" in Maugham's story, and critics have argued that her character "adds nothing to the story; it only enhances the film's surrealism" (Taubman 378) or that it is "too fantastic" (Plakhov 46).

I would argue, however, that this seemingly monstrous little girl functions in the film as Maria's "double." This child aids and abets all of Maria's actions in the film—she carries the fatal letter to Alexander, threatens him with scissors, witnesses his murder, even gives his dead body a few extra kicks. The little girl is also a deaf-mute, who communicates with Maria in sign language. The child's literal muteness further links Maria with the "native" woman, who speaks not a word—in any language—during the few moments she is present on screen. Clearly not of average height, nor average appearance, Maria's ward suggests a continuity of monstrous potential within all women—"civilized" or otherwise. The film's penultimate scenes suggest that this child is the equivalent of a "kitten" within whom lurks a tiger. As the lawyer remarks on the "barbaric instincts" lurking within even the most "decent" women, he picks up a kitten and begins to play with it. The camera then moves to focus on the child sitting next to him. She wears an emphatically feminine party dress—a pink and white froth of ruffles and lace—and hugs an armful of kittens. These same kittens are subsequently shown playing in a barn as the child enters, wearing a white furry coat and clutching yet another white kitten. As the camera pans up from the child's eye level, it reveals that the kittens are playing with the dangling shoelaces of Philip, who has hanged himself from the rafters. The association of the child with these kittens and the film's earlier odd scenes of Maria screaming while a tiger roars (who knows where? her mind's eye? her twisted psyche?) suggest that no cat is ever entirely domesticated, and no woman truly "civilized."[13]

Ornamental Orientalism

Appearances throughout the film, however, are deceptive, and the film calls attention to this fact. The film teases its spectators with visual detail that is impossible to organize into a stable system of signification. "Civilization," as the jailer insists, requires that "we" preserve our "external appearance" [*oblik*]. This "appearance" is repeatedly defined in the film in opposition to the "natives," yet the depiction of "native" customs is deliberately and markedly "generic." The "native" customs and costumes the film depicts are pulled from a wide variety of Central Asian cultural traditions—and frequently intermingled with "Western" behaviors and cultural attributes. Unfamiliar with Central Asian cultures, I cannot identify the "origin" of the various "native"/non-Western costumes, foods, accents, and behaviors—if, indeed, they have any specific ethnographic referent. What the untrained eye can see is that "authenticity" (in the spirit, for instance, of Hollywood films set in the "Orient"—*Gandhi, A Trip to India*, even *Apocalypse Now* come to mind) is demonstratively *not* a concern of this film's makers. One Russian critic has explained the "provisionally . . . Mongolo-Tibetan" look of the film as a result of Muratova's "probably intuitive" decision to "take a little from everywhere" [*s miru po nitke*] because of budgetary constraints—"in our circumstances she could never create a Singapore" (Plakhov 42–43). Others see the "busy" visual surface of the film as a continuation of Muratova's penchant for "ornamentalism" (Taubman 377).

One might also see the "ornamentalism" of *A Change of Fate* as "Orientalism," in the terms of Edward Said's influential study.[14] I would like to argue, however, that the film manipulates its viewers' Orientalist assumptions in order to undermine and denaturalize them. The film's eclectic décor both proposes and blurs the difference between "white" and "native" cultures. The lawyer's Asian clerk—the spokesman for the group that sells Maria's incriminating note back to her husband and lawyer—is shown praying in the daytime, presumably to Allah, but also eats with chopsticks and dresses in the style of old-fashioned Hollywood Asian villains—white suits, long hair, mustache, goatee, and glasses. When the clerk rises from his prayers in the lawyer's office to do a short serpentine dance, the juxtaposition mocks our partial and cinematically determined knowledge of "other" cultural traditions.

This deliberate play with "native" signifiers disrupts the fixity of colonial discourse in the film by foregrounding cinematic stereotypes of racial difference as such. Rather than asserting its authority to speak either for or about the "natives," the film takes as its subject what Edward Said has characterized as the "exteriority" of Orientalist texts—whether literary, scholarly, or cinematic. With its pastiche of Orientalist tropes, Muratova's film "makes strange" familiar Western cinematic conventions for depicting Asia, effectively reminding its viewer, in Said's terms, that any "statement about the Orient . . . relies very little, and cannot instrumentally depend, on the Orient as such" and is, rather, "a presence to the reader by virtue of its having excluded, displaced, made supererogatory any such *real* thing as 'the Orient' " (20–21).

Not only visual, but aural and "terpsichorean" codes as well are mixed and mismatched in this film. The central sequence of images that precedes the "white men's" journey into the "heart" of the "native" colony follows a scene in which a piano player, laughing maniacally, shifts between boogie-woogie riffs and Beethoven's "Moonlight Sonata." The aural pastiche is compounded when a "third" hand—that of a bystander of uncertain gender—contributes a few additional discordant notes. This scene sets the "tone" for those that follow, as the camera cuts to a woman in a strapless sequined gown picking her way in broad daylight across a muddy road filled with goats. As a "native" man pleads with the lawyer to help his brother—who is also in jail for murder—a youth of indeterminate gender and race, wearing a costume that only alludes to "native" dress, performs an ersatz "moonwalk" in the background.[15] The lawyer crosses this same goat-filled roadway in search of Philip—who is revealed in mid-waltz with the same gowned woman. Made wary by the film's reminders of my own ignorance, I hesitate to describe this woman as either "Oriental" or "Eurasian," although the setting suggests she may be a dance-hall girl or a prostitute of "local extraction," since Philip pays her at the conclusion of their dance. As they dance, Philip carries on a one-sided conversation with her, and the background music shifts again—from boogie-woogie to an Edith Piaf-like vocal.

Philip's speech here, repeated as a voice-over at the film's conclusion, is his defining moment in the film:

> I collect guns—old ones. At one time, it was the fashion, but the fashion passed, and I remained almost its sole adherent [adept]. I collect guns, their beauty fascinates me, the beauty of guns. There's nothing in the world more beautiful. A gun is the most beautiful thing. It's strange, isn't it, puzzling . . . strange—a terrifying, revolting purpose, and a beautiful, perfect shell and form. I myself don't shoot, I'm not a hunter. But I look [at them], it fascinates me. There are so many of us—by us, I mean, people—crowds of people, like crowds of stars.

These lines invite a psychoanalytic reading (or readings). Here, however, I will limit my comments to the deadly consequences of Philip's fascination with guns. He does not shoot. But his wife does. Maria kills Alexander with the revolver Philip has left with her for her protection while he goes—at her suggestion—to inquire about the purchase of a rare weapon from one of their acquaintances. When confronted with the existence of the incriminating note that summoned Alexander during her husband's absence, Maria tries to explain it as her attempt to get Alexander's advice about a "surprise" gift for Philip's birthday. She wanted, she says, to purchase a gun for him, but "doesn't understand" about weapons. Pleading stereotypically female helplessness, Maria is, in fact, far less helpless than her husband—whose preference for "looking" leads to his death.

The film thematizes the process of *looking* as it implies that Philip's fatal flaw may be the "fetishistic scopophilia" that Laura Mulvey has discussed as one of the principal ways in which the male unconscious copes with the castration anxiety provoked by the sight of woman (64–65). Significantly, throughout the scene in which Philip describes his fascination with guns—his pleasure in looking—it is not his gaze, but the gaze of his dance partner that the camera frames. The back of her head blocks the camera's view of Philip's face as he talks, then the camera focuses on her looking *at* him, coaching him soundlessly in the rhythm of the dance. Philip monopolizes *speech* in this scene—the woman does not speak—but not the "look," so central to psychoanalytic theorists like Mulvey who see visual pleasure as "split between active/male and passive/female" (62). When Philip thanks his anonymous partner for teaching him to waltz, his words merely underline what we might have guessed—it is the woman, not her male partner, who leads this couple's dance.

On another level, Philip's words, as they resonate with his wife's six shots into her lover's body, remind the viewer of the misleading, even treacherous appearance of those other things of beauty—women, whether "white" or "other"-wise. Indeed, Philip's encomium to the "beautiful, perfect form" and "terrifying, revolting purpose" of guns is equally applicable to his wife, the perfection of whose "form" he also praises. Inasmuch as the visual surface of the film, with its abundance of "exotic" props and extras, also "fascinates" the viewer, Philip's lines further remind us not to assume that we comprehend these "other" objects of our gaze.

The film maps the categories "woman" and "native" as equally "other" in relation to white men. Yet, while the film mocks rigid assumptions about the distinction between "nativeness" and "whiteness," this distinction breaks down most completely on the female side of the equation. Civilization with its rigid prescriptions of, in Philip's words, "what is funny, what is sad, how a husband should behave, and how a wife, what we should cry over, and what should make us laugh," is revealed as most insubstantial in its claims to regulate "white" women's behavior. While the film's characters insist on the fixity of ethnic distinctions, the film itself, in its construction of ethnic and sexual differences, suggests that the most "other" others are those of the opposite (female) sex. The film both asserts a distinction between "white" and "native" femininity and repeatedly collapses it.

The film plays with differences and divisions of all sorts. The worlds of both Maria and the "native" woman are radically separated in space and clearly demarcated from the world of men, who move more freely from one place to another. Maria's jail cell is a rough-walled and dank cavern. The jailer repeatedly promises to move her into another, more comfortable cell, "as soon as the whitewash dries" [*kak tol'ko pobelka prosokhnet*]—a detail that only reinforces the film's general depiction of "whiteness" as a superficial characteristic—at least in Maria's case.

In contrast to Maugham's story, in which the "native" woman lives in town above a store, the film takes its white male characters on a wild ride via jeep and primitive locomotive through vast barren hills to get to the "native" village where Alexander's mistress lives. As the clerk, their "native" guide, leads them on a mad race through a maze of mud-walled houses at the village, he encourages them to "breathe deeply," to "rest," exclaiming, "how good it is, that we've torn ourselves away from your stuffy office and out into nature." The white men, however, gasp for breath, and the lawyer starts to wheeze and cough. He is allergic to this "natural," "native" environment. The scene in which the note is purchased is a jumble of images—variously draped figures, the woman silent in the background, a close-up of Western shoes and pocket watch. Proximity to their "other" somehow deflates Philip and his lawyer. The terrain marks the village as radically different, and the journey there emphasizes its distance from the town, center of "civilization." But the electric iron the "native" woman is shown using, the pocket watch, and the child of markedly "non-native" appearance all indicate that neither distance nor difference is as absolute as the jailer, chief spokesman of colonial ideology, insists.

The "native" woman appears on screen for only the second time immediately after the second jailer repeats the first jailer's description of "native women" as "of course—strictly speaking—also white, but sort of yellowish." The woman holds her hands to her face in a gesture, perhaps, of sorrow, then the film cuts to a young girl in "native" dress, who looks at the older woman with what might be concern.

Although the juxtaposition of the jailer's words with the woman's face underlines the fact that her skin tones are neither "yellow" nor "white," the film strays very little from stereotypical depictions of "native" women as "silent" and "enigmatic." In this woman's only previous appearance on screen, the film cuts from the turbaned "break dancer" to heavy red hangings that part, veil-like, to reveal another veil of long dark hair. As the "native" woman parts her hair, her face fills the screen, but her eyes look up only once, briefly at the camera. In the next shot the woman sits on her knees with a deck of cards spread out before her. As she carefully places one card on top of another, it is impossible to determine whether she is telling fortunes or playing solitaire.

Our ignorance of her experience and intentions is, I think, the point. The film gives the "native" woman no lines and almost no expression, no *affect* that would explain her relationship with either Alexander, the child, or the men who have persuaded her to sell the note. The clerk describes her as "ignorant," and the film almost completely ignores her except as a device to motivate the plot, which centers on the "white" woman's "barbaric" pathology.[16]

The film suggests, in fact, that it is the "white" woman's voice—her access to language—that lies at the core of Maria's "corruption." The murder scene begins with Maria's high-pitched recital of an entry from her diary that suggests the fundamental narcissism of her passion for Alexander:

Since a certain happy time I have been visited by a spirit or a demon, or an incubus—I don't know what to call it—perhaps an angel. I am as happy as it is possible to be, even happier. And even if I am destined to know sorrow after happiness, I will always remember the degree of boundlessness attained by my bliss. My tender, passionate angel, who calls me an angel, my god who calls me a god. I don't know how to distinguish his body from his soul, in him everything is united and wonderful, like his wonderful eyes, like two angelic notes of two voices singing in unison.

The exalted and self-exalting tone of these lines suggest that the process of being *named* "an angel," "a god" is central to Maria's passion for Alexander—no other explanation of his attraction for her is ever either asserted or implied in the film. Her vague nomination of the "spirit, or demon, or incubus, maybe an angel" who visits her suggests that she is possessed by a demon of her own creation, a passion for "boundlessness" [*bespredel'nosti*] reminiscent of the eponymous hero of Lermontov's long narrative poem, "The Demon." Maria casts herself in the role of Tamara—the young nun whose nights are tormented by visits from the Demon, yet, in relation to Alexander, Maria plays the role of the Demon, whose "boundless" passion leads ultimately to Tamara's death.[17]

The only real "boundlessness" in the film, however, is that achieved by the horses of the two dead men—the deaths of both Alexander and Philip are followed by long shots of their respective saddle horses galloping across a vast and empty expanse of desert. The horses' hooves pound on almost too solitarily into the distance and across the low hills. Rather than representing some greater freedom allotted men in the world of the film, these free-running figures suggest that only after death is anyone free of the constraints of "civilization"—whether nominally "white" or "native." The horses are running, moreover, to their deaths. As Maria's "native" servants remark after Alexander's death:

> —Mr. Alexander's horse has run away, broken free. Impossible to catch her now. A bear will eat it, or a tiger.
> —Pity about the horse.
> —She was pretty.
> —Yes, pretty, not bad at all. Fat. Smart. A head like a snake. A broad chest, thin skin, good legs. Knew her name well, liked people.

The problem with Maria—who could be described in much the same terms—is that she does not recognize the name of "woman" as her own. Her craving for some other form of recognition, some other identity— "god" or "angel"—leads her to commit a crime of "diabolical passion" (in the lawyer's words). Muratova's explanation of the source of the film's title suggests that it is precisely the constraints placed on woman by "civilization"—whether "native" or "white"—that lie at the roots of Maria's act. According to Muratova, she found the term "a change of fate" in a book of legal speeches. It is the euphemism used to explain the behavior of a prisoner who suddenly kills his (or her) guard only six months before the end of a ten-year prison term. Muratova claims that such crimes are motivated by the prisoner's desire for change:

> [Muratova]: He [the prisoner] is tired of sitting there, and he kills a person who had not harmed him personally in any way—just so that an investigation would begin, a move somewhere, a prison again, but a different one. That's the whole point.
> [Interviewer]: So your heroine, as it were, moves from one cage to another?
> [Muratova]: You could call it a "cage," or—a place [*pomeshchenie*].
> (Bykov)

I would suggest that the one "place" Maria cannot escape in the film is that labeled "woman." As much as this film disturbs the boundaries that mark the difference between "white" and "native," it almost completely fails to shift the cultural signifiers that mark "woman"—regardless of ethnicity—as closer to "nature" than to "culture." The film frequently punctuates the scenes set in Maria's house and the "native" village with shots of unidentified "primitivist" paintings. Among the paintings that the camera dwells on longest, two stand out. One is obviously Eve handing Adam an apple. The other represents a naked woman with a fox flying up between

Encoding Difference

her thighs and some flying black creature gnawing at her breast. These paintings suggest that, within the film's system of signification, responsibility for the "original"—and for most subsequent—sin remains with Eve.

Notes

I am grateful to Nancy Condee, Helena Goscilo, Vladimir Padunov, and Mikhail Yampolsky for their comments on the first draft of this chapter, and to all the members of the Working Group on Contemporary Russian Culture for their support and encouragement of my work during the last three years. I would also like to thank Siobhan Somerville for referring me to articles by Homi Bhabha and Jane Gaines that I would not otherwise have found.

1. All transcriptions of dialogue from the film are my own, as are all translations from Russian sources into English. I have bracketed the words "to" and/or "it" in my translation of the woman's lines here in order to convey my sense that she is rejecting desire in general, rather than simply denying some particular, previously expressed wish.

2. A later "flashback" to a scene in the arboretum makes it clear that the perspective on all these scenes is that of the woman. As Jane Taubman has suggested, these opening sequences might also be interpreted as the woman's mental rehearsal of various versions of her final interview with the man (377).

3. Mulvey uses these terms as part of her larger argument about the ways that traditional narrative cinema "codes" women's appearance and "displays" woman as sexual object for exclusively male "visual pleasure." I do not propose to interpret Muratova's film as an exemplar of Mulvey's argument, however. *A Change of Fate*, as I see it, tends to question the kinds of male-dominant looking and narrative structure that Mulvey's influential essay critiques.

4. This speech, which has no prototype in the Maugham story on which the film is based, subverts a long tradition of Soviet insistence that "all peoples" must be "friendly" and "in solidarity" with one another.

5. Muratova's use of repetition, both verbal and visual, is too deeply embedded in her poetics to be explained exclusively in these terms. Other critics have noted, however, that repetition in her work often endows her characters' speech with a "phantom" quality that reverses or ironizes their surface meaning (Shepotinnik 7). Jane Taubman analyzes the frequently repeated texts in *A Change of Fate* as a form of "rehearsal" and suggests that the odd speeds and tones in which passages of dialogue are repeated foreground these texts as "quotations" (377).

6. For details of the film adaptations, see Madsen (199–205); Ringgold (104–5); and Morgan (250–52). In an interview with Jane Taubman, Muratova disavowed any knowledge of either film or stage adaptations, but Natal'ia Leble's performance as Maria, and, in particular, her appearance, occasionally recall the Bette Davis film.

7. Plakhov has suggested that *A Change of Fate* was influenced by Muratova's plans in the early 1970s to make a film of Lermontov's "Princess Mary" with two of the same actors—Natal'ia Leble and Iurii Shlykov—who appear in the later film (44–45). One wonders whether Muratova planned to use that story's setting in the Caucasus to explore the same colonialist themes that she emphasizes in her adaptation of Maugham.

Susan Larsen

8. For a discussion of the theme of miscegenation in Western "primitivist" texts, see Torgovnick 53–58, 146–47.

9. Earlier film versions portrayed the relationship between the two women as one of sexual rivalry—both the 1929 and 1940 films added a scene in which the Leslie Crosbie/ Maria character was compelled to go personally and bow before the "native" woman in order to retrieve the incriminating letter. In the 1940 version, moreover, in response to the Production Code's insistence that all malefactors be punished, the film concluded with a scene in which the "native" woman (in this case a "Eurasian," played by a white actress, Gale Sondergaard, in heavy makeup) stabs Bette Davis's Leslie Crosbie to death (Madsen 203).

10. I borrow the term "looking relations" from Jane Gaines's attempt to formulate a feminist film theory that analyzes the gaze in terms of both sexual *and* racial difference (12–26).

11. According to Taubman, this "performance" was originally filmed for Muratova's 1983 *Among the Gray Stones* [*Sredi serykh kamnei*], but fell victim to the many cuts imposed on that film. Muratova resurrected the sequence in *A Change of Fate* because she was "so fond of it" (Taubman 378). Maria's delight in this scene thus reflects the director's own "visual pleasure" in her creation.

12. The verb she uses [*vzbesit'sia*] derives from the word for "demon" [*bes*] and can mean either "to go mad," when applied to animals, or "to become furious."

13. Taubman also comments on this scene, but she offers a very different reading than that presented here (379).

14. Said discusses primarily written texts and devotes almost no space to Russian Orientalism in his now-classic analysis of Orientalist discourse, but his analysis seems particularly relevant to this film. U.S.-based scholars now working on Russian Orientalism include Monika Greenleaf, Katya Hokanson, and Harsha Ram.

15. I confess to some uncertainty on this point—there may be a "traditional" Asian dance form that looks like Soviet-style break dancing, which I encountered all over Moscow in 1987–88, the year *A Change of Fate* first came out. The many other dancing figures that appear in this section of the film, however, as well as the "multicultural" piano prelude, suggest that the incongruous appearance of this turbaned Michael Jackson wannabe is intentional. This scene is followed by another in which a male dancer performs a Ziegfeld Follies–style "Asian" dance in spangled tights and ostrich-plumed cap.

16. The 1940 film provides an interesting contrast to Muratova's version of this role, as its "native" woman exudes malevolence, "Dragon-lady" style, in her active pursuit of Leslie Crosbie (Bette Davis). Not only does she speak—in Malay or Chinese—but she does so with an air of regal hauteur, however menacing, that differs radically from the self-effacing and effaced presence of the "native" woman in Muratova's film.

17. I am grateful to Helena Goscilo for calling my attention to the Lermontovian subtext.

Works Cited

Bhabha, Homi K. "The Other Question: The Stereotype and Colonial Discourse." *Screen* 24, 6 (1983): 18–36. Rpt. in *The Sexual Subject: A Screen Reader in Sexuality*. Ed. John Caughie and Annette Kuhn. New York: Routledge, 1992, 312–31.

Bykov, Dmitrii. "Kira Muratova. Chto-to drugoe." *Literaturnaia gazeta* 16 December 1992.

Gaines, Jane. "White Privilege and Looking Relations: Race and Gender in Feminist Film Theory." *Screen* 29, 4 (1988): 12–26.

Madsen, Axel. *William Wyler, The Authorized Biography.* New York: Thomas Crowell, 1973.

Maugham, William Somerset. "The Letter." *Short Stories.* The Nonesuch Storytellers. London: The Nonesuch Press, 1990, 235–80.

———. *The Letter: A Play in Three Acts.* London: William Heinemann, 1927.

Morgan, Ted. *Maugham.* New York: Simon and Schuster, 1980.

Mulvey, Laura. "Visual Pleasure and Narrative Cinema." *Screen* 16, 3 (1975): 6–18. Rpt. in *Feminism and Film Theory.* Ed. Constance Penley. New York: Routledge, 1988, 57–68.

Muratova, Kira, dir. *Peremena uchasti (po rasskazu Somerseta Moema "Zapiska").* Soviet Union, 1987.

Plakhov, Andrei. "Peremena dekoratsii." *Iskusstvo kino* 7 (1988): 40–47.

Ringgold, Gene. *Bette Davis, Her Films and Career.* Secaucus, NJ: Citadel Press, 1966.

Said, Edward W. *Orientalism.* New York: Vintage Books, 1979.

Shepotinnik, Petr. "Opisanie rebenka prilagaetsia." *Iskusstvo kino* 7 (1992): 17–20.

Taubman, Jane. "The Cinema of Kira Muratova." *The Russian Review* 52, 3 (1993): 367–81.

Torgovnick, Marianna. *Gone Primitive: Savage Intellects, Modern Lives.* Chicago: U of Chicago P, 1990.

Wyler, William, dir. *The Letter.* U.S., 1940.

Seven

The ABC of Russian Consumer Culture
Readings, Ratings, and Real Estate

Nancy Condee and Vladimir Padunov

hi'er-o-glyph'ic—n. 1. A sacred character; a character in the picture writing of the ancient Egyptians, Mexicans, etc., or the mode of writing in such characters. 2. Any obscure or unintelligible symbol, sign, etc.; also, *pl.*, illegible writing.

> —*Webster's New Collegiate Dictionary* (1953)

An actor, for example, or even a clown . . . is a productive laborer if he works in the service of a capitalist (an entrepreneur) to whom he returns more labor than he receives from him in the form of wages; while a jobbing tailor who comes to the capitalist's house and patches his trousers for him, producing a mere use-value for him, is an unproductive laborer. The former's labor is exchanged with capital, the latter's with revenue. The former's labor produces a surplus-value; in the latter's, revenue is consumed.

> —Karl Marx, *Theories of Surplus Value*

However present and future historians of Russia describe and categorize the radical economic reforms introduced in early 1992—and these evaluations will span the range from theory-driven and impractical to market-responsive and politically reactive—one concrete and immediate consequence was the displacement of cultural objects by a wider range of consumer goods in the retail outlets that proliferated in Moscow during the period of 1992–93.[1]

Prior to the January 1992 reforms, these outlets had provided an ever-expanding network for the sale of such objects as dubbed audiocassette recordings of bards and rock groups, second-generation videocassettes of domestic and foreign films, posters and graphics, woodwork and folkloric artifacts, pins and games, appliqué t-shirts and sweatshirts, and joint venture and cooperative enterprise publications.

During the last two years of perestroika (1990–91) leading up to the

The ABC of Russian Consumer Culture

January reforms, many of these retail outlets—converted "Soiuzpechat' " kiosks; complexes of (illegally) constructed booths near major metro stations; separate sections or stands set up in already existing stores such as Dom knigi [House of Books] or Molodaia gvardiia [Young Guard (Bookstore)], Melodiia or Dom kompozitorov [Composer's House (Record Store)]—had even begun to establish their own informal distribution systems (wholesalers or jobbers), responsible for the regular delivery of these cultural objects either directly from the producers or from improvised storage facilities (garages, unoccupied rooms or corners of rooms in private and communal apartments, unoccupied spaces in soft-currency hotels).

After January 1992, however, most of these outlets for cultural objects were converted into mini–shopping stands, stocked with various brands of Western cigarettes, wines and spirits, chocolates and candies, after-shave lotions and colognes, and so forth. While many of these stands suffered acute supply problems during their first year of existence, by 1993 several informal distribution networks for consumer goods existed throughout Moscow, allowing the stands to maintain a steady stock of specific consumer goods, though not *yet* of brand names.

A is for Advertising: A Nation of Abecedarians?

Another programme to be launched in January [1993] is devoted to fashion. "Fashion Gallery" is . . . arranged in the form of an ABC with various topics (cloth, jewellery, perfume, etc.) discussed in an alphabetical order: atlas, accessories, "Armani," etc.

—Aleksei Egoshin, "TV Watch: Programming News"

This transformation of retail outlets is but one example of what might be described as a shift across the Moscow city landscape from a totalitarian culture in ruins to a consumer culture in disarray. Most visibly, this shift played itself out across the surfaces of the urban landscape—on the billboards, busses, dirigibles, and plastic shopping bags of the city. Out on the street, socialism's faux-leather briefcase, filled with canned goods and sausage, and its string-bags, topped with radishes and dillweed, have ceded their primacy to the commercial plastic bag [*paketik*], advertising Trekhgornaia manufaktura [Three-Hills Manufacturing Company] or Gzhel' porcelain. These new *paketiki* differ from socialism's thick, cloudy plastic bags, stamped with imitation woodcarving motifs in bile green or baby blue. The new *paketiki* are products of a different market. Their physical and aesthetic desirability is inextricably linked with their advertising function. They not only *are* something; they *do* something: they suggest what to buy next.

Nancy Condee & Vladimir Padunov

The new *paketiki* are different, too, from the slick, Soviet-era Berezka bags, carried for decades by stupid foreigners and proud *limitchiki*. While the *Berezka* bag alleged prior access to totalitarianism's hidden garden of delights, the new *paketiki* advertise participation in a new economic world order. Despite their shiny similarities, the Berezka bags and the new *paketiki* are radically different. The former was a nonnegotiable surface, an icon of central planning; the latter celebrates the act of commodification, presenting its surface, congenial to endless recommodification, as a portable billboard, which the consumer carries at no charge to the company. In fact, the consumer pays extra for the privilege of carrying it.

A similar service is performed by the consumer who displays other items of apparel from the marketplace's new wardrobe division. The t-shirts that first appeared in the mid-perestroika years (1987–89), satirizing Lenin by juxtaposing him with the major commercial icons of U.S. capitalism—first, Lenin and Coca-Cola; then, Lenin under the Golden Arches of McDonald's; most recently, Lenin reading *Pravda* [*Truth*] beside two large bottles of Pepsi—have ceased to be a way of coming to terms with the seventy-four years of Leninism. Instead, these images have become an ironic stance toward Coca-Cola, McDonald's, and Pepsi. They are counterculture's own advertising and, as with all countercultural images (as painters Komar and Melamid have repeatedly demonstrated), they are thoroughly indentured to the dominant culture—that is, whatever else they do, they advertise Coca-Cola, McDonald's, and Pepsi.

A major feature of Russia's rapidly expanding consumer culture is the proliferation of precisely these kinds of objects, whose chief characteristic is their circulation through the marketplace in dual capacities: as commodities-in-themselves and as advertisements, citations, or "training manuals" for a second commodity. Unlike simple commodities, which proceed through production (raw material, cloth, assembled product, decoration) and enter the marketplace to be consumed, the metacommodity performs heroic double duty: it enters the market simultaneously as an object and as a visual or aural signpost back to the marketplace.

While the most familiar U.S. examples are goods—the t-shirt, cap, or jacket bearing an advertising logo ("Hard Rock Café," "Pepsi," "Marlboro")— this phenomenon of metacommodification is by no means limited in the United States to consumer goods. It also extends to professional *services*, and is most tightly regulated in such areas as journalism, medical care, academic research, and political representation, where a clear (if wholly mythical) impartiality must be maintained. Existing legislation, industry standards, and other self-regulating tendencies protect such values as objectivity" and "sober judgment," ostensibly distinguishing the above professions from the partisan enterprises of, say, advertising, medical sales, corporate research contracts, and lobbying.

The temporary absence of these and other braking mechanisms in the Russian Federation contributes to a kind of "renegade capitalism," a market on the fringes of historical consciousness, belonging simultaneously to early capitalism, to its imagined future, and to its fantasies of a world unchecked by complex Western strategies of legislative denial.

In the absence of a sustained belief system, for example, that claims success in distinguishing among events for those that are "newsworthy," events themselves have been rapidly commodified—that is, they may become newsworthy as a result of a direct currency transaction between a corporation and a television journalist, acting as news "sales agent." Thus, according to one investigative journalist, while a thirty-second television news item may cost as much as a thirty-second advertisement, the news piece is often less expensive and provides greater credibility than the advertising format (Smucker).

A news piece on a Ministry of the Interior [MVD] agreement with Ford to purchase Ford vehicles as police patrol cars, for example, included an interview with Lev Dikar'ev, chairman of Avtoèksport [Auto Export], the Ford dealership for Ford's domestic Russian market. Denis Klimentov, the Ostankino news reporter who covered the event for the program *Utro* [*Morning*], happily and publicly admits to receiving a "gratuity" of 2,500 rubles [August 1992 rate] from Avtoèksport. In this environment, any effort to determine whether the MVD-Ford agreement was significant "in and of itself" is misspent. Money was paid; in return, the event became significant.[2]

In the same spirit, Aleksei Egoshin, who describes "Fashion Gallery" in the newspaper column "TV Watch" quoted above,[3] is neither a television executive, nor a television announcer, nor even an employee of a television company. He is the head of A + B advertising agency that arranges for the display of commodities through the medium of television. This display is packaged as a television program—that is, a commodity "interrupted" by advertisements, but not itself an advertisement—while in fact, the advertisement merely alternates its form, sometimes appearing under the pseudonym "Fashion Gallery," sometimes under its own name.

Is it the case then that, with the collapse of Communism, the secret weapons of Western multinational capital—an unwritten gentleman's agreement and obfuscating legislation—may now be deployed openly across the body of Russia? Not yet. For the time being, Young and Rubicam—the advertising agency that holds Moscow accounts for AT&T, Johnson & Johnson, Kodak,

6. Cover of comic book, *Once upon a Dime (Zhila-byla denezhka).*

and Sony—will successfully compete with Ladomir only if it overcomes its disadvantage of long-term experience in the Western advertising business.

Egoshin's abecedary of commodities, with its coy intermingling of generic description and brand name ("atlas, accessories, 'Armani' "), suggests that Russia has entered the elementary-school years of capitalism and, armed with good study habits, it will progress through the alphabet of commodities, finding the experience to be orderly, rewarding, and predictable. Egoshin is not alone in his pedagogic stance toward "the new" Russia or in his alphabetical methodology. These are recurrent tropes of Russia's new consumer culture. They are most developed in advertising and fine arts, areas of culture with the most to gain from an early market, absorbed with the rapid acquisition of material commodities. Shkola [School] Gallery, 1.0 Gallery, A-3 Gallery, Az'art (the fashion gallery), Al'fa Art (the art auction house), "A" Center (a cultural venue for eco-rock), like A + B Agency, all suggest a new beginning, an elementary, even alphabetical coherence to market culture.[4] A similar pedagogic undertone runs throughout new television game shows that "teach" about bonds and securities, sponsorship and

7a and 7b. Children's gambling games "Dicing Poker" and "Casino."

philanthropy; throughout the comic book series on finances—such as *Once upon a Dime* [*Zhila-byla denezhka*] (see Fig. 6)—adapted from publications of the Federal Reserve Bank of New York;[5] throughout new children's games such as Dicing Poker and Casino (both in Latin script, see Fig. 7), Art Theft [*Krazha*] and Arts Patron of the Arts [*Metsenat*]. All of these activities promote the message that Russia's task is to learn how to handle money.

Yet the handling of money is not as unfamiliar a task as the entrepreneur would make it appear. The housing official who markets his stamp, the army officer who sells the labor of the soldiers under his command, the television journalist who peddles his news, the visa officer from OVIR who sets a price on his services, the university official whose aid is provided for a fee "because" his salary is insufficient—these are hardly a scourge recently brought to Russia by the decadent West. The impulse to use one's position and connections as a basis to bring in money on the side [*podrabatyvat'*] rather than to live—accursèd—on one's own salary was no less endemic to real existing socialism than to newly emerging capitalism. The metacommodity— whether shirt cum ad or news cum ad—is a natural development of a culture accustomed to receiving multiple incomes (like prison sentences): one for nothing at all, another for doing what one was supposed to be doing in the first place.

High Culture and the New "New Economic Policy"

The Minsk communiqué of December 1991 provides historians with the political signpost marking the reversion of the Soviet Union back to Russia; the reforms of January 1992 provide them with the economic signpost marking the reversion of socialist labor and market practices back to capitalist ones. From this point of view, the announcement by the Ministry of Communications in mid-December 1991—that is, in the brief interval between the appearance of the political and economic signposts—that the cost of shipment and postage (even for printed matter) would increase by up to 300 percent beginning in January 1992 was the first indication that the entire existing, *state-financed*, economic basis of cultural production and distribution was about to be scrapped.

This announcement came several weeks after the completion of the 1992 subscription campaign by newspapers and periodicals in November 1991. Subscription prices for 1992 had already been substantially increased by all publishers in anticipation of increases in the cost of raw materials (paper and ink), production (typesetters and presses), and mailing. While these increased subscription prices resulted in a severe drop in the number of

1992 subscriptions nationwide,[6] publishers now discovered that they had significantly underestimated the scale of the rises in the cost of raw materials (the price per metric ton of paper rose 500 percent in the four months from October 1991 to February 1992),[7] minimum wages (300 percent to 500 percent during these same months),[8] as well as postage and shipment.[9]

As a result, virtually all publications found themselves on the verge of bankruptcy on the day the new economic policies went into effect. Ironically, those publications with the greatest number of prepaid subscriptions for 1992 (for example, *Moskovskii Komsomolets* [*Moscow Young Communist*] or *Ogonek* [*Little Flame*]) faced the greatest disparity between the actual costs of production and distribution per issue, on the one hand, and the cost projected per issue to prepaid subscribers, on the other. By April 1992, *Ogonek* alone was losing between eight million and ten million rubles for each issue despite a dramatic increase in the number of advertising pages (and a corresponding decrease in the number of stories and articles in each issue), forcing it to shift, for most of 1992, from weekly to semimonthly publication in an attempt to compensate for the differences in the retail cost per issue: sixty kopecks for subscribers compared with fifteen to twenty-two rubles in kiosks for single issues.[10]

Similar tactics—that is, increasing advertisement space without increasing the number of pages per issue and modifying publication schedules—were adopted by other publications throughout 1992. Many monthly journals switched (at least temporarily) to bimonthly publication (including, among others, *Druzhba narodov* [*Friendship of Peoples*], *Iunost'* [*Youth*], *Literaturnoe obozrenie* [*Literary Review*], *Moskva*, *Neva*, *Volga*, *Voprosy istorii* [*Problems of History*], and *Zvezda* [*Star*] or to a quarterly schedule (*Voprosy literatury* [*Problems of Literature*])); others ceased publication altogether for a while (*Pravda*); most publications postponed paying editorial salaries and honoraria to contributors for several months.[11] Even many of the newer, "market-financed" serial publications had to cease operation during much of 1992 because of the sharp rises in printing costs (for new issues) and distribution expenses (for issues published prior to 1992): for instance, *Konets veka* [*End of the Century*] (three issues), *Solo* (eight issues), and *Vestnik novoi literatury* [*Herald of New Literature*] (three issues).[12]

The collapse of the Russian currency was swift: 80 rubles to the dollar in December 1991; 125 in June 1992; 425 by October 1992; 1,000 by May 1993.[13] It was accelerated by the suspension of state subsidies in all fields of cultural production, of price subsidies on consumer goods, and of controls on the costs of raw materials. The collapse resulted in astronomical increases in the costs of both goods (to consumers) and raw materials (to producers). The rapid escalation of prices effectively wiped out the accumulated life savings of most of the Russian population, inexorably leading to a major redefinition of "essential" purchases and a corresponding change in spending patterns.

In the ensuing struggle of commodities to control the market's central space—geographically, economically, and socially—cultural objects were increasingly viewed as luxury goods, while imported Western packaged foods (including, ironically, European and American beers, as well as Smirnoff vodka) were seen as "survival kits." In June 1992, at tables throughout Moscow, books and packages of Western cigarettes sold at 65 to 120 rubles; recorded acoustic cassettes and Western beers sold at 100 to 150 rubles; recorded videocassettes and a kilogram of meat sold at 250 to 350 rubles, forcing shoppers to make a daily "devil's choice" between cultural objects and consumer goods.

By the end of the summer of 1992, the pattern of choices that could be traced throughout Moscow became clearer: virtually all central retail outlets that had previously specialized in cultural objects had been converted into kiosk shopping stands, which now sold a wide (and wild) assortment of consumer goods. While in December 1991 the central outlets of Al'ta Video had a catalogue of more than 900 films available for dubbing, and filled orders in forty-eight hours, by the summer of 1992 these had all become neighborhood "Night Shops." The central outlets for Soiuz Studio Tape Recordings, such as the kiosk across from the Melodiia store on Novyi Arbat, listed in December 1991 over 1,200 available tapes, with a twenty-four-hour turn-around period for tapes of foreign albums and a seventy-two-hour period for tapes of domestic rock concerts or performances; by the summer of 1992 these had become typical consumer goods stands. Appliqué t-shirt outlets at the Barrikadnaia and Novokuznetskaia metro stations, the almanac kiosks on Leningradskoe shosse, and the cooperative book publication kiosks around the Academy Hotel had all converted to ordinary consumer kiosks.

With similar results, but for different reasons, by May 1993 Moscow city authorities, in an attempt at "neighborhood gentrification," had cleaned up the city center, banning all street vendors on the Arbat (mostly sellers of nesting dolls [*matreshki*], military uniforms and medals, Soviet memorabilia) and all sales in the pedestrian underpass at Pushkin Square (unofficial serial publications and pornography). In both locations, the dozens of curbside peddlers, openly selling cultural objects displayed on improvised stands or spread out on blankets, were replaced by a handful of pensioners surreptitiously selling individual cans of food, bottles of alcohol, or

The ABC of Russian Consumer Culture

flowers from their dachas. At the same time, consumer goods stores [*kommercheskie magaziny*], selling foodstuffs, clothing, and electronic equipment, were opened all along the Arbat and even in the Pushkin underpass.

This geographic displacement of culture from the center of the city (that is, from within the Garden Ring Road) was not accompanied by an expansion of retail outlets specializing in cultural objects *outside* of the center. If in June 1992, for example, bookstands could be found on almost every street corner and in every underpass in the center of the city and every few blocks outside of the Garden Ring Road, then by May 1993 these same types of bookstands were located in specific and confined areas in the center: outside each official bookstore, in front of tourist hotels, around most tourist haunts, and every ten to twenty blocks in the periphery.

The two exceptions—two new bookstores specializing in avant-garde and high literature—can be seen as a market-driven response to the demand for quality fiction and poetry, but also as a formative moment in the continuing isolation and ghettoization of culture in the daily life of the citizenry. These two stores—Gileia at Znamenka Street 10 (formerly Frunze Street) and Salon 19th October at First Cossack Lane—reproduce this same process of geographic displacement: the former sells primarily material printed in Moscow and the provincial cities; the latter, material from St. Petersburg.[14]

By May 1993, consumer goods had not only displaced cultural objects geographically, they had also displaced them economically. Despite the across-the-board escalation of prices characteristic of daily life in Russia since January 1992, prices for most consumer goods rose *less* dramatically than prices for cultural objects, thereby ending the fragile equivalence of prices that had prevailed in June 1992 between these two types of commodities. A package of Western cigarettes (500 to 600 rubles in May 1993) was considerably cheaper than books at street-side bookstalls; books generally started at 1,000 rubles. Western beers cost 900 to 1,000 rubles, while audiocassettes (pirated or not) cost 1,500 to 2,000 rubles. A kilogram of meat started at 1,500 rubles, while second-generation videocassettes started at 6,000 and compact discs at 8,000 rubles.

The economic displacement of domestic culture in 1992–93 can be traced in all branches of the culture industry, at the same time that the flow of capital can be traced into the consumer goods sector. In the publishing industry alone, new "unofficial" newspapers and magazines virtually disappeared from the marketplace during 1992[15] (see Fig. 8). By 1993 many of the Russian-language, glossy, Western-style magazines that made their appearance between 1990 and 1991 (e.g., *Andrei, Moscow Magazine*) also

Nancy Condee & Vladimir Padunov

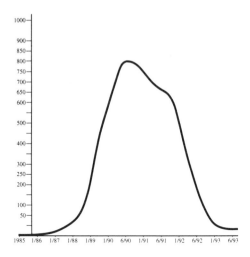

8. Graph depicting development of unofficial or nontraditional publications, 1986–93. Source: Archive of the Non-Traditional Press, Moscow, 1993.

ceased to appear. Nationwide subscriptions to journals and newspapers for 1992 and 1993 declined sharply. There was a striking drop in the number of continuing and new publishers, as well as a significant decrease in the number of new titles in stores and on the bookstands.[16] Not a single new printing combine was built in the entire country between 1986 and 1993 using state, joint venture, or private capital (Tokareva).

The Russian film industry was plagued by a reduction in the number of films produced domestically; by the growing number of Russian directors working abroad on joint venture production; by the disappearance of Russian films from most of Moscow's theaters; the flood of cheap, American action movies; a nationwide drop in per capita screening attendance; and the growing tendency to show new Russian films in specialty locations or repertory theaters (for example, at the Kino Center in the Krasnaia presnia district or the Revival Theater at the beginning of the Arbat). Similarly, the 1992–93 theatrical season failed to reverse the trend of playing to half-empty theater halls; there was a further drop in the number of new productions; the theatrical repertoire continued to be dominated by Western plays.

The broadcasting industry has experienced a proliferation of European and American television and radio broadcasts,[17] and a corresponding decrease in the transmission of Russian-language material. Political and/or socially outspoken materials such as pins, artifacts, and leaflets have begun to disappear entirely from the marketplace. Even the political *patreshki*

The ABC of Russian Consumer Culture

(nesting dolls of political leaders) languish on the stands of Izmailovo Market, while a brisk trade is carried on in *matreshki* bearing the images of the Ninja Turtles, the Beatles, Madonna, the Seven Dwarfs, Michael Jackson, and U.S. currency bills.

Viewed from the distance of Russia's entire history, the geographic and economic displacement of the culture industry from the central place it traditionally occupied in Russo-Soviet daily life is an unprecedented development in Russian cultural politics: the wholesale social displacement of the cult of high culture. This displacement has no parallel in post-eighteenth-century Russian social or cultural history. Even during the major "Romanov Thaw"—which extends from the immediate aftermath of the 1905 revolution (the legitimation of oppositional political parties, establishment of a national legislature, and restriction of censorship), through the Stolypin years (encouragement to capitalist accumulation, social reformation, and cultural tolerance) and the tricentenary of the Romanov dynasty (the sweeping amnesty to sociopolitical and cultural "deviants") to the onset of World War I—the Russian "cult of high culture" coexisted remarkably well with the resurgence of low (popular and mass) culture.[18]

Under Russia's present-day market conditions (its Klondike stage of capitalism), coexistence is not an available option in the cut-throat competition for display space, consumer demand, and cost. Just as bookstands have been displaced, for the most part, from the city center, high literature has been almost entirely displaced from the remaining bookstands.

As late as June 1992, the standard bookstand still displayed classics of the Silver Age (Anna Akhmatova, Mikhail Kuzmin, Osip Mandel'shtam) next to translations of Western detective fiction (James Hadley Chase, Raymond Chandler, Georges Simenon); books by émigré authors (Sergei Dovlatov, Aleksandr Solzhenitsyn, Vladimir Voinovich) next to translations of memoirs by Western capitalists (Dale Carnegie, Henry Ford, Lee Iaccoca); or literature of the "alternative" literary tradition (Andrei Bitov, Evgenii Popov, Vladimir Sorokin) next to books dealing with "alternative" realities (UFOs, astrology, herbal medicine).

By May 1993, most vestiges of high culture had been routed from the bookstands, whether they were located in the center or on the periphery of the city. Insofar as high culture was represented at all in 1993, it existed as a token presence: almost every stand displayed a stray token of one historical, philosophical, or theological book. One exception to this rout of high literature from the bookstands is the few stands that are in fact improvised retail outlets for specific publishers. Chief among these are the Gnosis/Progress bookstand on Zubovskii bul'var, specializing in books on

Nancy Condee & Vladimir Padunov

philosophy and semiotics (for example, Lotman), and the IMLI (Gor'kii Institute of World Literature) bookstand in the Institute itself.[19]

By comparison, bookstands located in areas of high tourist visibility (along Tverskaia Street, in front of tourist hotels, around tourist attractions) trade in and worship a different set of high cultural tokens: dictionaries and coffee-table art books.[20] Since most of these books are extremely expensive to the citizenry (2,000 to 40,000 rubles) and since many of the transactions occur in a non-Russian language and currency, these stands are, in a sense, capitalism's Berezka, selling hard-currency commodities difficult to obtain in the local market. The most striking feature of these tokens (erstwhile icons to high culture) is their indifference to high *literature*. No samples of classical or contemporary poetry, prose, or literary criticism are displayed on these bookstands. In a sense, the symbolic banishment of high literature from the tables of commerce is the market's revenge for the years of Soviet *cultural* imperialism—during most of which high literature occupied the place of honor in the pantheon of high culture—and Russia's *imperial* culture—during all of which high literature was the ever-present interlocutor in any high-minded "discussion of ideas."

Arts Patron: The Board Game

Object of the game: creation of the fullest, most valuable collection of paintings (not less than five) in one of the following areas: 1.) museum holding, 2.) national school, 3.) genre. The winner is the first to create a series not of separate pictures from all areas, but specifically a collection of canvases of only one of the above areas and, furthermore, the highest-priced collection.

—Rules of the game Arts Patron [*Metsenat*]

"You and your sponsor agree to make a movie. He borrows a considerable sum from a bank and lets you have a small portion of it. The rest he uses for profitable deals. Once you have walked, say, a quarter of the way, he will ask you whether the star actress is pregnant. This means you are supposed to stop shooting. It is easy to understand that he does not care at all about your movie and cinematography in general."

—Mikhail Ptashuk, Belarus film director

As the recent flood of publications amply documents,[21] the thirty-eight leading families of the Merchant Class were, by the early twentieth century, anything but merchants. Factory owners and railroad magnates, they occu-

The ABC of Russian Consumer Culture

9. Privatization voucher.

pied a place of higher status than ordinary merchants,[22] who engaged in buying and selling, but did not produce goods. Lowest of all were the *protsentshchiki*, money handlers of all sorts, largely those who lent money to the industrialists.

It is precisely the modern-day equivalent of the money handlers—those who speculate in gas, oil, minerals, armaments, property, vouchers (see Fig. 9), paintings, antiques, and other cultural objects of recognized material value—whose moment has now arrived, and the revival of the Merchant as object of reverence lends reflected glory to the labor of the *protsentshchik* and actual merchant, even as it conflates them with the industrialist. The Russian tendency to fuse Dale Carnegie, father of the entrepreneurial movement, with Andrew Carnegie, the Pittsburgh steel magnate, exemplifies this conflation.

One of the earliest cinematic representations of the Merchant was the 1913 film *Drama on the Volga* [*Drama na Volge*] by director-scriptwriter Nikolai Larin (about whom nothing else is known), an unknown cast, and producer Grigorii Libken (Christie). Libken was apparently one of many provincial entrepreneurs (Iaroslavl', in Libken's case) who correctly assessed the profits to be made from a rapidly expanding cinema industry that provided a newly urbanized population with scandalous visual material, a situation in some respects similar to the present day.[23]

Drama on the Volga tells the story of a wealthy Merchant's daughter, Nadia, who falls in love with the household steward, Egorushka, only to learn that she is to be married off to another wealthy Merchant, her father's crony. In an attempt to hide Egorushka, she accidentally suffocates him (signifi-

Nancy Condee & Vladimir Padunov

10. *Drama on the Volga (Drama na Volge)*, 1913. Director, Nikolai Larin.

cantly enough) in her bed, with its high pile of lace eiderdown and pillows. The rest of this fragmented film (two reels are blessedly missing) involves lengthy corpse scenes, a police investigation, and sexual blackmail by a servant-accomplice who had helped dispose of the body. The daughter's pyromaniacal revenge against her servant-blackmailer concludes this wrenching drama.

Larin's (and Libken's) *Drama on the Volga* was originally known as *Merchant Bashkirov's Daughter* [*Doch' kuptsa Bashkirova*] (see Fig. 10). Libken was apparently less concerned with the subtleties of Merchant culture than with blackmailing the wealthy Iaroslavl' Merchant Bashkirov, using evidence gathered from courtroom texts (Christie). We do not know the specific resolution of the Libken-Bashkirov "dispute." We would like to imagine that the Merchant gave in to the profiteer's cinematic blackmail, just as the Merchant's cinematic daughter gave in to her servant's sexual blackmail. But this is the critic's love of narrative shape. In any event, the film was released as *Drama on the Volga*, together with a disclaimer concerning the Bashkirov family.[24] The accompanying public interest was sufficient for Libken's Volga Company to succeed in selling the film internationally to Pathé Frères.

The ABC of Russian Consumer Culture

The film's significance, then, is not its substance, but its production and, by implication, its producer, whose self-portrait might be discerned in the very work he underwrites. What was Libken: a producer? a blackmailer? To which social layer did he belong, even granting him the problematic title of "producer": merchant? *protsentshchik?* A pitiless entrepreneur who profited by exposing the alleged sins of the Merchant's daughter, Libken transformed the Iaroslavl' Merchant from flesh into silver nitrate, a shift (paradoxically) in cultural power *away* from the conservative, tradition-bound Merchant class toward the rash new profiteer. Libken's film provides a fragmentary glimpse into the future, a time when Libken's double commodity—cinema and blackmail "evidence"—would be appreciated, even admired. The Radishchev of new Russian capitalism, Libken sounded an early clarion call to *protsentshchiki* eighty years hence. While the biography of director Nikolai Larin and that of the film's cast has sunk into obscurity, two stories survive in fragments—Libken's own and the story he chose to tell: how the Merchant's progeny murdered its servants.

As culture turns from the Soviet bureaucratic patron—chiefly, in one form or another, the Ministry of Culture—to the mercantile patron, its reimagining of the Merchant past again becomes a task of major significance and urgency. The recent Moscow celebrations marking the respective centenaries of Eliseev's and GUM were more than mere historical acknowledgment. They were ceremonies that reaffirmed old alliances and lineages within the merchant profession and the Merchant class (whose motto "For the Merchant Corps" adorned the original GUM when it opened in 1893), and between Russian and foreign capital, whose GUM outlets include Benetton, Galeries Lafayette, SoapBerry Shop, and Christian Dior.

The rediscovery of the *metsenat* as an object of curiosity and reverence swept through much of cultural production in 1992–93.[25] The Tret'iakov Gallery exhibit "Savva Mamontov and Russian Art" (June 1992) brought over five hundred of Mamontov's collected paintings, sculptures, photographs, and other works of decorative and applied art from the Russian Museum, the Historical Museum, the Tret'iakov Gallery, and private collections. The exhibit included all four major portraits of the railroad and factory industrialist by Repin, Tsorn, Serov, and Vrubel'. In early 1993, a similar exhibit, occupying nearly twenty halls of the Art Museum in Iaroslavl', was devoted to the collection of Saint Petersburg shipbuilder-scholar Vladimir Ashik (*Nezavisimaia gazeta* [*Independent Gazette*] 18 May 1993).

In the same spirit—but in a radically different outpost of cultural production—the board game Arts Patron challenges its players to engage in a late-twentieth-century version of Merchant patronage, buying and selling

11. Board game, "Arts Patron" (*"Metsenat"*).

tiny cardboard paintings—including "works" by Cézanne, Monet, Van Gogh, and Renoir—so as to acquire a collection with the highest currency value. Facilitating (and hindering) this process are the game's mafia, art fairs, security services, Patrons' Club, auction houses, antique shops, appraisers, and even a Foreign Arts Patron [*Inostranets-Metsenat*], who, with an unlucky roll of a six on the die, can disappear together with your Cézanne (see Fig. 11).

"Arts Patron," too, is the name given to two recently established annual prizes (one to a CIS patron, one to a Foreign Patron [*Inostranets-Metsenat*]) awarded for outstanding cultural patronage by the newly founded International Association for the Promotion of Culture, funded by Ostankino, *Izvestiia* [*News*], and *Delovoi mir* [*Business World*].[26] A recent special issue of the almanac *Pamiatniki Otechestva* [*Monuments of the Fatherland*], entitled "Patrons and Collectors" [*Metsenaty i kollektsionery*], was followed up by a lengthy discussion in the newspaper *Nezavisimaia gazeta* by the almanac's editor-in-chief, Sergei Razgonov, with Academician Boris V. Raushenbakh and Savelii V. Iamshchikov, director of an unnamed collectors' club, on the cozy theme "Patrons Aren't Born: Sometimes Even Good Examples Are Infectious" [*Metsenaty ne rozhdaiutsia: inogda i dobrye primery zarazitel'ny*] (*Nezavisimaia gazeta* 18 May 1993).[27]

Here, amidst sage utterances ("The right to be a patron is an honor" [*Pravo byt' metsenatom—èto pochetnoe pravo*]) and homey, patriarchal wisdom ("The best of the contemporary entrepreneurs understand that philanthropy is the requisite companion [f.] of sound business" [*Luchshie iz sovremennykh predprinimatelei ponimaiut, chto blagotvoritel'nost—obiazatel'naia sputnitsa solidnogo biznesa*]), the elusive distinctions between *"metsenat"*—with its positive connotations—and *"sponsor"*—usually, in such comparisons, with negative connotations—were once again debated.[28]

And, finally, just when we can stand no more, the television series *Russkii metsenat* [*Russian Patron*] was registered with the Ministry of Print and Information on 11 January 1993 by Evgenii N. Lisitsyn, President of Panerma Television Company (*Svidetel'stvo 02158*). Premiering on Russian State Television in July 1993, the television series is devoted to "the rebirth of Russian culture, art, education based on the traditions of patronage and the broad elucidation of philanthropic work." Conceived as a combination of discussion group, game show, arts fund-raiser, and educational program on the history of arts patronage [*metsenatstvo*], the show introduces the public to prominent entrepreneurs and artists in a studio hung with portraits of famous Russian patrons and encourages potential entrepreneurs to enlist in their effort (*Tsenarii-plan*).

In addition to directing Panerma, Lisitsyn is the head of the foundation Russian Patron [*Russkii Metsenat*], funding, among other projects, the reconstruction in northern Moscow of the Church of Our Savior of Filipp, Metropolitan of Moscow. Russian Patron is one of scores of new philanthropies that have come into existence in the early 1990s with the purpose of reestablishing the tradition of cultural patronage.[29]

One of the more interesting such foundations, still in its infancy, is the Higher Non-Party School [*Vysshaia Bespartiinaia Shkola*], formerly the Foundation for the Support of the Young Creative Intelligentsia [*Fond v podderzhku molodoi tvorcheskoi intelligentsii*], headed by *Literaturnaia gazeta* [*Literary Gazette*] journalist Iurii Shchekochikhin. Registered on 18 February 1993, and beginning its work on 29 April 1993 (*Ustav*), the Higher Non-Party School has already received funding for two awards: the Gorbachev stipend, awarded to the young historian who writes the best history of the perestroika period; and the Nixon stipend, to be given to a young scholar working in the area of interethnic conflict resolution (*Literaturnaia gazeta* 5 May

1993). The foundation is unusual, even at this early stage, in its explicit support of younger artists, scholars, and scientists, for whom the cutoff age of eligibility is thirty-three years.

A foundation whose council is largely composed of liberal democrats, the Higher Non-Party School is the philanthropic entity most intelligible to Western understanding of foundations. Members of its council have all been prominent figures in the perestroika period; many were well-known sixties figures [*shestidesiatniki*] or have had extended cultural contacts with the Western élite dating from the mid-Thaw years: the scholar Galina Belaia, political commentator Igor' Kliamkin, writer Bulat Okudzhava, editor and publisher Mariia Rozanova, Minister of Culture Evgenii Sidorov, critic and writer Andrei Siniavskii, director Oleg Tabakov, actor Mikhail Ul'ianov, poet Andrei Voznesenskii, and others.

These cultural credentials are the greatest strength and weakness of the Higher Non-Party School. The generation whose own youthful energies spanned the (now) forty-year period since the death of Stalin is proposing to support contemporary culture in a business environment not in the slightest amenable to their noble idealism, led by a president known for his journalistic battles against the Russian mafia. Once again simultaneously behind and ahead of the times, they are a group with enormous Western credibility, mad enough to publicize an endorsement by Gorbachev (29 April 1993), and optimistic that it is possible, reasonable, and even necessary to ask where the money comes from.[30] Whether it is possible for a cultural foundation to maintain both fiscal rectitude and economic viability under the current market conditions remains to be seen.

Unlike the Higher Non-Party School, with its emphasis on youth and the contemporary avant-garde, most of the new foundations are conceived as institutions aimed at resurrecting legitimacy by restoring the cultural monuments of older, established patronage systems: Russian Patron supports the reconstruction of its church; the Diagilev Center supports the reconstruction and screen adaptation of three Fokin choreographies (*Petrushka, Firebird,* and *Schéhérazade*) (*Nezavisimaia gazeta* 6 July 1993); a group of Nizhnii Novgorod patrons donate money to fund sculptor Viacheslav Klykov's statue of Avvakum; entrepreneur and "citizen of Russia Kononykhin," as he chooses to be called, provides funds for another Klykov statue to Cyril and Methodius on Moscow's Slavianskaia Square.

The Cyril and Methodius statue was one of the first Moscow monuments to be erected after August 1991—that is, in the post-Communist era. It marks a return to the statuary of the human body, away from the metonymic statuary of the late perestroika era, such as the large rock from the

The ABC of Russian Consumer Culture

prison camp system on Solovetskie Islands, unveiled not far from Lubianka Square on 30 October 1990. This rock, literally the gulag's rubble, was Soviet statuary's penultimate oeuvre (*Report* 36). A short walking distance and a short time away, two interconnected incidents in statuary history would soon be enacted—the toppling of Feliks Dzerzhinskii and the unveiling of Cyril and Methodius, an end and a beginning, *izhitsa* and *az*, the wiping away of Soviet hieroglyphics and the setting down of a new Russian alphabet.

Aesthetic versus Property Values

If before the artist depended on party bosses, on government bureaucrats, now it is the neo-millionaire who calls the tune.

—Sergei Razgonov, Editor-in-Chief of *Pamiatniki Otechestva*

As money becomes increasingly worthless, many rich people are willing to invest in art.

—Liudmila Lunina, "Art without Commerce"

For a brief period in 1991–93, under the evolving rules of emerging capital, it seemed as if the "final and decisive battle" between factions in the arts organizations was being fought out over control of the buildings that had housed their respective institutions. These included property battles in August and September 1991 between the liberal Moscow Writers' Union and the conservative Russian Writers' Union; the subsequent battles over the Central House of Littérateurs between Timur Pulatov's International Society of Writers and Artem Anfinogenov's Union of Russian Writers;[31] the battle over the mansion on Gogol' Boulevard between Eduard Drobitskii's International Federation of Artists and Oleg Savostiuk's International Confederation of Artists' Unions; the battle over the House of Arts in Kuz'minki among several different arts organizations; the battle over the Marx-Engels Museum between the Russian Club of the Nobility and industrialist Peter Ludwig's proposal for a museum of modern Western art; Iurii Liubimov's battles over the Taganka Theater (Matizen, Nikolaevich, Minkin); and the battle over the Kino Center between the Union of Cinematographers and the shareholders' organization of the Kino Center led by Stanislav Govorukhin.

These property battles, fought in earnest by late 1991, followed hard upon the "founders' battles," fought out over the previous eighteen months to establish the founder [*uchreditel'*] of cultural entities (and thus provide the basis for a claim to property).[32] But unlike the founders' battles, the very fact of property battles caused considerable alarm in the cultural community. The sight of artists (or so they were called)[33] fighting over property values rather than aesthetic ones contradicted prevailing myths of both socialist and bourgeois societies about the artist as "free" from economic ambitions.

In social arenas other than culture, the acquisition of property has had its own legitimizing discourse—for the businessman, an exercise of entrepreneurial skill; for the church, an affirmation of spiritual tradition; for the research institute, a matter of institutional survival. For the artist, however, the acquisition of property continually threatens to be a self-negating act of philistinism. With no multigenerational community of artists who have owned property, who were born to property, or who inherited property, Russia now has a multigenerational community of artists who has reason to believe that the control of property is the control of culture, that the real battleground is real estate.

Indeed, until the Russian currency is stabilized, until the ruble becomes something more than a metaphor for social disintegration, property is undeniably a reliable measure of wealth. Legal ownership papers (a changing concept in itself) are arguably the closest corresponding currency to dollar bills. These two paper icons—the dollar sign and the ownership stamp—have preserved a delicate if fluctuating balance that has long warranted daily listing in Western newspapers: the U.S. dollar versus a three-room renovated apartment within the Garden Ring. Against this currency, the dollar is steadily dropping.

It is not surprising, therefore, that painting—of all areas within the culture industry—is unusually revealing of the current social urgency to acquire property. It has become, to quote a familiar source, "the most important of all the arts" because its "need" for property is the most explicit and manageable[34] at all stages of its production, distribution, and consumption. Painting, the territory of cultural activity across which property relations are played out most evidently, not only requires property, it is itself material property that can neither be reproduced nor mass-produced without losing value. At the moment when property becomes the key issue in redefining social relations, painting—like film in 1922 (according to Lenin) and certainly again in May 1986 (despite Lenin), like statuary in August 1991—is an ideal playing field for those relations.

Insofar as painting is closely linked in the popular imagination with the brief but important Merchant tradition, the associative triangle "merchant/property/painting" (as in Shchukin/the Trubetskoi Palace/Matisse) sustains a vision of Russia's new future better than any heretofore proffered alternative (e.g., the restoration of the Romanov dynasty, a return to agrarian peasant culture). In other words, not only the Merchant, but also the Merchant's objets d'art have the power to articulate a prescriptive future for Russia in the modern world. Thus, at the moment when élite culture is in danger of perishing at the buzz saw of history, the Merchant-*protsentshchik* reappears—*Maecenas ex machina*—as, of all things, the conservator of cultural heritage. Not without a price, but a conservator nevertheless.

Just as cinema negotiated a space for change in May 1986, and was joined by the writers as early as June 1986,[35] so painting—in both a figurative and a literal sense—negotiated a space in 1993. The patronage of painting has significant implications for the patronage of high culture in general, at least for the near future: allocation of space, the distribution of philanthropy's funds throughout the culture industry, the vested interests of the philanthropic network, and so forth.

So while it may be true that, in general, the real battle is over real estate, property is rapidly becoming too valuable to be left undisturbed in the hands of culture. Increasingly, the cultural institution is the impoverished landlord of a wealthy tenant: the publishing house Moskovskii rabochii [Moscow Worker], the journal *Voprosy literatury*, the Institute for the Study of Cinema Art are among many cultural institutions that have constricted their own working areas so as to lease office space to foreign companies. This "temporary solution" is squeezing culture out of the property market altogether; it can afford to occupy space only as a corporation's tax write-off in legislation that is yet to be drafted.[36]

This legislation will of necessity address the "bright future" of consumer culture (philanthropy, tax incentives for cultural support, distinctions between profit and nonprofit cultural enterprises), as well as the "darker side" of legislating culture (definitions of libel and slander; geographic zoning of eroticism; standards for literature, theater, rock, journalism, and other fields). These two categories of legislation—one that facilitates the survival of élite culture, the other that constricts the proliferation of erotic culture—are closely interconnected. Apparent opposites, they are both "border communities" that define the shape of the culture industry.

Forbidden Zone: The Culture of Titillation

Taken together, the disappearance of high culture from most retail outlets in the city center and the segregation of high cultural objects in commercially designated trading zones (specialty bookstores and bookstands, specialty movie theaters) marks the ironic victory of pornography and the culture of eroticism over traditional high culture. If, during the last two years of perestroika (1990–91), erotic literature was effectively banished from most "above-ground" retail outlets—taking refuge instead in underpasses and in metro stations—and was on the verge of being subjected to a variety of zoning laws,[37] then during the first year of the "capitalist marketplace," high culture is experiencing a similar kind of banishment and ghettoization.

In the same way, just as pornography was the first type of printed commodity that joyfully ignored any attempt at maintaining the pretense of a list (or retail) price, opting instead for a "negotiable price" [*"tsena po dogovorennosti"*], all cultural objects today are priced at what the market will bear.[38] In this respect, pornography is no longer the "guerilla commodity" it used to be between 1990 and 1991. Instead, in its antagonistic relationship to high culture, it has become a pathfinder, a trendsetter commodity in Russia's capitalist marketplace, forcing high culture to reproduce its own marginalized status.

Paradoxically, however, just as the culture of eroticism has now successfully expanded into all branches of Russia's culture industry (the increased use of sexually explicit and erotic language in literature, the obligatory depiction of sexual encounters on the screen, nudity on the stage, profane speech in rock lyrics, the appearance of sex shops and "personal columns") and has effectively begun to marginalize high literature, new hard-core pornographic books have virtually vanished from the marketplace and the number of hard-core newspapers has sharply dropped.[39] While it is possible that publishers of hard-core pornography have simply relocated their activities beyond even the periphery of Moscow, it is more likely that, at the moment of its victory, pornography has itself been changed.

In other words, as the aesthetic novelty of obscenity faded between 1990 and 1993, and as the culture of eroticism penetrated Russia vertically (through the culture industry) and horizontally (through all of society), pornography significantly "softened." And this softening, in turn, has been instrumental in opening up the Russian cultural marketplace to a new influx of multinational publishing capital and a new generation of Western erotic publications. Chief among the latter is the appearance in 1993 of a Russian-language edition of *Penthouse* magazine (see Fig. 12). While the Russian *Penthouse* maintains almost all of the standard rubrics (letters, articles, stories) and offers as many breast-shots, it differs from the American edition in two respects: the absence of unobstructed vaginal photographs and the greater number of rear-view images.[40]

The "coyness" or "softness" of the Russian *Penthouse* is characteristic of

12a, 12b, and 12c. First three issues of the Russian edition of *Penthouse*.

13a, 13b, and 13c. Three popular scandal sheets, *Criminal Chronicle,*
Nonsense, and *Scandals.*

the present-day state of eroticism in Russia, which is moving away from graphic explicitness to a kind of gleeful titillation. Redefined in this way, the literature of titillation totally dominated the publishing industry in Russia in 1993. Not surprisingly, scandal-sheets—*Kriminal'naia khronika* [*Criminal Chronicle*], *Kliukva* [*Nonsense*], *Ochen' strashno* [*Very Scary*], *Skandaly* [*Scandals*] (see Fig. 13)—are both the newest entrants in the competition for newspaper readership and have had the greatest increase in circulation and print runs. Translations of steamy bedroom novels (especially popular at the moment are Jacqueline Susann's *Valley of the Dolls* [1966], *Love Machine* [1969], and *Once Is Not Enough* [1973]; and Jackie Collins's *Hollywood Wives* [1983] and *Lucky* [1985]) dominate the display space on the bookstands. Suspense thrillers (especially translations of Michael Crichton and Stephen King) and political thrillers qua exposés (most notably Valentin Stepankov and Evgenii Lisov, *The Kremlin Conspiracy* (*The Investigator's Version*) [*Kremlevskii zagovor (versiia sledstviia)*]) are beginning to break the readership monopoly that detective fiction has maintained since early 1989 (see Fig. 14). Indeed, this last publication is such a "scandal thriller" that it has placed the entire political situation of the country into jeopardy. Written by the procurator-general of the Russian Federation and his deputy (that is, by the men directly responsible for conducting the trial of the ringleaders of the abortive August 1991 putsch), the book—a description of the events leading up to and during the attempted coup that finds all of the defendants "guilty as charged"—was published several months before the beginning of the trial. While this insured that the book enjoyed a remarkable succès de scandale, it simultaneously prejudiced the government's case against the accused, forcing the trial to be postponed yet again.[41]

Officials and agencies of the Russian government, as well as of the governments of Belarus and Ukraine, have proven unprepared and unequipped to deal with the explosion of the culture of eroticism and titillation, resorting to Soviet-era methods in attempting to control its spread. The Belarus Government Committee of Experts in Evaluating Works of Literature, Art and Journalism, Mass Media and [Cultural] Objects for the Existence of Elements of Pornography, the Cult of Violence, and Cruelty officially banned the sale of Nikolai Daneliia's innocuous collection of poems and illustrations because of the presence of "uncensored expressions and 'obscene' words," and because neither the author nor the " 'works' have any relationship whatsoever to Belarus"—despite the fact that the title page of the collection indicates Minsk as the city of publication (see Figs. 15 and 16). While it is possible that Daneliia's book is not for sale in Belarus—his book was readily available in Moscow—it is much more likely that this official

Nancy Condee & Vladimir Padunov

14. Dust jacket cover for *The Kremlin Conspiracy (Kremlevskii zagovor)* by
Valentin Stepankov and Evgenii Lisov.

ban is unofficially ignored both by cultural consumers and by the government agencies regulating the economic transformation of the culture industry.

In Russia, at least, this is certainly the case. It is not surprising, for example, that the decision by the mayor of Moscow in February 1993 to ban all "foreign-language only" advertising in the city was still being ignored, for the most part, at the end of May 1993.[42] At issue here is neither so-called "traditional Russian lawlessness" (as intellectual historians might claim) nor a conspiracy by democrats and Western capitalism (as the linguistic purists and ultranationalists already claim). Instead, at issue is the government's inability to adopt a consistent policy in the face of increasing visualization of Russian culture in the marketplace.[43]

If the political branch of the government proved to be quite adept at

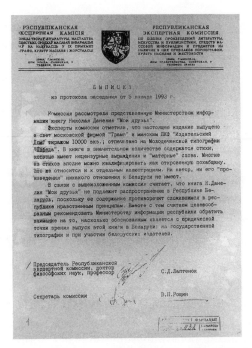

15. Document issued in Belarus banning the sale of Nikolai Daneliia's
To My Friends (Moim druz'iam).

16. Cover of Daneliia's *To My Friends.*

manipulating public opinion by its use of images in the mass media (especially television) during the referendum of 25 April and in the aftermath of the bloody May Day parade; and if the economic branch of the government continues to provide incentives for additional capital investments and to open the Russian market to "brand name" goods (most recently demonstrated by the transformation of GUM into a miniature urban mall, housing a variety of boutiques specializing in Western consumer goods); then the cultural branch of the government continues to concentrate almost exclusively on verbal texts and messages, thereby condemning itself to be ignored. The struggle to maintain linguistic purity and/or to uphold the former dominance of the written text makes little sense at a time when the majority of the population spends less time reading than watching dubbed versions of foreign soap operas, MTV, English broadcasts on CNN, or the "CBS Nightly News with Dan Rather",[44] or listening to the non-Russian music—and, with increasing frequency, non-Russian disc jockeys and announcers—that rule the airwaves. Consumer culture, for better or worse, has arrived in Russia and has brought with it the dominance of the visual, the erotic, and the West.

While the visualization of the Russian culture industry had not yet led to major changes in the book publishing industry during the summer of 1992, by May 1993 its impact was visible in every bookstore and on every bookstand in Moscow: newly published books were being packaged differently. Unlike earlier times, when books were published with monotone covers and with almost no images on the bindings, most new books (hardcover or paperback) now feature cover art that is brightly colored and shiny, and that frequently makes use of raised-letter printing; many hardcover books now come with dust jackets (in the past reserved exclusively for expensive art albums) that reproduce the covers. The appearance of dust jackets is such a recent development that it has even outstripped the packaging technology available to the publishing industry: unfolded dust jackets are now "issued" separately to customers when they purchase a book.

This revived attention to packaging and cover art—significantly altering the "look of Russian literature"—can be traced through the entire spectrum of new publications in Russia: in high literature and in the literature of titillation; in the large publishing houses and in the small presses; in the reprints of prerevolutionary experimental writing and in contemporary experimental literature; and in the new generation of journals.[45] Indeed, there is a growing trend among the new commercial publishers and small presses to package manuscripts of experimental and avant-garde literature in nontraditional ways to emphasize a publication's "visual objectness" by defamiliarizing its existence as a "book."

The ABC of Russian Consumer Culture

This trend has two essential substreams: publications that dismantle the book and publications that resist reading. Recent notable examples of the former include Lev Rubinshtein's three boxed, index-card narratives *Small Nocturnal Serenade* [*Malen'kaia nochnaia serenada*], *Mama Was Washing the Frame* [*Mama myla ramu*], and *Appearance of the Hero* [*Poiavlenie geroia*]; Aleksandr Brener's and Roman Baembaev's envelope of cards (*Japanese God* [*Iaponskii Bog*], a euphemism for "prick"); and Igor' Ioganson's stapled signatures (*Intersonnetia: Four Notebooks* [*Mezhsonet'e: chetyre tetradi*]). Examples of the latter—publications that shift a reader's attention from the verbal text to the "text as visual object"—include an invertible book (Andrei Turkin's *Lyrics* [*Stikhotvoreniia*] and A. Dzhikiia's *Pictures* [*Kartinki*]); Oleg Grigor'ev's collage book of poems *Mit'ki and Verse* [*Mit'ki i Stikhi*]); the miniature *Anthology of One-Dot Poetry* [*Antologiia odnotochnoi poèzii*]; as well as the series of pamphlets published by Sergei Sigei, which are accompanied by visual block-print poems.

The spread of visualization—together with the culture of titillation described earlier—has now affected every branch of the Russian culture industry and has extended across all of society. And predictably, each branch of the culture industry has responded and adjusted to these two new dominants. Virtually every cultural event—book publication, printing of a new journal, release of a new film or album, premiere of a stage production, exhibit opening, unveiling of a monument—is celebrated by a ritual referred to as *prezentatsiia*. While the precise meaning of this term is slippery (literally, it means "presentation"), the event is much closer to an informal party than to a formal ceremony: after a few brief remarks (celebrating the appearance of a new cultural object) and toasts (addressed as much to the successful mass-producers of the object as to the original artist), guests and hosts intermingle; cocktail party conversations take the place of speeches; and the consumption of food prefigures the consumption of the cultural object.

These *prezentatsii*, in fact, constitute a point of intersection for the process of visualizing culture and for the culture of titillation: both are based on spectacle; both are based on the presentation of surface; and both bear an aversion to high culture. *Prezentatsii* require a kind of theatrical space, within which they can be enacted, collapsing all distinctions between audience and actors, spectators and participants. Every *prezentatsiia* is its own visual event and in turn yields its own events, descriptions, and recollections. And yet, despite the underlying aversion to high culture—or perhaps, because of this aversion—most *prezentatsii* are staged in the now emptied temples of high culture: the Central House of Artists, or Composers, or Filmmakers, or Littérateurs; the Kino Center; a theater or a square; a museum or a gallery.

In effect, the ritual of *prezentatsii* presents high culture with an eviction notice, forcing its representatives to vacate a piece of choice property, if only for one night. On the night of 27 May 1993, for example, the enormous House of Littérateurs simultaneously hosted—that is, was rented out for—two *prezentatsii*. On the side of the Povarskaia [formerly Vorovskogo] Street entrance, the publishing house and journal *Ogonek* presented the publication in book form of Mikhail Liubimov's *The Life and Adventures of Alex Wilkey, Spy* [*Zhizn' i prikliucheniia Aleksa Uilki, shpiona*]. Liubimov's spy thriller—a classic example of the culture of titillation—was very popular when serialized by *Ogonek* in 1992. The novel is based on the author's experiences as an agent of the KGB, and describes actual cases and operatives. Attended by many (former) members, spouses, and widows of the Soviet intelligence community—according to Oleg Kalugin, earlier a general in the KGB (and author himself), every third person at the *prezentatsiia* was a former colleague—this event was conducted with impeccable middle-class gentility.

At the same time, but on the opposite side of the building (facing Herzen Street), IMA-Press and the *Mit'ki* staged their own presentation of Grigor'ev's collection of verse collages. This *prezentatsiia* was a kind of countercultural "happening," organized around a rock band, dancing crowds, stands selling counterculture books, tapes, and posters.

Immediately in front of the House of Littérateurs on the Povarskaia Street side was a thriving meat and poultry market; on the Herzen Street side sat a man playing an accordion—the traditional Russian folk instrument of the countryside—and singing raucous peasant songs.

With their "Club"—as the House is commonly referred to (Garrard 2)—besieged both inside and outside its walls, where were the erstwhile representatives of Russian high literature? They had retreated into its inner fortifications, huddled over coffee in the basement snack bar or dining in the Club's restaurant, sandwiched between the two events. Their presence at the *prezentatsii* was unnecessary; their property was essential.

Notes

Research for this chapter was supported in part by a grant from the International Research & Exchanges Board (IREX), with funds provided by the Andrew W. Mellon Foun-

The ABC of Russian Consumer Culture

dation, the National Endowment for the Humanities, and the U.S. Department of State (Title VIII). Additional financial assistance was provided by a research grant from the Hewlett International Small Grants Program at the University Center for International Studies and the Graduate School of Public and International Affairs at the University of Pittsburgh. An early draft of the essay was presented at the conference "Postcommunism: Rethinking the Second World," sponsored by the Center for Cultural Studies at the University of California at Santa Cruz. We would also like to express our appreciation for the advice, support, and assistance we have received from David Birnbaum, Helena Goscilo, and other members of the Department of Slavic Languages and Literatures at the University of Pittsburgh and the members of the Working Group, as well as Nadezhda Azhgikhina (*Ogonek*), Janusz Einhorn (Einhorn Associates), Vivian Foley (ProMedia, Moscow), Aleksandra N. Ivanova-Anninskaia, Vasilii Kravchuk, Colin MacCabe (British Film Institute), Irina Shilova (Institute for Cinema Studies, Moscow), and Greta Slobin (University of California at Santa Cruz). None of the above-mentioned organizations or individuals is responsible for the views expressed in this article.

The quotation by Mikhail Ptashuk, which appears as an epigraph to the *Metsenat* section of this chapter, was drawn from Georgy Melikyants, "A Plea for Help."

1. For examinations of cultural economics and politics in the production, distribution, and consumption of cultural objects in Russia through the summers of 1990–92, see the first three articles in this series: "*Makulakul'tura*," "Perestroika Suicide," and "Pair-a-Dice Lost."

2. One might better debate whether the news piece cum advertisement was intended to sell Fords or to send a message about whose "company car" will police the outposts of capital.

3. The fact that the piece from *Moscow News* was included in the regular column "TV Watch" with a headline reading "Programming News" further underscores its status as "newsworthy" information, rather than as advertising agency business.

4. Learning is also the legitimizing discourse behind Russia's first official strip school, the Erikom Striptease School, located (of course) in a dormitory of the Academy of Sciences. Its staff, Evgenii and Vera Lavrovskie and Aleksandr Mikhailov, are a promising professional combination: respectively, an exgynecologist, a magician's assistant, and a clown. "Striptease has to be taken seriously and studied," Lavrovskii explains in an interview with journalist Fiona Fleck. Their best student, blessed with the name of Angela Kalashnikova, has set her sights on a specific target audience: her dance specialties are a Japanese hara-kiri act and a cowboy number (Fleck 33).

5. Most recent in this series are *The Story of Money* [*Chto takoe den'gi*] 3; *The Story of Banks and Thrifts* [*Chto takoe bank i sberegatel'nye kassy*] 4; *The Story of Electronic Money* [*Chto takoe cheki i èlektronnye den'gi*] 5; and *Once upon a Dime* [*Zhila-byla Denezhka*] 6 (Moskva: NACHALA-Press, 1992). All of these comic books are adapted from the series published by the Federal Reserve Bank of New York.

6. The 1993 subscription campaign proved to be even more disastrous for Russian newspapers and journals. See Bohlen, "Few Russian Papers Thriving."

7. The May 1993 cost per ton of cardboard was 40,000 rubles; for newsprint, 90,000 rubles; and for No. 1 Offset paper, 110,000 rubles. See "Po slukham i ofitsial'no."

8. According to an undocumented report filed by the Moscow Bureau of the émigré newspaper *Novoe russkoe slovo* [*New Russian Word*], the average monthly income in May 1993 for a midlevel Moscow journalist was close to 100,000 rubles. If in January 1993

Nancy Condee & Vladimir Padunov

the average payment to authors was 700 to 800 rubles per typed page, by May 1993 the average was 1,500 to 3,000 rubles. See "Pressa podnimaet tseny. I gonorary."

Most striking in this report is the emergence of a new standard of payment in the Russian publishing industry: "per typed page." The traditional standard was—and in some parts of the industry remains—the printer's sheet [*pechatnyi list*], which was between 22 and 26 typed pages. Clearly, the transition from "hot type" to "soft type" (offset, camera-ready) printing is affecting more than just the modes of production and the linguistic codes; it is already altering systems of measurement and payment for labor. Even *Novyi mir* [*New World*] has made this transition. In a recent issue, the editors published an announcement declaring a competition for the best short story or novella written by a student at the Literary Institute; stories were limited to 48 typed pages, novellas to 120. See *Novyi mir* 5 (1993): 2.

9. See Filipp Urban's examination of the economic unfeasibility of undertaking any form of publishing venture in Russia because of growing hyperinflation.

10. By 1993 *Ogonek* had resumed a weekly publication schedule, though it reverted to semimonthly publication for the summer months. While the price of a single issue of *Ogonek* was 40 rubles at kiosks in May 1993, the cost per issue to subscribers remained substantially lower: a subscription for the first six months of 1993 cost 390 rubles.

11. It should be stressed that the threat of impending bankruptcy affected all branches of the publishing industry in Russia, journals (new and old, "thick" monthlies and irregular glossies) as well as books (former state publishing houses, cooperatives, and joint ventures). Not surprisingly, many of these turned directly to the West with appeals for "hard-currency" capital investments, "hard-currency" prepublication financing, and "hard-currency" subscriptions. See, for example, the advertisements soliciting contributions to "Save *Novyi mir*" (*AATSEEL Newsletter*, February 1993: 17); to finance the publication of the *Bakhtinskii sbornik* [*Bakhtin Collection*] (*AATSEEL Newsletter*, November 1991: 23); and to preorder the forthcoming publication by Khudozhestvennaia literatura [Artistic Literature] of the two-volume edition of Vladislav Khodasevich (*AATSEEL Newsletter*, February 1993: 27).

12. Each of these periodicals has been re-energized in 1993. The recent Booker Prize awards of £2,500 to be shared by the journals *Solo* and *Vestnik novoi literatury* undoubtedly helped both of them to stabilize their distribution problems, as well as to undertake the publication of new issues (see "2,5 tysiachi funtov sterlingov na dvoikh"). Since this award, both *Solo* and *Vestnik novoi literatury* have published new issues, with the former also dramatically changing its appearance (paper, binding, layout, etc.). Similarly, while *Konets veka* failed to publish its fourth issue until 1993, the publisher began to issue a number of books in 1992; most notable among them is Iurii Borev's *Fariseia: Poslestalinskaia epokha v predaniiakh i anekdotakh* (Moskva, 1992), a companion volume to his earlier collection of anecdotes and apocrypha about Stalin and his immediate circle of associates (*Staliniada* [Moskva: Sovetskii pisatel', 1990]).

13. On 8 June 1993, ITAR-TASS reported that the rate of inflation for the first five months of 1993 alone had reached 164%; see Keith Bush.

14. For a discussion of the state of book publishing and retailing in Russia through the end of 1992, see David Lowe.

15. The Archive of the Non-Traditional Press is directed by Aleksandr Suetnov, who has closely followed and documented the "unofficial" press since the end of the stagnation period. In 1992, Suetnov published an impressive two-volume bibliographical guide to "unofficial" serial publications in Russia between 1985 and 1991: *Samizdat: bibliograficheskii ukazatel' (katalog netraditsionykh izdanii)*, izd. 2-oe, dopolnennoe (Moskva: Tsentr

The ABC of Russian Consumer Culture

17. Cover of Aleksandr Suetnov's *Samizdat.*

obrazovatel'nykh programm instituta Novykh tekhnologii obrazovaniia, 1992, (see Fig. 17). For a detailed review of this publication, see T. Blazhnova, "Samizdat na samokhranenii," *Knizhnoe obozrenie* [*Book Review*] 14 May 1993.

16. According to Russian government statistics, in 1992 there were 28,716 books and pamphlets published in the Russian Federation, with a total print run of just over 1.3 billion copies. These figures represent a drop of 5,334 titles (15.7 percent) and 317 million copies (19.4 percent) in comparison with 1991. See Platova.

17. In fact, 1992 may be remembered in Russia as the year of the Western soap opera [*myl'naia opera*]. By far the most popular program on Russian television during 1992 was the Mexican soap opera *The Rich Also Cry*; second most popular was another Mexican soap *Nobody But You*; third was a Russian soap *The Trifles of Life*; and fourth the U.S. soap *Santa Barbara*. See Kikoin.

18. See Simon Karlinsky's impassioned—and highly tendentious—paean to this period in his review of Laura Engelstein's *The Keys to Happiness: Sex and the Search for Modernity in Fin-de-siècle Russia* (New York: Cornell UP, 1993).

19. This stand is the major outlet for all of the literary criticism published by Nasledie [Heritage]—the publishing arm in literature of the Russian Academy of Sciences, which has effectively taken over publishing material that earlier would have been handled by Nauka (Moscow) Publishers. In 1992, Nasledie published the first three volumes of the *Akhmatovskie chteniia*, collections of articles by Russian and Western scholars of Akhmatova: *Tsarstvennoe leto*, *Tainy remesla*, and *Svoiu mezh vas eshche ostaviv ten'*, compiled and edited by N. V. Koroleva and S. A. Kovalenko (see Fig. 18). While in earlier years, such a publication would have appeared in a print run of at least 10,000 copies and would have disappeared from the citywide marketplace almost overnight, these three volumes were printed in runs of 2,000 copies (the first issue) and 1,000 copies (the second and

Nancy Condee & Vladimir Padunov

18. Covers of the first three volumes of *Akhmatova Readings*
(*Akhmatovskie chteniia*).

third), were for sale in only one location in the city, and half a year later were far from sold out. Also available at this bookstand was Mikhail Golubkov, *Utrachennye al'ternativy. Formirovanie monisticheskoi kontseptsii sovetskoi literatury. 20–30-e gody* (Moskva: Nasledie, 1992), another book that—because of its subject and cover art—would have been sold out before it reached the marketplace during the early perestroika years.

20. Dictionaries and reference works of all kinds seem to be experiencing a major publishing boom at the moment. There is even a new edition of "Ozhegov,"—the most commonly used Russian-Russian dictionary, both domestically and abroad—*Tolkovyi slovar' russkogo iazyka* (Moskva: Az' Ltd., 1992). This new edition differs from earlier ones in two essential respects: in addition to S. I. Ozhegov, it lists N. Iu. Shvedova as a coeditor and it contains entries on "*govno*" [shit] and "*zhopa*" [ass]. While this edition lists no other "unprintable words"—it does not even contain "*kher*" (both the old name of the consonant "*kh*" and a euphemism for "*khui*" [prick]), though it includes all other earlier and present consonant names ("*az*" for "*a*," "*buki*" for "*b*," and so forth)—the inclusion of "*govno*" and "*zhopa*" into household dictionaries is a significant publishing moment in Russian society.

In the last few years, publishers have issued a large number of dictionaries that are devoted to Russian-language subcultures. In addition to pirated reprints of the major Western dictionaries and reprints of earlier Soviet ones—for example, S. M. Potapov, *Slovar' zhargona prestupnikov (blatnaia muzyka)* (Moskva: Narodnyi Komissariat Vnutrennikh Del, 1927)—the following new dictionaries have also appeared: D. S. Baldaev, V. K. Belko, and I. M. Isupov, *Slovar' tiuremno-lagerno-blatnogo zhargona (rechevoi i graficheskii portret sovetskoi tiur'my)* (Moskva: Kraia Moskvy, 1992); Iu. P. Dubiagin and A. G. Bronnikov, *Tolkovyi slovar' ugolovnykh zhargonov* (Moskva: Inter-OMNIS and ROMOS, 1991); A. Fain and V. Lur'e, *Vse v kaif (materialy k slovariu molodezhnogo slenga)* (n.c.: Lena Production, 1991); Lev Mil'ianenkov, *Po tu storonu zakona (èntsiklopediia prestupnogo mira)* (St. Petersburg: "Damy i gospoda," 1992); A. Sidorov, *Slovar' blatnogo i lagernogo zhargona (iuzhnaia fenia)* (Rostov-na-Donu: Germes, 1992). Mil'ianenkov's dictionary provides the single best visual encyclopedia tracing the history and meanings of Soviet prison tattoos (see Figs. 19 and 20).

The ABC of Russian Consumer Culture

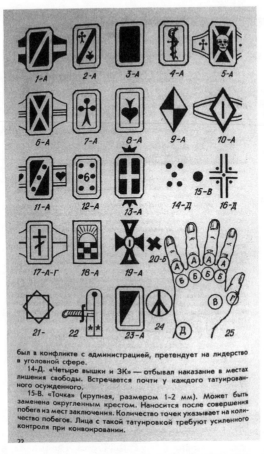

19. Illustration from Lev Mil'ianenkov's *On the Other Side of the Law*
(Po tu storonu zakona). Meaning and location of ring tattoos.

21. Among recent works on merchant culture, are P. A. Buryshkin, *Moskva kupeche-skaia* (Moskva: Stolitsa, 1990) a reprint (now with a foreword by, of all people, Petr Pala-marchuk) of the Chekhov Publishers edition from 1954); Natal'ia Dumova, *Moskovskie metsenaty* (Moskva: Molodaia gvardiia, 1992); and Savva Morozov, *Ded umer molodym: doku-mental'naia povest'* (Moskva: Rubikon, 1992), a memoir about the author's grandfather, Savva Timofeevich. For further reading on Merchant culture, see Edith W. Clowes, Sa-muel D. Kassow, and James L. West, eds., *Between Tsar and People: Educated Society and the Quest for Public Identity in Late Imperial Russia* (Princeton: Princeton University Press, 1991); Kiril Fitzlyon and Tatiana Browning, *Before the Revolution: Russia and Its People under the Czar* (Woodstock: Overview, 1978): especially 35–38; and Beverly Whitney Kean, *All the Empty Palaces: The Merchant Patrons of Modern Art in Pre-Revolutionary Russia* (New York: Universe, 1983).

22. For the sake of clarity, "Merchant" denotes a member of the Merchant class, whether

Nancy Condee & Vladimir Padunov

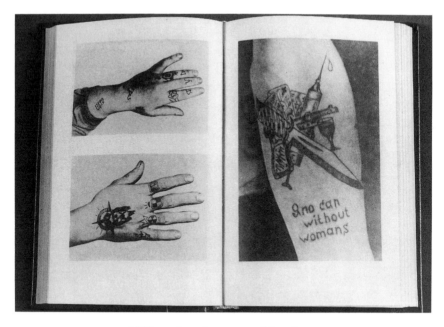

20. Mil'ianenkov, forearm and hand tattoos.

or not the individual engages in merchantry; "merchant" denotes an individual engaged in the buying and selling of goods.

23. In deference to Peter Kenez, we will not pursue this historical red herring.

24. "We have been asked to announce that the film *Merchant Bashkirov's Daughter* is to be released under the title *Drama on the Volga*. As is known, the film is the work of the Volga company and has been acquired by Pathé Frères. The title has been changed because the heroine's surname is identical to that of some well-known merchants in a certain town on the Volga—by sheer coincidence, of course." *Sine-Fono,* 4 (1913): 30, quoted in Yuri Tsivian 182–85.

25. Film has yet to render up a significant cinematic *metsenat.* One would surmise that cinema—with its reputation of being the most important of all arts (however tendentious and, now, outdated that position is), its "natural" proclivity for creating larger-than-life characters, and its developed subculture of money-laundering—would soon lend itself to a major cinematic enactment of this myth, whether constituted as historical biography (a mercantile "hagiography") or as contemporary *film-à-clef.*

26. *Humanitarian Aid and Philanthropy in the Ex-USSR* March 1993: 1. This publication of Interlegal International Charitable Foundation is based on information from the news agency *Postfaktum.*

27. This is one of several recent articles in *Nezavisimaia gazeta* reviving the mystique of the industrialist-*metsenat.* See also Polunina on A. P. Bakhrushin.

28. Nowhere do we find any recognition that the word "metsenat," having entered the language earlier, creates the illusion that the money, too, must be older and "therefore" a more reliable source of wealth. The emerging distinction seems to be that "pa-

tron" [*metsenat*] differs from "sponsor" [*sponsor*] in that the former does not insist upon the advertisement of a specific product in exchange for funding. See, for example, the discussion in Alapaevskii.

We would also like to call attention in passing to the use of the feminine noun *blagotvoritel'nost'* in describing the philanthropic act of giving and its matrimonial or erotic pairing with the masculine construction "sound business" [*solidnogo biznesa*], whose activity, by contrast, is the *taking* of money; together they constitute a kind of wedding-cake construction of capitalism—and indeed, the shaky, risky first steps of the honeymoon period, volatile and intense, constitute an apt description.

29. Other recent foundations include the Fellowcountryman [*Sootechestvennik*] Foundation; the Enlightenment [*Prosveshchenie*] Charitable Foundation; the Moscow Education Foundation, which works to bring the television program *"Teleklass"* into the classroom; Academician Gennadii Mesiats's Demidov Foundation (Ekaterinburg), which distributes awards in the sciences and humanities with funds provided by the Urals branch of the Academy of Sciences, the Novaia Gil'diia Joint Stock Company, and Acme Investment and Industrial Corporation; the Tartar Business Club and Charity Foundation; and Academician Andrei Gonchar's Fundamental Research Fund, which supports pioneer research projects. Somewhat more dubious organizations include the People's Academy of Culture and Human Values, headed by President Toshpulat Tozhiddinov. A significant player in the advancement of the so-called Third Sector (nongovernmental and noncommercial) is the Interlegal International Foundation. Its May 1993 seminar, "Recognizing the Third Sector," was attended by over thirty U.S. governmental and nongovernmental organizations, joined by Russian counterparts to discuss organization, structure, management, taxes, accounting procedures, legal, and business strategies for charitable activity. See *Humanitarian Aid and Philanthropy in the Ex-USSR* May 1993: 2. Not under discussion here are those new institutions that promote humanitarian aid (such as the Russian Red Cross Society), charity (such as Human Soul, Moscow Charity Home, or the Charity Foundation for the Social Protection of Russia's Film Actors), contests (Belosnezhka Fund for Russia's Talented Children), international or foreign foundations (such as the International Monetary Fund Program of Aid to Scientists of the Former U.S. S. R., and the Russian-American Cultural Initiative Fund), fundraising, or social welfare organizations.

30. "Learning that the foundation is associated with Shchekochikhin, the well-known fighter with the mafia in Russia, many commercial structures were ready to transfer money to ensure that the editor that [sic] heads the paper's investigative reporting would leave them in peace. But Shchekochikhin did not accept the mafia's gifts. The foundation's money will be clean. Within the framework of the foundation a grant for specialists studying America has been set up by R. Nixon" (Sergei Smirnov-Dobushev). U.S. readers might find an implicit contradiction between the last two sentences.

31. See Voinovich's parody of this state of affairs.

32. Some of the relevant publications on these battles include Celestine Bohlen, "Amid Soviets' Changes, Who Owns the Papers?" *The New York Times* 11 June 1990; Vera Tolz, "Adoption of the Press Law: A New Situation for the Soviet Media?" *Report on the USSR* 6 July 1990: 9–11; Aleksandr Podrabinek, "Glasnost' ili svoboda pechati?," *Novoe russkoe slovo* 12 July 1990; "Zhurnal 'Ogonek' budet aktsionernym obshchestvom," *Novoe russkoe slovo* 21–22 July 1990; *Report on the USSR* 27 July 1990, 17 August 1990, 7 September 1990, 14 September 1990; Editorial Board, "Svobodnaia tribuna pisatelei: neobkhodimoe ob"iasnenie s chitatelem," *Literaturnaia gazeta* 18 November 1990; I. Samofal, "'Niva', 'Veche' i drugie," *Literaturnaia Rossiia* [*Literary Russia*] 30 November 1990; Julia

Wishnevsky, "Press Law Makes Trouble for Writers' Unions," *Report on the USSR* 2 November 1990, 16 November 1990; and "Reshat' po zakonu," *Literaturnaia gazeta* 26 December 1990.

33. This term, no longer useful because it is too sweeping in its generality, is replaced by the more particularized nomenclature for arts administrators. This greater terminological specificity can be noticed in both Russian and U.S. journalistic accounts of Russian culture. Imagine, for example, such a newspaper headline today as the following from the *New York Times* of 10 January 1989: "Soviets Designate a U.S. Dealer for Their Artists." Here subject, direct object, and indirect object would all demand much greater differentiation (both in journalistic reporting and in self-designation) than in 1989.

34. Theater, ballet, and opera still present overwhelming problems of organization, management, and acquisition of goods and services; they are correspondingly less "manageable"—that is, a poorer investment—than the visual arts. A recent indication that this may be slowly changing is Inkombank's decision to underwrite Oleg Tabakov's studio-theater at 1 Chaplygin Street. In return (or not), the theater intends to revise its profile so as to produce more of the "eternal classics": Chekhov, Gogol', Gor'kii, and so forth. An exception among the 1993–94 offerings is Jean-Claude Brisville's play "Le Souper," a two-hour dialogue between Talleyrand and Fouché about the division of power at the time of the Premier Empire. "But the production must not have any cheap hints at our political situation," promises director Andrei Smirnov *(Moscow News* 18 June 1993). Capital, apparently, deserves more expensive Aesopian language than its predecessor.

35. We have in mind the Fifth Congress of the U.S.S.R. Cinematographers' Union and the Eighth Congress of the U.S.S.R. Writers' Union.

36. It is becoming increasingly evident that such legislation will be drafted in coordination with Russia's entry into the General Agreement on Tariffs and Trade (GATT), to which the Russian Federation submitted its application on 9 April 1993; the NASDAQ stock market exchange, which now lists Petersburg Long Distance as the first Russian company; and other international facilitating institutions. Within the business community, the range of expertise includes the Fuqua School of Business (Duke University) affiliate institution, the Fuqua Center for Manager Development (St. Petersburg), funded by R. J. Reynolds Tobacco International; the U.S. Telecommunications and Electronics Consortium in the Newly Independent States (US TEC-NIS); the United States–New Independent States Chamber of Commerce; and Soros Foundation funding for internships of Russian entrepreneurs at U.S. firms.

37. For a more detailed discussion of the state of pornography during this earlier period, see Condee and Padunov, "Perestroika Suicide."

38. And, not surprisingly, under conditions of Klondike capitalism, the market "can bear" the most astonishing contradictions in terms of costs. To cite but one extreme example: a copy of Andrei Voznesenskii's coffee-table/visual-poetry book, *Videomy* (Moskva: Kul'tura, 1992), published in a "limited print run" of 1,000 copies, was sold at an auction in February 1993 for 225,000 rubles; a ticket to attend the *prezentatsiia* [publication celebration] was auctioned off for 25 rubles. Despite expectations that this book would become an immediate bibliographic rarity (because of the author, the print run, the auction, the price), *Videomy* was still widely available in May 1993 for 5,000 rubles at some of the bookstands or even for the mere list price of 1,387 rubles in bookstores. For more information about *Videomy*, see "Videomy—za 225 tysiach," *Literaturnaia gazeta* 10 February 1993; "V gostiakh u novoi knigi," *Literaturnaia gazeta* 24 February 1993; Yana Maerzon, "Voznesensky: A Challenge to His Own Popularity," *We/My* 5 March 1993.

The ABC of Russian Consumer Culture

39. The most frequently encountered erotic newspapers are still *Info-SPID* [*Info-AIDS*] and *Eshche* [*More*]. While *Eshche* is published in Latvia, it has begun to acquire a reputation in Moscow for the quality of its fiction, reproducing in some respects the myths that surround *Playboy* magazine in America (which is "read," as often as not,—or so it is claimed—for the quality of its interviews and stories).

40. The Russian edition of *Penthouse* has not yet become a monthly publication, though the publishers hope to begin publishing a new issue each month by the end of 1993. Interestingly, while the price for each issue has increased apace with the national level of inflation (the first cost 875 rubles, the second 1,650 rubles, the third 2,300 rubles), the price of each back issue has remained unchanged.

41. The trial was postponed on 18 May 1993 when the presiding judge ruled in favor of the defendants' motion challenging the impartiality of the prosecutors. The judge, Anatolii Ukolov (in Russian, "Injection"!), appealed to the Constitutional Court and the Supreme Soviet to review the case and to decide whether the prosecutors are "genuinely independent"; see N. G., "Events," *Moscow News* 21 May 1993; Natalya Gevorkyan, "The Trial of Emergency Committee Members May Fall into Abeyance," *Moscow News* 28 May 1993; Anna Ostapchuk, "Pervaia pobeda obviniaemykh: sud udovletvoril khodataistvo ob otvode gosudarstvennykh obvinitelei," *Nezavisimaia gazeta* 19 May 1993; Valerii Rudnev, "V sviazi s delom GKChP vozmozhna otstavka General'nogo prokurora Rossii," and "Sud otvel nyneshnii sostav gosudarstvennykh obvinitelei," *Izvestiia* 19 May 1993.

42. The Moscow ruling—following a similar decision made in St. Petersburg in December 1992—was scheduled to go into effect on 1 April 1993; see "Moskovskie vlasti zapretili reklamu na inostrannykh iazykakh," *Novoe russkoe slovo* 1 March 1993.

43. For a discussion of the visualization of Russian culture, see Condee and Padunov, "Pair-a-Dice Lost," 75–77.

44. In addition to his CNN broadcasts in Moscow, Ted Turner has also purchased Channel 6 in Moscow, the last of the available VHF channels in the country; see "Turner Channel for Moscow," *New York Times* 30 December 1992; "First Commercial TV Station Airs Movies, CNN News," *We/My* 24 January 1993.

45. An interesting contrast in possible relations to cover art is provided by three new high culture journals, *De visu* (three issues), *Novoe literaturnoe obozrenie* [*New Literary Review*] (two issues), and *Zdes' i teper'* [*Here and Now*] (two issues; see Fig. 21). While *De visu*—a monthly journal that is devoted to Russian literature and culture from the 1890s through the 1930s—features a cover that is strikingly simple and uncluttered in its layout (white background, black lettering along the top, no illustration apart from the Latin lettering of the title), *Novoe literaturnoe obozrenie*—a bimonthly journal devoted to all of Russian culture—uses a cover and format that are more traditional for the "thick journals," and *Zdes' i teper'*—a quarterly devoted to Russian philosophy, literature, and culture—varies its cover (colors, design, layout) from issue to issue.

Works Cited

"2,5 tysiachi funtov sterlingov na dvoikh." *Literaturnaia gazeta* 20 January 1993.

Alapaevskii, Vladimir. "Mamontov vernulsia i drugikh zovet." *Novoe russkoe slovo* 3 August 1993.

Antologiia odnotochnoi poèzii. Moskva: Gumanitarnyi fond, 1991.

21a and 21b. Covers of three new journals *De visu, Novoe literaturnoe obozrenie,* and *Zdes' i teper'*.

Brener, Aleksandr, and Roman Baembaev. *Iaponskii Bog.* Moskva: Nenayobnaya [*sic*] ptitsa, n.d.

Bush, Keith. "Monthly Inflation Rate Picks Up." *RFE/RL Daily Report* #108 (9 June 1993).

Christie, Ian. Notes. *Early Russian Cinema.* Vol. 4. *Provincial Variations: "The Wedding Day" and "Merchant Bashkirov's Daughter."* British Film Institute, 1992 (10 volumes in video-cassette).

Condee, Nancy, and Vladimir Padunov. "*Makulakul'tura:* Reprocessing Culture." *October* 57 (1991): 79–102.

———. "Pair-a-Dice Lost: The Socialist Gamble, Market Determinism, and Compulsory Postmodernism." Russian translation in *Iskusstvo kino* 9 (1992): 72–81.

———. "Perestroika Suicide: Not by *Bred* Alone." *New Left Review* 189 (1991): 67–90 and *Harriman Institute Forum* 5, 5 (January 1992): 1–15.

Daneliia [Gudvin], Nikolai. *Moim druz'iam, 1959-+1985.* Minsk: Tramp—Izdatel'skii Dom, 1992.

Dzhikiia, A. *Kartinki.* Moskva: IMA-Press, 1991. Invertible book with Turkin (below).

Egoshin, Aleksei. "TV Watch: Programming News." *Moscow News* 20–27 December 1992.

Fleck, Fiona. "Russia's Strip School." *Elle* February (1993): 32–34.

Garrard, John, and Carol Garrard. *Inside the Soviet Writers' Union.* New York: Free Press, 1990.

Gorbachev, M. S. Letter to the Higher Non-Party School. No date (received at *Literaturnaia gazeta* by fax 29 April 1993). Personal collection.

Grigor'ev, Oleg. *Mit'ki i Stikhi.* Moskva: IMA-Press, 1991.

Humanitarian Aid and Philanthropy in the Ex-USSR March 1993.

Humanitarian Aid and Philanthropy in the Ex-USSR May 1993.

Ioganson, Igor'. *Mezhsonet'e: chetyre tetradi.* N.c.: Mysh', 1992.

Janecek, Gerald. *Zaum' tudei: sovremennaia zaum'.* Ed. Sergei Sigei. Eisk: Al'fa i omega, 1993.

Kalugin, Oleg. *Korzina vtoraia.* Moskva: PIK, 1991.

———. *Vid s Lubianki: "Delo" byvshego generala KGB. Mesiats pervyi.* Moskva: PIK, 1990.

Karlinsky, Simon. "Liberating the Sexes: The Freedoms that Vanished with the October Revolution." *Times Literary Supplement* 11 June 1993.

Kikoin, A. "Novoe pokolenie vybiraet 'mylo'." *Novoe russkoe slovo* 24 November 1992.

Literaturnaia gazeta 5 May 1993.

Liubimov, Mikhail. *Zhizn' i prikliucheniia Aleksa Uilki, shpiona.* Moskva: Ogonek, 1993.

Lotman, Iurii. *Kul'tura i vzryv.* Moskva: Gnosis, Izdatel'skaia gruppa "Progress," 1992.

Lowe, David. "The Book Business in Postcommunist Russia: Moscow, Year One (1992)." *Harriman Institute Forum* 6, 5 (January 1993).

Lunina, Liudmila. "Art without Commerce." *Moscow News* 15–22 March 1992.

Matizen, Viktor. "Sukiny deti v kino, teatre i zhizni." *Novoe russkoe slovo* 18 March 1993.

Melikyants, Georgy. "A Plea for Help to Save the Arts in Russia." *We/My* 29 June–12 July 1992.

Minkin, Aleksandr. "Esli by znat'!" *Ogonek* 38 (September 1993): 24–26.

Nezavisimaia gazeta 18 May 1993.

Nezavisimaia gazeta 6 July 1993.

Nikolaevich, Sergei. "Teatr na Taganke: posledniaia mizantsena." *Ogonek* 38 (September 1993): 14–23.

Platova, Marina. "Knigoizdanie v 1992 godu." *Knizhnoe obozrenie* 4 June 1993.

"Po slukham i ofitsial'no." *Knizhnoe obozrenie* 4 June 1993.

Polunina, Nadezhda. "Portret kollektsionera." *Nezavisimaia gazeta* 19 May 1993.

"Pressa podnimaet tseny. I gonorary." *Novoe russkoe slovo* 15 June 1993.

Razgonov, Sergei, Boris V. Raushenbakh, and Savelii V. Iamshchikov. "Metsenaty ne rozhdaiutsia: inogda i dobrye primery zarazitel'ny." *Nezavisimaia gazeta* 18 May 1993.

Report on the USSR 9 September 1990.

Rubinshtein, Lev. *Malen'kaia nochnaia serenada. Mama myla ramu. Poiavlenie geroia.* Moskva: Renaissance, 1992.

Sigei, Sergei, ed. *KAZMA (Kazimir Malevich: pis'ma k Shutko).* Eisk: Eiskii istoriko-kraevedcheskii muzei, 1992.

———, ed. *KRUCHENYKH (Aleksei Kruchenykh: arabeski iz Gogol'ia).* Eisk: Al'fa i omega, 1992.

———, ed. *Zaum'.* See Janecek.

Smirnov-Dobushev, Sergei. "'Vysshaia bespartiinaia shkola' nachinaet priem." *Vechernii Klub [Evening Club]* 6 May 1993.

Smucker, Philip. "Payments to Air 'News' Increase in Russian Broadcasting." *We/My* 10–23 August 1992.

Stepankov, Valentin and Evgenii Lisov. *Kremlevskii zagovor (versiia sledstviia).* Moskva: Ogonek, 1992.

Svidetel'stvo o registratsii sredstva massovoi informatsii 02158. Personal collection.

Tokareva, Elena. "Dvulikii ianus knizhnogo razvala." *Literaturnaia gazeta* 9 June 1993.

Tsenarii-plan pervoi peredachi teletsikla "Russkii Metsenat." Personal collection.

Tsivian, Yuri, with Paolo Cherchi Usai, Lorenzo Codelli, Carlo Mantanaro, and David Robinson. *Silent Witnesses: Russian Films 1908–1919.* London: British Film Institute and Edizioni Biblioteca dell'Immagine, 1989.

Turkin, Andrei. *Stikhotvoreniia.* Moskva: IMA-Press, 1991. Invertible book with Dzhikiia (above).

Urban, Filipp. "The Picnic Is Over: How the Publishing Business, Which Was Profitable Just a Little While Ago, Has Become a Losing Proposition." *Nevskoe vremia [Neva Time]* 77 (232), 18 April 1992. Tr. H. M. Olmsted, Research Services, Harvard College Library.

Ustav Fonda v podderzhku molodoi tvorcheskoi intelligentsii 8 February 1993 (registered 18 February 1993). Personal collection.

Voinovich, Vladimir. "Better Read than Red." *The Washington Post. Book World* 7 March 1993.

Notes on Contributors

VICTORIA E. BONNELL is Professor in the Department of Sociology at the University of California, Berkeley. She is the author of several books on the prerevolutionary Russian labor movement and is currently coediting, with Ann Cooper and Gregory Freidin, a volume of eyewitness accounts of Russia's August 1991 coup. She is also completing a study of Soviet political art.

KATERINA CLARK is Professor of Comparative Literature and Slavic at Yale University. She is author of *The Soviet Novel: History as Ritual* (U of Chicago P, 1981) and, with Michael Holquist, *Mikhail Bakhtin* (Harvard UP, 1985).

NANCY CONDEE's work includes coauthored articles with Vladimir Padunov in the *Harriman Institute Forum, October,* the *Nation, New Left Review,* and *Framework,* as well as the Russian journals *Iskusstvo kino, Znamia,* and *Voprosy literatury.* Her work has appeared in *Slavic and East European Journal, Slavic Review, Germano-Slavica, Wide Angle,* the *Wilson Quarterly,* and the *Washington Post.*

GREGORY FREIDIN is Professor in the Department of Slavic Languages and Literatures at Stanford University. He is the author of a critical biography of Osip Mandelstam and has written extensively on modern Russian culture and politics for scholarly and large-circulation publications. He has also translated into English Khrushchev's memoirs and, into Russian, *The Federalist Papers.* He is the editor of *Russian Culture in Transition: Selected Papers of the International Working Group for the Study of Contemporary Russian Culture* (Stanford 1993). He is currently completing a study of Isaac Babel', *A Jew on Horseback: Isaac Babel in Russia and America.*

HELENA GOSCILO, currently the chairwoman of the Slavic Department at the University of Pittsburgh, specializes in contemporary Russian literature and culture, Slavic women's writing, the novel, and Romanticism. Her most recent publications include articles on Tat'iana Tolstaia and on recent Russian women's prose, as well as *Skirted Issues: The Discreteness and Indiscretions of Russian Women's Prose* (M. E. Sharpe, 1992) and *Fruits of Her Plume:*

Essays in Contemporary Russian Women's Culture (M. E. Sharpe, 1993). She is completing a monograph on Tolstaia's fiction, writing a study of Liudmila Petrushevskaia, and coediting with Beth Holmgren a collection of essays on Russian women's popular culture.

JOHN KACHUR is a Ph.D. candidate at the University of Pittsburgh, with interests in twentieth-century Russian literature and culture. His dissertation topic examines the writings of Vladimir Makanin and traces Makanin's unique development during the period of stagnation and perestroika.

SUSAN LARSEN is an Assistant Professor in the Slavic Department at Yale University. Her previously published work includes articles on Russian theater, contemporary Russian film and gender issues, as well as several translations of plays (Andrei Platonov's *Hurdy-Gurdy* and Nikolai Koliada's *Slingshot*). Current projects include a study of the "new women's prose" in Russia and a book on the novelist and playwright Mikhail Bulgakov.

ERIC NAIMAN, Assistant Professor of Comparative Literature and Slavic Languages and Literatures at the University of California, Berkeley, is completing a book on sexuality in early Soviet culture.

ANNE NESBET, Assistant Professor of Slavic Languages and Literatures at the University of California, Berkeley, is the author of articles on Bakhtin, Mandelstam, Platonov, and Nabokov. She is currently working on a book on violence in Soviet culture.

VLADIMIR PADUNOV teaches at the University of Pittsburgh. Together with Nancy Condee, he has written on contemporary Soviet and Russian culture and cultural politics.

MIKHAIL YAMPOLSKY has worked in Moscow as a researcher at the Institute of Cinema Studies and the Institute of Philosophy (Russian Academy of Sciences). He now teaches at New York University. He has published extensively in film, European cultural history, and visual anthropology. Together with Alexander Zholkovsky, he is currently completing a book on Isaac Babel'. His other projects include a book on the representation of death in European culture.

Index